SHORT FRENCH FICTION
Essays on the short story in France
in the twentieth century

SHORT FRENCH FICTION

Essays on the short story in France
in the twentieth century

Edited by
J.E. Flower

UNIVERSITY
of
EXETER
PRESS

First published in 1998 by
University of Exeter Press
Reed Hall, Streatham Drive
Exeter, Devon EX4 4QR
UK

British Library Cataloguing in Publication Data
A catalogue record of this book is available from the British Library

Paperback ISBN 0 85989 570 X
Hardback ISBN 0 85989 569 6

Typeset in Caslon by Kestrel Data, Exeter

Printed and bound in Great Britain by
Short Run Press Ltd, Exeter

Contents

Introduction

J.E. Flower

As historians of literature have widely recognized, the short story in France has a long and distinguished pedigree. Most critical studies devoted to it suggest as a starting point the earliest recorded collection, *Les cent nouvelles nouvelles* (1456–67), inspired in particular by the translation of Boccaccio's *Decameron* which had appeared forty years earlier. But we might also think back beyond these stories to the medieval *fabliaux* and to the romances of writers like Chrétien de Troyes for examples of fiction which already possessed that blend of narrative drive and focus which would become hallmarks of much traditional and successful short-story writing later. Surveys of the evolution of this particular form of fiction in France are sufficiently available to make any detailed account in the Introduction to a volume of this kind redundant; in particular, attention should be drawn to the excellent introduction by J. Gratton and B. Le Juez to their *Modern French Short Fiction*.[1] Let us simply recall, however, that from that distant starting point nearly six centuries ago to the present there has been a multiplicity of changes in content, tone and style. Even before the short story came into its own around 1830, and came to rival other established forms of imaginative writing, it was a far from insignificant literary form. Within the constraints imposed by publishing, much short fiction enjoyed considerable success—the sentimental and moral tales in Marguerite de Navarre's *L'Heptaméron* (1558–9), the longer, more complex stories of love and court society in the seventeenth century, the *contes philosophiques* produced by the likes of Voltaire and Diderot a century later still, Perrault's fairy stories, erotic tales, fables. . . .

The principal reasons for the marked increase in the production of short stories in early nineteenth-century France, it is generally agreed, were two-fold. The first was a widespread rise in the level of literacy, though we should not forget that compulsory primary education would not appear in France for another half century; the second was the rapid growth in the printing and publishing industries with the resultant appearance on the market of new newspapers and literary periodicals such as the *Revue de Paris* and the *Revue des deux mondes*. Such commercial expansion was not only of general public benefit, of course. As in more recent times, some authors began to realize that by publishing their work in the pages of these new periodicals they enjoyed a higher profile. They discovered as well that short-story writing (or the serialization of longer works) was a convenient way of boosting their income.

From around 1830 a number of writers—in the main novelists —readily turned their hand to this form, with the result that within a relatively short period it became increasingly refined and gained currency as a literary genre every bit as prestigious and valid as the novel. Indeed, it is from this period that compilers of international anthologies tend to select their 'representative' French short stories —Balzac's 'La Grande Bretache', Mérimée's 'Mateo Falcone', Maupassant's 'Une ficelle' for example, make regular appearances. Nor should we forget that for all their efforts in other literary forms, some of these authors—Mérimée and Maupassant are the prime examples—are today recalled first and foremost as writers of short stories.

Having reached this level of eminence it is somewhat surprising to find therefore that in the twentieth century the short story in France has tended to be neglected as if it were in some way inferior to other forms of prose fiction. In the most general of terms one reason for this eclipse, in the beginning at least, was the renewal of interest in the novel. Tradition played its part in this. The cyclical novel (the *roman-fleuve*), incorporating multiple volumes, recalled Balzac's *Comédie humaine* or Zola's *Rougon-Macquart* series, and was best illustrated by Roger Martin du Gard's *Les Thibault*, Jules Romains's *Les Hommes de bonne volonté* and Duhamel's *La Chronique des Pasquier*. More significant was the emergence of the *roman*

2

psychologique. Proust's *A la recherche du temps perdu* was not without similarities to the *roman-fleuve*, of course, but it introduced a whole new dimension of subjectivity into prose fiction, an exploration of the role of memory and the question of transforming observation into art. Such developments as these, together with the kinds of experiments and issues with which someone as influential as Gide was preoccupied, dominated prose fiction for most of the first half of the twentieth century.

This is not to say that some writers, far better known as novelists, did not try to reflect such concerns in short stories. Mauriac, for example, was one such, with his anguished trilogy *Un homme de lettres*, *Coups de couteau*, *L'Insomnie*. But it was not until around the middle of the century that the short story began to re-emerge with some vigour, to stand alongside, if not challenge, longer fiction. The publication of Sartre's collection *Le Mur* (1939) was an important event; so was that of Camus's *L'Exil et le royaume* (1957). Other writers too, some of whose stories are discussed in this volume, have been influential in their own particular ways—Paul Morand, Alain Robbe-Grillet, Daniel Boulanger, Jacques Perret, Marguerite Yourcenar, Jean-Marie Le Clézio, Marguerite Duras, André Stil to name but a handful. Even so, whatever the intrinsic quality of their short fiction, most if not all of these writers—unlike Mérimée or Maupassant—continue to be thought of as novelists, poets or playwrights. There have been very few writers in recent years whose reputations rest entirely, or nearly entirely, on the quality of their short stories. Despite the success of novels like *Travelingue* or *Uranus*, Marcel Aymé may be considered one, with such delightful collections of stories as *Le Passe-muraille* or *Les Contes du chat perché*; Marcel Arland may be another with, for example, *Les Vivants*, *Les Plus Beaux de nos jours* or *A perdre haleine*. But if indeed they have achieved this status they are exceptions rather than the rule.

Moreover, as René Godenne has claimed with some justification, the general plight of the short story has also been due at least in part to many writers' *own* perception that the genre is somehow qualitatively inferior.[2] There are few who seem to wish to claim the *nouvelle* as a genre in its own right, though one notable exception to this is Michel Tournier whose commitment to the short form, whether for children or adults, is as great as it is to his longer works. Commercial concerns also have a part to play. Having failed in their attempts to

3

launch *collections* of short stories, some major publishers such as Gallimard or Julliard will now only publish such volumes on condition that the author is already well known. (In fact the same conditions prevail elsewhere, certainly in the Anglo-Saxon world.) And for all his skill in this particular form of writing even someone like Tournier remains best known and most vigorously promoted as the author of *Le Roi des aulnes* or *Vendredi*; similarly Camus is best known for *L'Étranger* and *La Peste*, Sartre for *La Nausée* or *L'Etre et le néant*, and Simone de Beauvoir for *Le Deuxième Sexe*. Furthermore, in the context of the works studied in this volume, the individual stories by at least two of the authors are almost always thought of as belonging to the collection in which they first appeared, as though that collection—Sartre's *Le Mur*, Camus's *L'Exil et le royaume*—had the status of a quasi-novel. An extreme, more recent example of this is Perec's *La Vie mode d'emploi*.

This is not to say that the short story is unpopular with the reading public in France. Maupassant's stories continue to attract a large readership[3] and there is as much if not more demand for those by certain foreign authors—Chekhov, Borges, Mansfield, for example —as there is for those produced by modern French writers. One reason for this state of affairs may simply be habit, but another may lie in the fact that in France the question of nomenclature and hence definition has never been resolved. In the Anglo-Saxon world 'short story' (both with and without a hyphen), 'short fiction' or 'tale' (even 'novella') have seldom caused problems except for professional critics. But in France *conte* (with its variations *de fée, populaire* etc.), *nouvelle* (seemingly interchangeable with *conte* for Maupassant), and in more recent years *nouvelle-historique, nouvelle-histoire, nouvelle-instant, récit court* or *nouvelle-monadique*, for example, underline a problematic which remains unresolved and constantly evolving. To quote Cottenet-Hage and Imbert in the Introduction to their recent anthology *Parallèles*, the definition of the *nouvelle* 'ne cesse de s'ouvrir et de se métamorphoser'; between it and the *conte* 'les frontières (sont) poreuses'. And, they continue: 'Ductile et protéiforme, la nouvelle continue à narguer les efforts d'un appareil critique qui a quelquefois été désireux de l'immobiliser dans un carcan de définitions génériques et rigoureuses.'[4]

The Introduction to this volume is not the place to attempt to follow the niceties of the debate around this issue of definition, which has taken place largely in the work of British and North American critics. Let us recall, though, that for no little time Poe's view, first expressed in 1842, held sway: that the short story should proceed 'step by step to its completion with the precision and rigid consequence of a mathematical problem', and that of 'the greatest importance' was 'the unity of effect or impression'.[5] The debate has been ongoing and, during the last two decades in particular, modern critics have repeatedly shown how inadequate are Poe's requirements for the genre, albeit without arriving at a neat, working definition themselves. Some appear to regard the task as impossible. Ian Reid in 1977 wrote that the short story had 'no monotypic purity' and that it was 'almost any kind of fictitious prose briefer than a novel';[6] six years later Valerie Shaw commented that: 'there are so many different kinds of short story that the genre as a whole seems constantly to resist universal definition';[7] in 1991 Allan Pasco argued that while a single all-embracing definition would appear to be that 'a short story is a *short, literary prose fiction*', on reflection such a formulation 'covers a library of controversy'.[8]

Elsewhere, however, attempts to arrive at an assessment of the essential quality of short stories focus, perhaps inevitably, on the need for 'intensity', 'vigorous compression', 'speed' or 'tiny moments, seen [. . .] telescopically'; not surprisingly some critics have considered short stories to be 'closer in spirit to poems' than to novels.[9] In the immediate past, in their efforts to make some sense of such general uncertainty, Gratton and Le Juez, in the Introduction to their anthology of French short fiction, have proposed three guiding principles which they categorize as 'delimiting', 'focusing' and 'economising', and which together lead to a 'total efficiency'.[10] In the context of their discussion of the evolution of the short-story form in France in the late twentieth century, with authors' increasing experimentation and the production in some cases of stories only two or three pages in length,[11] these principles seem admirable. (Gratton develops some of these issues in Chapter Eight of the present volume.) They also underline the power which even the shortest of stories—'showing more by telling less'[12]—can have to engage the reader's participation in such a way that he or she builds on the text, teases out its implied meanings,[13] and begins to measure what I would tentatively define as its mass: in other words, its potential for interpretation which, as in all good art, far outstrips any imposed purely formal limitations. There is a weight, a density, an energy awaiting release, often in ways not intially anticipated.

The essays constituting the first seven chapters of this book deal in turn (and, in the main, chronologically) with stories which belong to the regular 'canon' of modern French short fiction. They make no claim to be exhaustive in their analyses but each has something new to say and invites the reader to go beyond the immediate context or circumstances of what is related. As a result the reader is drawn to pursue reflections of a philosophical, religious or political nature, to reconsider gender relations, to ponder on the individual's relationship with society and the question of collective responsibility, or to consider how fact (reality) and fiction can intertwine and become inseparable. In ways that recall works by Boccaccio or Constant, Diderot or Maupassant the essays also illustrate just a few of the many ways in which short stories may be narrated. Yourcenar's 'Le Lait de la mort' frames story within story, 'La Femme rompue' turns on the form and style of the *journal intime*, Duras's 'La Mort du jeune aviateur anglais', with the extraordinary subtle and explosive quality of its writing, heralds some of the experimentation of late twentieth-century fiction. Some stories—'La Pierre qui pousse' and 'L'Enfance d'un chef' are both good examples—form part of collections which, to use Godenne's phrase, benefit from an 'unité organique' with the consequence that they may be more rewardingly studied if there is a knowledge of the whole volume from which they have been taken. Others, even if they bear the impression of some of their author's recognizable preoccupations ('Les Suaires de Véronique' or 'La Carte') are more free-standing. The tone and register of these stories range widely, as the essays remind us: internalized reflection, anguished introspection, parody, humour, irony, oral-style delivery, impersonal third-person narrative and private diary, for example, are all represented. With the exception of Aymé's 'La Carte', all of the stories examined in these first chapters are, of course, quite lengthy and, in the case of 'L'Enfance d'un chef' in particular, stretch some of the elementary notions of the short story to the full, reminding us once again of the difficulty in arriving at a single, all-encompassing definition for this form of writing.

The final chapter is deliberately different. In it Gratton introduces the reader to the most recent changes and experiments which have taken place in short fiction in France and which, in some ways, are a form of coda to those which have occurred over the last fifteen years or so in particular in the longer 'nouvelle fiction'. Most of the writing that is the subject of this last chapter is of such a brief nature that the value of concentrating on a few illustrative texts, to the degree that the earlier chapters are able to do, would have been strictly limited. What is striking—and what Gratton so clearly demonstrates —are the ways in which this new style of writing overlaps, to a much greater degree than almost all earlier short fiction, with poetry, autobiography or the novel, in what he neatly defines as 'systematic slippage' and 'post-modern genre hopping'.[14] While it is quite different in kind from the preceding chapters therefore, the last one is in no way simply a postscript. It charts a process which has gathered and continues to gather pace and, in the realm of fiction, may well reflect a society which, as the millennium approaches, is increasingly in a state of rapid change and even dislocation.

*　　*　　*

All but the last of the essays in this volume began their existence as a series of public lectures generously sponsored by the Simon Cohen Memorial Trust and given at the University of Kent in the early months of 1996. I would like to thank all the contributors for their willingness to rework their material and for having considered what must undoubtedly at times have seemed unnecessary queries and comments.

1

Jean-Paul Sartre
'L'Enfance d'un chef'

William Bell

Contextual note

'L'Enfance d'un chef' is one of a group of five stories written by Sartre between 1936 and 1938. They were published in book form in 1939, under the title *Le Mur*. A sixth story, 'Dépaysement', which had been written with a view to inclusion in the volume, was judged by Sartre to be a failure and discarded. (The text of this last can be found in the Pléiade volume, J.-P. Sartre, *Œuvres romanesques*, Appendice I, pp. 1537–57.) In the original edition, and in all subsequent French editions, the stories were printed in the order: 'Le Mur', 'La Chambre', 'Érostrate', 'Intimité', and 'L'Enfance d'un chef'. The effect of this arrangement is to create a book in which crime (*le fait divers*) and scenes of private life are framed by stories which have contemporary history as their field of reference.

Prose fiction represents a significant category within the body of Sartre's work. The volume of stories followed closely on the heels of a highly original first novel, *La Nausée* (1938), and was itself closely followed by the trilogy *Les Chemins de la liberté* (a trilogy originally conceived as a tetralogy: volumes I and II were published in 1945; volume III in 1949; the fourth volume exists only as a fragment). After 1949, Sartre abandoned fiction for other forms of writing: plays, essays, biography, philosophy, journalism.

It could be argued that generic distinctions were never very important to Sartre. What mattered was to convey ideas by whatever means were likely to prove most effective. Such an attitude might seem to imply a lack of interest in formal questions. This is not true of Sartre, however. By 1939, he had established himself as an intelligent theorist of form in the novel and a sophisticated practitioner.

Sartre's output was vast and one would not wish to make any exaggerated claim for the importance within it of 'L'Enfance d'un chef'. It is, however, a highly satisfying autonomous work of art, employing narrated monologue (*style indirect libre*) to relate the formative years of a member of the bourgeoisie and incorporating into his story a satiric perception of some of the major intellectual fashions of the inter-war period: psychoanalysis, surrealism, right-wing nationalism. The novella has a strong autobiographical dimension, a trait which it shares with other examples of Sartre's fiction. It also has what might be called a *fonction annonciatrice*, the portrait of the hero seeming to prepare the ground for such later works as *L'Etre et le néant* (1943), *Réflexions sur la question juive* (1946), and *Les Mots* (1963). Moreover, additional interest derives from the circumstances of its publication, some seven months from the outbreak of war and seventeen from the collapse of the Third Republic.

Questions of method

'L'Enfance d'un chef', then, is one of the first literary texts to be published by Sartre. I stress the word *literary*: there are earlier philosophical texts but *La Nausée* and the group of stories known as *Le Mur* represent the first significant block of literary work. How should one approach these texts? Should one treat them as closed structures or read them in the light of their relationship with other texts in the Sartrean corpus? There is something contrived about the former method. It involves a discounting of knowledge; worse, it involves a pretence that knowledge consciously withheld has not contributed to our understanding of the supposedly closed structure. If, however, we adopt a synthetic approach and allow cross-referencing to become a major resource, we inevitably create a sense that the early texts have been overtaken—in some way displaced or devalued—by subsequent texts.

Take Lucien, hero of 'L'Enfance d'un chef'. Lucien worries about his image. People see him in a particular way and immediately he asks: Is this how I am? Is this me? If this is me, can I bear to be me? (I am trying here to convey the gist of what we are told about Lucien.) If these are indeed the main features of Lucien's behaviour, then the character is intelligible in general moral terms. He is a comic type, a normal person (someone like us!) in whom the propensity for anxious self-regard has become a vice. But Lucien is more than a comic type and Sartre, whether or not we think he is more than Molière, is not Molière. To the informed reader, what Lucien exemplifies is a theory as to the Self and the extent to which a sense of self is mediated by other people. Where is that theory set forth? The role of the expert is to deploy the relevant intertext and to provide a reference—to *L'Etre et le néant*, in the present case.[1] We follow up the reference and what we find is a whole elaborate account—*le regard d'Autrui*, key-holes, facticity—which 'explains' the behaviour of Lucien.

In some respects Sartre invites this kind of treatment. He said in an interview in 1938 that, ideally, he would like to express his ideas in literary form: 'J'aurais rêvé de n'exprimer mes idées que dans une forme belle—je veux dire dans l'œuvre d'art, roman ou nouvelle'. But some things are too technical; they do not lend themselves to discussion in layman's terms: 'Aussi je me vois obligé de doubler, pour ainsi dire, chaque roman d'un essai.'[2] *Doubler chaque roman d'un essai* . . . Does this imply two kinds of discourse, equal in status and which complement one another? Or does it imply a limping kind of discourse and a prop? I am reminded of the line from *Henry V*: 'Piece out our imperfections with your thoughts . . .'.[3] Is the fiction—novel or story—imperfect? Does it need piecing out with the thoughtful essay? Clearly, that way of understanding the relationship does no service to the literary text. For that reason, I have tried, in what follows, to be especially circumspect in the use which is made of cross-referencing within the body of Sartre's own work.

Titles and the inferences we draw from them

Titles of novels function like names of people: they identify and carry an implication of uniqueness. They may also, in varying degrees, signify. 'L'Enfance d'un chef', I would argue, is an example of a title that signifies. I shall try to make my point via a consideration of novel titles generally (and here I use the word *novel* loosely, to designate works of fiction, in prose, of whatever length).

Are the titles of novels eloquent? Is there a general rule? If I were to formulate a rule, it would be something like: Any novel which we have read and enjoyed, we perceive as having an eloquent title. Example: *La Nausée*. The facts are well known. *La Nausée*, which was written and rewritten over a period of years, was first referred to as 'un factum sur la contingence'. Then it was called *Melancholia*—a reference to the Dürer etching. Then it was called *Les Aventures extraordinaires d'Antoine Roquentin* and Sartre had a scheme whereby it would be published with a wrapper which said: 'Il n'y a pas d'aventures'. Then, finally, when it was with the Gallimard publishing house, Gaston Gallimard proposed that it be called *La Nausée* and Sartre accepted. Anyone who rehearses these facts does so in order to arrive, sooner or later, at the thought: Great title! But anyone who rehearses the facts and makes the judgement will first have read the book.

Second example: 'La Pierre qui pousse'. Was Camus's story ever called anything else? I do not know, but it seems to me that this is a good title, an eloquent title. It is interesting in the way that a conundrum is interesting: How come the stone grows? It is pertinent in that it focuses on a central detail of the story: the local legend of a stone with miraculous properties. And it is allusive; it points on the one hand to a Christian myth, and on the other to a humanist myth of Camus's own devising; on the one hand, Peter: 'Thou art Peter, and upon this rock I will build my church',[4] and on the other (*pierre qui pousse, pierre qu'on poussse*), Sisyphus: 'Il faut imaginer Sisyphe heureux'.[5] So the title is eloquent, but once again, eloquent in retrospect.

Is the converse also true? What would one think of a rule which said: No title of a novel which one has *not* read is ever eloquent? One response might be to say that we have no view: there are too many novels that we have not read. Another might be to concur on the grounds that titles take their meanings from books, not books from titles. The fact remains, however, that we are constantly entertaining titles in advance of reading the books to which they belong. Therefore it is reasonable to ask whether the meaning of a title is always, by definition, deferred, or whether in some cases—perhaps in every case to a greater or less extent—it might not be immediately construed.

Consider the five stories of *Le Mur*: what meanings can be wrung from their titles on the supposition that we have not read them?

'**Le Mur**'. Which wall? *Mur des fédérés, mur de Berlin, mur du son, raser le mur, sauter le mur, mettre au pied du mur, se cogner la tête contre le mur*: as soon as one looks in the direction of idiomatic language, one begins to see the possibilities. It is on the idiomatic and associative use of language that Sartre builds when he takes the title of the first story, 'Le Mur', and extends it metaphorically to the whole group. The 'prière d'insérer' which accompanied the first press copies of the book says the following:

> Personne ne peut regarder en face l'Existence. Voici cinq petites déroutes—tragiques ou comiques—devant elle . . . Toutes ces fuites sont arrêtées par un Mur; fuir l'Existence, c'est encore exister. L'Existence est un plein que l'homme ne peut quitter.[6]

Capitals underscore the point. *Wall* is a figure for the impossible. *Wall* is frustration: 'O wicked wall! through whom I see no bliss . . .'

'**La Chambre**'. Roomy titles come with qualifiers, as a rule—*Room with a View, A Room of One's Own*—; this one is plain to a fault. It is true that *chambre*, 'bedroom', is particular where 'room' is general, but not much can be built on the literal sense. Could it be a metaphor? Metaphor for claustration? I am cheating, of course, pretending that my attention had never been called to the sequence of titles: 'La Chambre', *Huis clos, Les Séquestrés d'Altona*, and the thematic continuities which it might imply. If I play the game properly, I should want to claim that 'La Chambre', as a title, is relatively mute.

'**Erostrate**'. A title which is much more difficult to interpret if we are not classicists and very old. It tells us perhaps about the *public virtuel* of the 1930s. But if, at that time, a certain kind of culture could be taken for granted, why did Sartre have recourse to *mise en abyme* in order to justify his title? In the course of the story, the terrorist hero, Paul Hilbert, talks with friends about Lindbergh who has just flown the Atlantic (1927). The friends are enthusiastic, Hilbert not: 'Lindbergh est un héros blanc. Il ne m'intéresse pas'. Hilbert reserves his admiration for a different kind of hero, *le héros noir*. His friends object:

'Alors, ce serait un détraqué.'

Mais Massé, qui avait des lettres, intervint à ce moment: 'Je le connais votre type,' me dit-il. 'Il s'appelle Erostrate. Il voulait devenir illustre et il n'a rien trouvé de mieux que de brûler le temple d'Ephèse, une des sept merveilles du monde.'[7]

Massé, qui avait des lettres . . .[8] Which of us could claim as much? So here is another uncommunicative title.

'Intimité'. We get a sense, but do we get the right sense? The term has a currency in French which it does not have in English. Noun and adjective describe those areas of life which are withdrawn from public view: *dans l'intimité de la conscience, intimité conjugale, la vie itime, privée*. English usage is more restricted. It does, however, include the connotation: 'Intimacy, *euphemism* for illicit sexual intercourse' (*Shorter Oxford English Dictionary*). Panther Books, in the 1960s, marketed a paperback edition of *Le Mur* in which the stories, translated by Lloyd Alexander, were printed in a different order, with 'Intimacy' being placed first and the title of the volume changed accordingly. Was Sartre consulted? Did he approve? One should not dismiss the possibility. Presenting *Le Mur* in the Pléiade edition, Michel Rybalka reminds us that 'le volume a obtenu d'emblée une réputation de scandale . . . Les principaux reproches adressés au recueil ont été ceux d'obscénité, de "goût de l'horrible" et même de pornographie'.[9]

'L'Enfance d'un chef'. If one wanted to argue that titles can be prospectively eloquent, this is the one to work with, not 'Intimité'. Not only does it identify a subject-matter, it tells us that an approach to the text has to be made via biography and our sense of the models which obtain in that particular genre. *Childhood of a Leader*: a human type and a narrative paradigm which explores the relationship between origins and achievement. The function of the title is to appeal to a cultural norm which the story then subverts.

A human type

Bear in mind that *chef* in French designates not only one who leads (*personne qui est à la tête, qui dirige, commande, gouverne*) but one who is fitted, by character and deportment, to perform the role of leader (*personne qui sait se faire obéir*—example: *un tempérament de chef*).

Sartre's novella focuses on this latter, extended sense of the word. It is largely taken up with questions of fitness: Does Lucien display, is he able to discover in himself, *un tempérament de chef*? Bear in mind, too, that *chef* figures as a title or descriptor of office in a series of expressions of the kind: *le chef de l'Etat, chef de cabinet, chef d'entreprise.* Such expressions have their military equivalents: *chef d'état-major, chef de bataillon,* etc. Summarizing, one can say that the word carries notions of status and responsibility and that it has its primary applications in the field of civil and/or military government.[10]

Biography: model and parody

Childhood of a Leader . . . A certain kind of biography sets out to show by what route the public man or woman has become what he or she is or, as it may be, was. What were the origins, the influences, the decisive moments? What combination of talent, ambition and circumstance made for the subsequent achievement? It is likely that the narrative will present itself, in greater or less degree, as an explanation. It is likely, too, that the narrative will conform to one or other of two types: either it will insist on the disadvantages that have to be overcome before greatness is achieved, or it will insist on the powers, the qualities of heart and mind, that mark the individual out for greatness. Great despite or great because of: either way, the biographical subject is celebrated.[11] An example of the first type would be Joan of Arc; of the second type, Napoleon. Both names are invoked in 'L'Enfance d'un chef'—for satiric or comic purposes, as we shall see.

Biographers can, of course, fiddle with the paradigms. Make much of the voices and what one sees in the life of St Joan is God's triumph, not the triumph of a girl. Make much of the Corsican origins of Napoleon and what one sees is either a triumph of revolutionary principle or a scandal and an enigma. Chateaubriand took the latter view: 'Absurde en administration, criminel en politique, qu'avait-il donc pour séduire les Français, cet étranger?'[12]

I offer these remarks on biography not for their own sake but in order to lay a foundation for the claim that 'L'Enfance d'un chef' is a variant on a familiar biographical model: a comic variant, a parody. We *place* the title. And having placed the title, we notice—ought perhaps to notice—that neither does it modify nor is it modified by a proper name. Not 'De Gaulle: l'enfance d'un chef', not 'Mitterrand: l'enfance d'un chef', just 'L'Enfance d'un chef'. The status of the biographical subject is affirmed but, in the absence of a famous name, it is not corroborated. As a result, the story which we are about to read is open-ended. The retrospective illusion does not obtain.

What do I mean by 'retrospective illusion'? The idea is brilliantly formulated in *Les Mots*. When the great man dies, says Sartre, we take possession of his life. We can read it from front to back or back to front. We can pick it up in the middle, travel upstream or down, whichever: 'c'est que l'ordre chronologique a sauté'.[13] By way of illustration, Sartre imagines a moment in the life of Robespierre. It is 1789: Robespierre is an obscure provincial lawyer but our under-standing of that fact is vitiated by a knowledge of what lies ahead—Jacobin dictatorship and the manner of his death:

> Dans les salons d'Arras, un jeune avocat froid et minaudier porte sa tête sous son bras parce qu'il est feu Robespierre, cette tête dégoutte de sang mais ne tâche pas le tapis; pas un des convives ne la remarque et nous ne voyons qu'elle; il s'en faut de cinq ans qu'elle ait roulé dans le panier et pourtant la voilà, coupée, qui dit des madrigaux malgré sa mâchoire qui pend.[14]

There is a comic verve here which is irresistible. But Lucien is not a historical figure and 'L'Enfance d'un chef' is not a true biography. When, therefore, Sartre says of Lucien, 'ce personnage, au fond, ne *prend* pas comme un personnage de roman; on ne se dit pas: Qu'est-ce qui va lui arriver?', I am not convinced. What is there to inhibit a reader's curiosity? The title creates certain expectations. Whether or not the expectations are fulfilled, only a reading of the story will tell.[15]

The initial question

Geneviève Idt suggests that, if one wants to understand the logical structure of a story, one should ask: What is the question which is posed at the beginning and how is it answered at the end? As a way of opening up a text, it works reasonably well. 'Lucien sera-t-il un chef?': here is the question. 'Lucien est un chef parmi les Français': here (perhaps) is the answer.[16] The original question is posed not once but repeatedly throughout the narrative. It arises within the framework of the father-son relationship:

> Une fois, au retour de la promenade, papa prit Lucien sur ses genoux et lui expliqua ce que c'était qu'un chef. (. . .) 'Est-ce que je deviendrai aussi un chef?' demanda Lucien. 'Mais bien sûr, mon bonhomme, c'est pour cela que je t'ai fait.' 'Et à qui est-ce que je commanderai?' 'Eh bien, quand je serai mort, tu seras le patron de mon usine et tu commanderas à mes ouvriers.'[17]

The child is in the world for a purpose: to become a leader is his destiny. There are the boots. Is he big enough to fill them? What follows is a story about status—the difference between *n'importe qui* and *quelqu'un*—and a story about character, about moral qualities and how they are revealed in action.[18]

Roman d'apprentissage

The story has momentum. It drives forward, or at any rate it seems to do so: childhood, adolescence, the threshold of maturity. Sartre's next work of fiction will be called *L'Age de raison*. It has a different hero, but the story of Mathieu Delarue picks up at roughly the point where Lucien's story ends. In this respect, it has been suggested, the novel constitutes a kind of sequel to the novella. Youth, followed by maturity: *l'adolescent et l'homme fait*.

In its forward momentum, the novella approximates to the novel of education, *roman d'apprentissage, Bildungsroman*. The novel of education, standard model, displays a process whereby wisdom is distilled from experience. Travels and travail—and a residue in the shape of improved powers of survival and maybe a nugget of truth, a golden rule: 'Il faut cultiver son jardin'; 'A nous deux maintenant!'; 'L'homme se corrompt partout'; 'C'est là ce que nous avons eu de meilleur!'; 'Il faut suivre sa pente, pourvu que ce soit en montant'; 'Mon fils sera crémier'.[19] Terse statements which purport to convey the lessons of a lifetime. The story of Lucien exhibits this characteristic feature of the novel of education. But the revelation, in his case, is accompanied by a gesture, and the description of the gesture marks the revelation as false even before it is put into words:

> Il éleva doucement, précautionneusement sa main jusqu'à son
> front, comme un cierge allumé, (. . .) et les mots vinrent
> d'eux-mêmes, il murmura: 'J'AI DES DROITS!' (p. 243)

The adverbs (excessive), the simile (grotesque), the capitals (wilfully crude): so many features casting doubt on the quality of the insight which has been achieved.

Heroes in novels of education are abused—by life, by the author —and as a consequence, late in the day, they are disabused. Sartre's hero, despite appearances to the contrary, is neither abused nor disabused.[20] Lucien changes but he does not progress. He makes mistakes and claims that he learns from his mistakes. In fact, he learns nothing. What Sartre has done is to invoke the conventions of the novel of education and direct them against his hero. But there is a refinement which we ought to notice. If Sartre exploits the novel of education for satiric purposes, it is because he is logically constrained to do so. Novels of education are grounded in the belief that there is a wisdom born of experience. Sartre pours scorn on such a notion. In *La Nausée*, in the figure of Dr Rogé, he draws a savage portrait of the man of the world, the man who has seen everything and who knows it all:

> Les belles rides; il les a toutes . . . Voilà un homme qui a de la
> chance: du plus loin qu'on le voit, on se dit qu'il a dû souffrir et
> que c'est quelqu'un qui a vécu. Il mérite son visage, d'ailleurs,
> car il ne s'est pas un instant mépris sur la façon de retenir et
> d'utiliser son passé: il l'a empaillé, tout simplement, il en a fait
> de l'expérience à l'usage des femmes et des jeunes gens.[21]

Retenir et utiliser son passé: how else would one describe the skills of the apprentice hero? It follows that Lucien's failure lies not so much in a falling short, relative to the traditional hero of the novel of education, as in a coming close. He is a deluded apprentice, an undeserving survivor. Then again, perhaps (when you boil it down) that is what the novel of education amounts to: a celebration of the art of survival. 'Ils ont essayé de me détraquer mais ils ne m'ont pas eu' (p. 208).

Introspection

Idt postulates, at the beginning of this story, a question of the kind: 'Lucien sera-t-il un chef?'[22] The same question is posed explicitly by Lucien: 'Est-ce que je deviendrai aussi un chef?' (pp. 164–5). There is, however, another question which runs very strongly in the text. Posed at a later point in the narrative, it is logically prior to any question about leadership. That question is: 'Qui suis-je?' Lucien, a pupil at the Lycée Condorcet by this time, sits about on a Sunday, self-preoccupied and trying to decide whether or not he is conceited: 'Est-ce que je me gobe?' Suddenly, something clicks; he wakes up: 'A la place de cette stupeur qui lui était si douce . . . , il y avait maintenant une petite perplexité très réveillée qui se demandait: "Qui suis-je?"' (p. 175). The formula is immediately repeated and then, in the next paragraph, two questions are offered in parallel. First question: 'Mais qu'est-ce que je vais devenir?' Second question: 'Qu'est-ce que je suis, *moi*?' *Devenir . . . être*: the story is dynamic in the extent to which it is organized round the first question and the first verb, static in the extent to which it is organized around the second question and the second verb.

'Qui suis-je?' The question has a pedigree: an ethical pedigree (Rousseau, Montaigne, Socrates) and an epistemological pedigree (Descartes). *Connais-toi toi-même . . . Je pense donc je suis . . .*: Lucien wrestles with the moral imperative and with the Cartesian first principle. He wrestles, and from a sense that introspection leads nowhere, he grows weary. You look for *caractère* and what you find is *comédie*: '"Mais moi aussi je suis un comédien," dit-il en battant des paupières' (p. 197). You look for essence and what you find is fluidity: *nuage capricieux et fugace; brume blanche qui s'effiloche; transparence gélatineuse qui tremblote sur la banquette d'un café.* What is true of Lucien is true, Sartre would have us believe, of all of us.

I say that introspection leads nowhere. That is to overstate the case. Introspection allows Lucien to approach the truth. There is even a moment when, like Sartre, he thinks about writing a *Traité du Néant*. But then he turns away: 'Je suis trop scrupuleux, pensa-t-il, je m'analyse trop' (p. 212). Better men than Lucien have turned away: 'Qu'un autre vous réponde, ô sages de la terre!/Laissez-moi mon erreur . . .'.[23]

Le regard d'autrui

> 'Je suis adorable dans mon petit costume d'ange.' Mme Portier
> avait dit à mamam: 'Votre petit garçon est gentil à croquer. Il
> est adorable dans son petit costume d'ange.' (p. 151)

The opening sentences of the novella are studiously vacuous. They
nevertheless contrive to express the idea that identity might be a
function not of self but of others. Beauty in the eye of the beholder!
But not just beauty, size: 'Lucien Fleurier est une grande asperche'
(p. 167). It is typical of the 1930s Sartre to imply that, when it comes
to truth, the toilet door has more to offer than Montaigne or
Descartes. It is not of course true that Lucien is a vegetable (though
he may be a bean-pole). What is true is that he has a body and that
he is perceived by others as tall. So the idea of facticity presents itself;
the idea that the Self as object is no less real than the Self as subject.
So too the idea that our sense of identity, of who or what we are,
is mediated by other people—Barataud: *une punaise*; Fleurier: *une
asperche*. A rose by any other name . . . ? Not a bit of it. Change the
name and you change the nature of the beast: *type énorme, chic type,
grand garçon raisonnable, as des as*. Or alternatively: *bourgeois, comédien,
pédéraste, mufle*.

The two preoccupations, introspection and the look which defines,
converge in the final scene, when Lucien takes stock:

> 'Première maxime, se dit Lucien, ne pas chercher à voir en soi;
> il n'y a pas d'erreur plus dangereuse.' Le vrai Lucien—il le savait
> à présent—, il fallait le chercher dans les yeux des autres . . .
> (p. 242)

The first maxim is absurd, the second a half-truth.

Contingency

The grotesque metaphor of the asparagus spear is introduced in order
to insist: (1) on the reality of the bodily self; (2) on the defining role
of others. Sartre keeps the metaphor in play, however, and builds it
into an eloquent passage in which the idea of contingency is conveyed.
It is the summer vacation. Lucien is back home in Férolles. He goes
for a walk[24] and as he walks, he thinks positive thoughts: 'I've grown

up', 'I'll show them!' Then his mood changes. He feels lonely and anxious. He tries to imagine himself in the company of friends but it doesn't work:

> ils étaient loin, très loin et il lui semblait que le vrai Lucien était perdu, il n'y avait qu'une larve blanche et perplexe. 'Qu'est-ce que je suis?' Des kilomètres et des kilomètres de lande, un sol plat et gercé, sans herbes, sans odeurs et puis, tout d'un coup, sortant droite de cette croûte grise, l'asperge, tellement insolite qu'il n'y avait même pas d'ombre derrière elle. (p. 212)

No question of being there for a purpose: *fait pour devenir chef, fait pour commander*. Just an overwhelming sense of being there—figure in a landscape, *larve blanche*, [*présence*] *insolite, asperge*.[25] Implicit in the description is the thought which is formulated two pages later: 'Son existence était un scandale' (p. 214).

Recapitulation

Stories have a chronological structure and they have a logical structure. The logical structure is best understood in terms of an enigma posed at the beginning and solved by the end. In the present case, Idt suggests, an appropriate formula for the enigma might be: 'Lucien sera-t-il un chef?' And for the resolution: '[Lucien est] un chef parmi les Français'. If, however, the enigma were to be formulated as the question: 'Qui suis-je?', then the answer would come in several parts. One can assemble the parts from the ideas reviewed above. They are: that we are contingent beings; that we are not just minds but also bodies; that we have no fixed identity. These simple ideas can be amplified. Contingent, i.e. not, as Lucien's father would have it, *faits pour* [*quelque chose*], but either lacking in finality or pursuing ends which we have chosen and whose value exists as a function of our choice. Not just minds . . . , i.e. not describable in traditional idealist terms; not one thing but a mixture of things: subject and object, introvert and extrovert, autonomous self and mediated self (the terms deployed by Sartre in more technical writing are *pour-soi* and *en-soi*). No fixed identity, i.e. unstable in our thoughts and moods, victims of external circumstance, defined by our acts and therefore, like boxers, no better than our last fight; but also (again the notion of the hybrid) creatures who are capable of self-transcendence and of whom the only true description has the form of a paradox: 'un être qui est ce qu'il n'est pas et qui n'est pas ce qu'il est'.[26] Here is the answer to the question: 'Qui suis-je?' The paradox is not formulated in 'L'Enfance d'un chef'; it is unlikely that we shall formulate it of our own accord. But if we fail to recognize in Lucien any of the traits which might call forth and justify the paradox, we shall have missed much.

Un pré-engagement

In the preceding paragraph I have allowed my commentary to drift in the direction of a set of ideas which might figure in any account of Sartre's ontology. Could this have been avoided? I think not. Contat and Rybalka tell us that the conception of *L'Etre et le néant* dates from 1939 and the period of Sartre's military service in Alsace. This fact—essay following closely upon novella—is sufficient to explain a conceptual overlap. My purpose is, however, to write about 'L'Enfance d'un chef' for its own sake. I shall, therefore, devote the space remaining to ideas which, if they are not exclusive to the novella, nevertheless attain an importance there which they do not have in any other work by Sartre. The first of these, the concept of leadership, I have already discussed, but without exhausting the subject. The second, the concept of rights, appears late but forcefully in the novella.

What Sartre has to say on the subject of leadership and rights would be interesting at the best of times. It is, however, especially interesting for having been said at the worst of times. Consider the following brief chronology:

1938 March	The *Anschluss*: Austria becomes a province of Germany.
July	Sartre finishes writing 'L'Enfance d'un chef'.
30 September	Munich: the triumph of appeasement. Chamberlain proclaims his belief in 'peace in our time'.
1939 January	Volume publication of *Le Mur*.
February	Recognition by France of Franco's government.
March	Germany occupies all of Czechoslovakia.

23 August	The Nazi-Soviet pact: Russia promises neutrality in the event of war.
1 September	Germany invades Poland.
2 September	General mobilization. Sartre is conscripted into the Army.
3 September	The ultimatum is delivered. Hitler's government makes no reply. Britain and France declare war.
1940 April	*Le Mur* wins the 'Prix du roman populiste'.
10 May	Germany invades Holland and Belgium. Churchill becomes Prime Minister.
14 May	The French front is broken on the Meuse.
14 June	The Germans enter Paris.
16 June	The Third Republic votes itself out of existence. Pétain assumes power.
18 June	De Gaulle broadcasts from London.

The effect of juxtaposing literary and world events might be to imply the small significance of Sartre's novella. That is not my intention; nor is it my intention to attack Sartre on the grounds of irresponsibility. It is a commonplace that his practice in the 1930s was very different from the theory and practice which he developed in the post-war years. If, however, one wants to make a case for a kind of *pré-engagement*, a stirring of interest before history invades the private space, then it is to 'L'Enfance d'un chef' that one will appeal.[27] The image of leadership reflects negatively on generals in uniform 'ou autres chefs d'État moustachus'.[28] The negative depiction of the anti-semite alerts the reader to the thin line which separates prejudice from violence:

> L'antisémitisme de Lucien était d'une autre sorte: impitoyable et pur, il pointait hors de lui comme une lame d'acier, menaçant d'autres poitrines. (p. 241)

Pointait . . . comme une lame d'acier: the hybrid figure, metaphor anticipating simile, works not only in terms of Sartrean catagories—permeable/impermeable, viscous/hard—but in terms of the history of the period. The import of the work is, then, broadly anti-fascist.

Cohen-Solal argues that, when Sartre's literary career takes off in the spring of 1937 and when, a few months later, he enjoys further success (the move from provincial lycée to the Lycée Pasteur in Neuilly), it has the effect of integrating him into the community. Without making him an establishment figure, it brings to an end the sort of marginalization which is reflected in *Les Aventures extraordinaires d'Antoine Roquentin*: 'Pour l'heure, accueilli, reçu, légalisé, Sartre regarde le monde, mais en acteur désormais . . .'[29] If that is so and if 'L'Enfance d'un chef' is symptomatic of a greater involvement, the derisive, contemptuous way in which notions of leadership and rights are handled in the novella is all the more striking.

Leadership

Lucien is not a leader; the bourgeoisie has no God-given right to rule. Beyond that, what is Sartre telling us? Is he saying that a society of free men would have no use for leaders? That all leaders are megalomaniacs, ordinary folk who mistake themselves for somebody else?[30] That powers of leadership have their source in the credulity and fear of those who are led?[31] Or is he saying that, inasmuch as we cannot explain it either by destiny (a myth) or by character (an alternative form of the same myth), the concept of leadership is strictly unintelligible? I think that he is saying all of those things, saying them in a spirit of provocation and out of a belief in the salutary virtues of disrespect.[32] Readers will react according to their temperament and convictions. For my part, of the various propositions which I attribute to Sartre, I judge the last to be the most interesting.

As I reflect on the possibility that leadership is not a quality but at best a set of institutional arrangements, I find myself turning to a work of fiction written by a near contemporary of Sartre's, Drieu la Rochelle.[33] In 1934, Drieu published, also with Gallimard, a volume of stories very similar in length and type to the ones gathered in *Le Mur*. Six stories, with the title of the first, 'La Comédie de Charleroi', doubling as the title of the volume. In that first story—a long short story or novella (84 pp.)—a young man revisits the battlefield where he has fought in the early weeks of the Great War. (The dates of narrative present and past are given precisely: 2 July 1919, 24 August 1914.) He relives the battle in memory and, as the narrative unfolds, we witness a process whereby a youth not unlike Lucien—'mince bourgeois intellectuel'—transforms himself into a hero. The process is captured in the fragments of text assembled below.[34]

> J'entrais dans le vif de la guerre, dans le vif de la société, la question du commandement.
> Nous étions là trente hommes dans un creux. Qui commandait? Il y en avait qui avaient des galons, d'autres qui n'en avaient pas. Des professionnels et des civils. Il y avait ce lieutenant, un bourgeois, un civil. Il entrevoyait ce qu'il fallait faire, mais il aimait mieux ne pas le voir au point de devoir le faire. Et pour le sergent, le fait qu'il ne voyait rien, c'était sa pauvre force. Or, moi tout de suite je voyais clair—je savais—et je bouillonnais. (p. 47)

> 'Il faut que quelqu'un . . . On a besoin de quelqu'un. Il faut que quelqu'un se lève le premier, il faut que quelqu'un fasse que la chose soit. Quelqu'un. Celui-là là-bas qui se lève à demi? Non, il se recogne. Alors qui? Quelqu'un, voyons. Pas moi, toi ou lui. Moi, pauvre soldat, pourquoi moi?'
> J'écoutais d'abord inconscient la rumeur. Et puis soudain. Ah mais, il y a moi. Après tout, il y a moi. (p. 64)

> Or, maintenant dans cette plaine je m'ébrouais. Toutes mes forces surgissaient à l'espoir. Et cet espoir, c'était que l'événement allait faire justice de la vieille hiérarchie imbécile, formée dans la quiétude des jours. Dieu allait reconnaître les siens; cette plaine c'était le champ du jugement. La guerre m'intéressait parce que j'allais me faire capitaine, colonel—bien mieux que cela, chef. (p. 67)

> Tout d'un coup, je me connaissais, je connaissais ma vie. C'était donc moi, ce fort, ce libre, ce héros. C'était donc ma vie, cet ébat qui n'allait plus s'arrêter jamais. (p. 67)

> J'étais un chef. Je voulais m'emparer de tous ces hommes autour de moi, m'en accroître, les accroître par moi et nous lancer tous en bloc, moi en pointe, à travers l'univers. Tout dépendait de moi, toute cette bataille—et les batailles de demain, les révolutions de demain—pesait sur moi, me sollicitait, me suppliait, cherchait sa résolution en moi. Tout dépendait de moi. Il me suffisait de vouloir et tout se précipitait en un point, tout se réalisait, tout se signifiait.

Il me suffisait de me lever, de me lever sur le champ de bataille—et tous ces mouvements et ces plissements apercevaient leur sommet; tout ce séisme humain, voyant tracée sa ligne de faîte, y bondissait.

Je tenais dans mes mains la victoire et la liberté. La liberté. L'homme est libre, l'homme peut ce qu'il veut. L'homme est une partie du monde, et chaque partie du monde peut, à un moment de paroxysme, à un moment d'éternité, réaliser en elle tout le possible. La victoire.

La victoire des hommes. Contre quoi? Contre rien; au-delà de tout. Contre la nature? Il ne s'agit pas de vaincre la nature, ni même de la surmonter, mais de la pousser à son maximum puisque la puissance est en nous. Il ne s'agit pas de vaincre la peur par le courage—mais de fondre la peur dans le courage et le courage dans la peur, et de s'élancer à l'extrême point de l'élancement. (p. 68)

There is so much here that is of interest from the point of view of a comparison with Sartre. The centrality of the term *chef*. The sequence: 'On a besoin de quelqu'un. (. . .) Ah mais, il y a moi. (. . .) J'étais un chef.' The assertion that leadership—*la question du commandement*—is at the heart of military and civil society. The shift of meaning whereby *chef* is dissociated from formal expressions of rank and hierarchy—*vieille hiérarchie imbécile*—and presented instead in terms of self-knowledge: 'Tout à coup, je me connaissais . . .', and self-affirmation: 'C'était donc moi, ce fort, ce libre, ce héros.' The suggestion that it is within the power of any man to accede to the status of leader, a pure expression of liberty: 'Tout dépendait de moi. (. . .) Il me suffisait de me lever . . .' Finally, the suggestion that what are traditionally known as acts of valour do not in fact originate in a moral quality but in something much more obscure: instinct or impulse, a kind of *élan vital*.

Had Sartre read 'La Comédie de Charleroi'? There is, to my knowledge, no explicit testimony to that effect. But Simone de Beauvoir, describing their style of life in 1932, says of herself and Sartre: 'nous lisions tout ce qui paraissait'.[35] Everything? If not literally everything, then certainly the products of the maison Gallimard. So is it possible that Sartre, having read 'La Comédie de Charleroi' when it first appeared, set out consciously to reply to Drieu? There are grounds for thinking not. For one thing, Sartre

directs his satire, in 'L'Enfance d'un chef', against a range of targets
—psychoanalysis, surrealism, Action française—by comparison with
which a story by Drieu is insignificant. For another, if Drieu had
been targeted, one would expect the text to announce that fact in
some unmistakable way. But if Sartre had no thought of Drieu when
he composed the novella, the points of convergence are all the more
remarkable. They lose none of their interest when we consider the
subsequent history of the two authors.[36]

Rights

'J'AI DES DROITS!'—that is the wisdom which Lucien distils from
experience, the self-evident 'truth' which fills his mind at the end of
the journey. The reader is bound to ask: What kind of rights are
founded in the hurts done to the passer-by and the fellow guest?
When Lucien and his chums beat up the *petit bonhomme olivâtre*
whom they meet in the rue Saint-André-des-Arts, they commit what,
in any society ruled by law, is a crime. Their actions constitute an
abuse of freedom; they could, at a pinch, be described as an expression
of freedom, but never as a right. What, therefore, Lucien means by
his statement 'J'ai des droits!' is that he personally is above the law,
or that he is a member of a class which, because it makes the law,
can also make exceptions to the law, or that the protection afforded
by the law is so capricious and uncertain as to render meaningless
the whole notion of the rule of law.[37]

Remember the context in which the episode occurs. Lucien, in this
last stage of the maturing process, has been introduced to the thought
of Maurice Barrès. In Barrès, he has found both the explanation of
his malaise—'je suis un déraciné'—and the remedy: 'la terre et
les morts'. *La terre et les morts*: Barrès in a nutshell! A deterministic
theory of the human being whereby moral identity is bound up with
the history of a place and a community, and moral well-being requires
that we behave in conformity with that fact. Sartre announces this
latest enthusiasm of Lucien in discreetly ironic terms: 'voilà donc que,
de nouveau, on lui offrit un caractère et un destin' (p. 225). *De
nouveau*: not for the first time; *offrir*: a quick fix, a solution handed
to him on a plate. Barrès, as Susan Suleiman remarks, 'is simply the
last in a long line of mediators, all of whom function as both authors
and authorities for Lucien'.[38]

Barrès celebrates regional identity: the *déracinés* of his novel hail from Nancy and the ancient dukedom of Lorraine. Sartre mimics this feature of Barrèsian writing—Lucien has his roots in Férolles and 'le doux paysage de l'Ile de France'—but he makes no sustained attempt to construct a regional identity for his hero. His satiric verve focuses on France, not on the Ile de France. The *caractère* and *destin* of Lucien—*faux caractère, faux destin*—are discovered in the cultural traditions of the nation-state, in the Catholic tradition on the one hand— 'c'est moi la cathédrale'—and the Republican tradition on the other—'J'AI DES DROITS!' (p. 243). Cathedrals and Rights: medieval France and modern France. The trouble is that both traditions have decayed. What remains of the one is visceral anti-semitism. What remains of the other is an empty shibboleth.

Sartre's indictment of Lucien is an indictment of the Third Republic. France, *pays des droits de l'homme*, is a myth. The historical reality of the inter-war years is that of a régime committed to the defence of power and privilege. But if that is true, to what does Sartre appeal when he conveys so powerfully the sense that Lucien's treatment of the Jew is wrong? Is it perhaps to some ideal thing— 'Quelque chose dans le genre des triangles et des cercles; c'était si parfait que ça n'existait pas . . .' (p. 243)—the same notion of Universal Rights as was appealed to by those who drafted, in the summer of 1789, the *Déclaration des droits de l'homme et du citoyen*?[39]

Lucien, at the end of the story, goes off to grow a moustache—a useless gesture and comic proof of the wonderful pseudo-Cartesian dictum: *Je ne pense pas donc je suis une moustache*, which waits like an uncovered manhole in one of Roquentin's monologues in *La Nausée*.[40]

2

Marcel Aymé
'La Carte'

Christopher Lloyd

When Marcel Aymé (1902–67) first published his story 'La Carte' in the weekly newspaper *La Gerbe* in 2 April 1942 and then eighteen months later in the collection of ten stories entitled *Le Passe-Muraille* (Gallimard, 1943), his reputation as a novelist and storyteller who combined popular appeal with literary merit was already well established. His fourteenth novel, *La Vouivre*, was also to be serialized in *La Gerbe* from 22 July to 9 December 1943, while *Le Passe-Muraille* was his fourth collection of stories; nine were to appear altogether, including two posthumous collections, comprising about one hundred tales.

Although the selection of one short text for study from such a large choice of material may seem somewhat arbitrary, in fact 'La Carte' is of considerable interest, both inherently, in terms of narrative form and content, and because it is highly typical of Aymé's production as a story-writer. From a purely quantitative point of view, at slightly less than 6,000 words in length (or twenty-three pages in the Livre de poche edition),[1] the story manifestly fulfils the generic requirement of brevity and is also closest to the average length of the ten stories in *Le Passe-Muraille* (they range from fourteen pages to forty-four, with the average being twenty-four). More significantly, 'La Carte' is also highly entertaining and demonstrates Aymé's mastery of the short form both to amuse and instruct. While the plot depends initially on an imaginative conceit, it also sheds considerable light on living conditions in France during the German Occupation, as seen by an inside observer. And finally, the tale raises important questions concerning the responsibility of the writer as an observer, moralist and participant in moments of social and historical crisis.

'La Carte' appeared at a bleak moment in French history, the middle year of the Second World War. A fortnight after it features in *La Gerbe*, the collaborationist Premier Laval returned to power as head of the Vichy government, on 18 April 1942; the whole of France was to be occupied from 11 November 1942, which effectively removed any remaining illusions about the country's economic, political and military independence from the occupying forces. While most of the tales in *Le Passe-Muraille* make no direct reference to such events, three stories do in fact deal specifically with the privations caused by the Occupation: these are 'La Carte', 'Le Décret' and 'En attendant'. All three stories focus on the notion of time, unsurprisingly no doubt, when the war and the queues it brought for essential goods seemed equally interminable. 'En attendant', for example, refers to 'la guerre de 1939–1972' (p. 225) and describes how people standing in a queue discover that one of their number has expired. But whereas 'En attendant' remains within the confines of a more stylized realism, 'La Carte' and 'Le Décret' use temporal manipulation of a more overtly fantastic variety for allegorical and satirical purposes.

'La Carte' is a first-person narrative, in the form of a diary written by an aspiring writer called Jules Flegmon, which covers the period from 10 February to 6 July in an unspecified year. This journal recounts how the wartime government decrees that time will be rationed, so that unproductive consumers will be entitled only to fifteen days' existence or less each month. The decree is put into practice, but market forces rapidly distort its intended effects, producing flagrant abuses, and the venture is abandoned. As this summary suggests, the story combines comic fantasy with a veiled critique of the inequity (and iniquity) of rationing, government interference, social privilege and individual egotism. Presumably it passed German censorship and the editorial control of *La Gerbe* and Gallimard because it was perceived as an entertainment. Making light of shortages, or deriding those who exploited them, was, in fact, not uncommon during the Occupation, as popular songs like Georgius's 'Elle a un stock' (Rawson/Georgius, 1941) and Fernandel's 'Les Jours sans' (Dervaux/Pelsenaire, 1942) amusingly demonstrate. Rationing cards were introduced in France from 1940 and were to remain in force for ever a decade. The card in Aymé's story rations not commodities, but life itself; the tickets it contains are each worth twenty-four hours' existence. Hence, perhaps, the narrator's sentimental reaction to their colour, 'd'un bleu très tendre, couleur de pervenche, et si doux que les larmes m'en sont venues aux yeux' (p. 67).

Aymé's use of the fantastic thus acts as a channel and a diversion for social comment: while allowing him to draw attention to injustices tolerated by the Occupation authorities, at the same time the displacement of reality to an imagined, parallel universe effectively attenuates the satirical impact of the tale. Out of the hundred or so stories which he produced during his career, about fifty contain some element of the fantastic or marvellous, whether expressed as children's fables, contemporary fairy tales, philosophical allegories or social satire. Indeed, the fantastic arguably is the defining feature of Aymé's work as a storyteller, and therefore merits closer initial attention. The critic J.-L. Dumont notes that 'le merveilleux ayméen, qu'il soit fantastique ou féerique, s'achemine toujours vers le rire'.[2] In other words, the writer is more interested in using humour to comment on the vagaries of human nature and society than in mere fantasy. The fantastic does not mark a threshold leading to unknown fears or horrors (as it does in the work of certain nineteenth-century story-tellers like Poe or Maupassant), but rather, to quote another commentator, 'naît du réel et se nourrit de ses conflits avec le possible', in a dialectic 'du quotidien et du fantastique', operating in a sort of ludic fourth dimension.[3] The fantastic element in Aymé story is, typically, given in a matter-of-fact fashion and the plot then recounts how characters adapt to new circumstances in a world where normal laws and desires otherwise continue to operate.

Thus Aymé's fictional world in 'La Carte' and many other stories (such as the famous title-piece of Le Passe-Muraille) is a paradoxical mixture of fantastic elements with observed reality, where the initial modification of the real disrupts the conventional order of things in one specific area; from the resulting disorder, a new order is eventually established. As far as 'La Carte' is concerned, there is another, more troubling, paradox in the fact that this iconoclastic tale was first published in La Gerbe, an avowedly pro-Nazi, collaborationist organ. Unsurprisingly, Marcel Aymé's reputation suffered after the

Liberation of France in 1944 because he had, throughout the Occupation, voluntarily published articles, stories and novels in such collaborationist newspapers.

It is worth spelling out the context in which *La Gerbe* came into being. It was established by the writer Alphonse de Châteaubriant (1877–1951) from 11 July 1940. Châteaubriant's political sympathies (as well as his lack of judgement and pompous, bombastic manner) are demonstrated by his presentation of Hitler as 'le Messie conduisant son peuple vers la terre promise' in his book *La Gerbe des forces* (1937).[4] After the defeat of France in 1940, he headed a group called 'Collaboration', urging the building of a fascist Europe in the same dithyrambic tones; he left the country at the Liberation, spending the rest of his life in exile. While it is important to stress that Marcel Aymé never expressed any sympathy for Nazism or its more jejune advocates such as Châteaubriant (although he does seem to have regarded Marshal Pétain, the tituler head of the French state, as a legitimate figure of authority), nonetheless his willingness to publish supposedly innocent texts in *La Gerbe* or *Je suis partout* (where the stories 'Légende poldève' and 'Les Sabines' from *Le Passe-Muraille* also appeared) illustrates the same blinkered opportunism which a story like 'La Carte' ostensibly sets out to criticize. A glance at the issue of *La Gerbe* which contains 'La Carte' (on page five, Thursday 2 April 1942) reveals that this self-proclaimed 'Hebdomadaire de la volonté française' strikes on its other seven pages a fervently *maréchaliste* and anti-Allied note; in addition, there are direct attacks on the Jewish politicians Mendès, Zay and Blum (all three of whom were imprisoned by the Vichy régime, with Zay eventually being murdered by the Milice). Similarly, the issues of *Je suis partout* containing 'Légende poldève' and 'Les Sabines' (2 October 1942, and 8–22 January 1943) are unequivocally pro-German and contain explicit anti-Semitic denunciations of named individuals. However politically neutral they may themselves be, it is hard to avoid the conclusion that, in such a context, one obvious function of Aymé's stories was to serve as a sweetener to encourage readers to swallow some very nasty propaganda.

These generic and ideological issues supply a literary and historical context for the understanding of Aymé's story, although of course the tale is perfectly comprehensible to a reader who has none of this information. Our discussion of 'La Carte' will focus now on more obviously intrinsic elements relating to its structure, characters and themes, before returning to this wider perspective. Structurally, the story is most interesting in two ways. Firstly, in its use of the diary form to betray the foibles of the narrator without explicit con- demnation (his narrative reveals him, no doubt involuntarily, to be an egocentric and ambitious man-of-letters, even if his immediate acquaintances are equally self-seeking and egotistical). Secondly, with its regular enunciation of dates contrasted with the novel notion of chronological elasticity and instability, the story allows a ludic, or even metaphysical, exploration of time as both an existential and social phenomenon.

To see 'La Carte' simply as a comic allegory about the rationing of commodities in short supply is therefore unduly restricting. Perhaps because we are so used to being governed by time, we tend to forget that it is socially imposed on us and overlook its daily pressures (although a trip on an urban motorway in the rush hour or during a bank-holiday offers a painful reminder of how we submit with resigned conformity to the regular division of work and leisure). Moreover, such pressures are, in many cases, the relatively recent inventions of industrialized societies. For instance, until the coming of the railways in the nineteenth century, local time was set by the meridian and thus varied noticeably between communities even within a relatively small country like France. Conversely, the totali- tarian Third Reich switched France, after its humiliating defeat in 1940, on to Central European time (where it remains to this day); hence the word-plays favoured by some writers on the notion of 'La France à l'heure allemande'.[5] As M. J. Attali rightly observes, 'le calendrier est le premier instrument du pouvoir'.[6]

The main character of 'La Carte' is both a victim of and commentator on the chronological manipulations inflicted on the nation. One critic finds the personality of the diarist Flegmon to be simply odious.[7] Perhaps it would be more charitable to describe him as vain, self-seeking and at the same time ludicrous (his amorous and professional aspirations are unappealing and also frustrated). The protagonist's name invites us to regard him with a certain derision from the beginning. Alain Juillard offers a complex onomastic interpretation in a recent book on *Le Passe-Muraille*:

> Le nom de Jules Flegmon [. . .] est une sorte de mot-valise
> fort bien venu: il réunit le prénom Jules (allusion à deux grands
> <diaristes>, Jules de Goncourt et Jules Renard, la syllabe —*mon*
> faisant allusion à Ed*mon*d de Goncourt), le *flegme* d'un
> observateur désabusé de la comédie sociale, et la purulence du
> *phlegmon*.[8]

To this might be added that the name Jules can also mean a
chamberpot or a pimp, while the word 'phlegmon' means a pustulant
abscess in French and English. To be called Jules Flegmon is thus
as absurd a combination of names as those of other fictional characters
such as John Thomas, Lance Boyle or Ernest Everard.

Juillard's reference to diarists, however, may seem somewhat
tangential, though late nineteenth-century chroniclers like the
Goncourt brothers and Renard certainly mingle witty social observation with egocentric grumblings like the fictional Flegmon. It is worth
noting that *generically* the diary was a significant literary form during
the Occupation (famous examples being those kept by André Gide,
Jean Guéhenno and Ernst Jünger). Flegmon's private philosophizing
and account of public indignities are matched (in more serious vein),
for example, by Guéhenno when he recounts his experience of
queuing for an *Ausweis* from six o'clock in the morning on 11 August
1941 and of the 'commerce des tickets' which began from late 1940,
with the result that 'Les plus pauvres vendent aux plus riches leur
droit à vivre, à manger'.[9]

Flegmon's journal in 'La Carte' covers a period of twenty-one
weeks, from February to July of an unspecified year (presumably 1941
or 1942). Over these six months, there are forty-five entries, the
rhythm of which reflects Flegmon's changing attitude to and experience of time-rationing. Each month brings a surprising
development or reversal, which serves as a source of comedy and as
a sign of Aymé's inventiveness in his dialectic of the fantastic and
everyday. The first two entries (10 and 12 February) introduce
Flegmon's discovery of the restrictions, which are rumoured to involve
'la mise à mort des consommateurs improductifs: vieillards, retraités,
rentiers, chômeurs, et autres bouches inutiles' (p. 63). There are
obvious echoes in this sinister project of the Nazis' 'final solution',
the implementation of which was abetted by their vassal states;
exclusion of unwanted categories of citizens from public life and

political rights was the first stage in the process, not only in the Third Reich, but also under the Vichy régime, which introduced statutes severely curtailing the rights of Jews in October 1940 and June 1941. Flegmon, however, is at first unperturbed by the moral implications of the measures, which indeed he heartily approves of, sanctimoniously urging his seventy-year-old neighbour, Roquenton (who has a twenty-four-year-old wife), to adopt the appropriate spirit of self-sacrifice. Subsequently, Flegmon learns from the administrator Maleffroi that existence is to be rationed rather than suppressed. This notion seems rather less poetic when he discovers on 13 February that writers are considered 'inutiles' and to be allowed only fifteen days a month ('une infamie!' [p. 64]).

After this explanatory prologue, subsequent entries in the diary record a second phase (running from 16 February to 1 April) which reveals the practical consequences upon Jules Flegmon and other people of the time-rationing decree, which becomes effective from 1 March. Like old Roquenton (allowed six days) and Mme Roquenton (allowed fifteen), Flegmon discovers he has become a member of an underclass. Within this underclass there are marked gradations: if prostitutes are rationed to seven days, Jews are allowed only half a day per month of existence. Flegmon further discovers that he is ignored by those unaffected by the decree (thus he becomes 'un demi-vivant, un fantôme' to his concierge [p. 65]) and treated with callous brutality by those who operate it. For example, after queuing for ration tickets, he records 'Les nombreux agents commis au service d'ordre nous traitaient avec beaucoup de mépris, nous considérant évidemment comme un rebut d'humanité' (p. 67). (It is, again, worth recalling that the infamous mass round-up of thousands of Jews now known as 'La Rafle du Vel d'Hiv' was carried out by the Parisian police in July 1942, only three months after 'La Carte' first appeared.) Aymé teasingly shows several of his Montmartre associates to be present in the queue, including the writer Céline, whose notorious, paranoiac anti-Semitism is derided in his complaints that the whole business is a further sign of Jewish hegemony. The social scale of the phenomenon can be extrapolated from the figures given by the diarist: if 2,000 people are collecting their ration cards at the Mairie du XVIIIᵉ, then 40,000 Parisians could be affected and up to one million nationally.

The period between 24 February and 16 March shows Flegmon's

efforts to make the best of his situation. He gains an extra day's ration and intensifies the rhythm of his existence, indulging in extended writing, sex and eating. His complacent listing of the black-market produce which he greedily consumes, together with his account of 'consoling' Lucette Roquenton for the disappearance of her spouse, evidently make Flegmon's claim to be 'un parfait stoïcien' (p. 68) seem ridiculously hypocritical. Flegmon, who wishes to supplant the smug Perruque, also reveals that academicians are exempted from the decree. Finally, he describes at length the disappearance of Lucette and then his own (16 March).

The grim humour of the story is reinforced by the fact that the third phase begins on 1 April, when all those subject to time-rationing return to life, after a two-week hiatus in the case of the diarist. From this point, Aymé moves beyond the purely sociological aspects of his story to raise philosophical questions concerning our experience of time. The central issue is whether it is an absolute, constant constraint, or rather something experienced variably by different subjects. The problem has, of course, long since beguiled philosophers and scientists as much as artists. Aymé's contribution typically avoids academic ponderousness; he rarely felt the need to justify his imaginings by deferential or learned reference to supposed authorities. On the contrary, when Flegmon turns elsewhere for advice on his experience at the end of his journal, the 'célèbre philosophe Yves Mironneau' fobs him off with largely unintelligible subtleties (p. 85), the implication being that such rhapsodic theorizing is certainly of no practical use and quite probably specious.[10] In any case, considerable ambiguity remains about the exact nature of the experiences recounted in 'La Carte' (due in part to its brevity, and in part to Flegmon's unreliability as a narrator or Aymé's reluctance to overload his plot with analytical detail). We do learn, however, that those whose existence is suspended have no awareness of their absence and apparently 'save' the days during which they disappear. Hence Flegmon's observation that 'la distinction entre temps spatial et temps vécu n'est pas une fantaisie de philosophe. [. . .] En réalité, le temps absolu n'existe pas' (pp. 71–2).

April (the second month of rationing) further develops some of the themes outlined so far. The *ménage à trois* established between Flegmon, Mme Roquenton and her suspended husband shows the diarist's dubious amorous success; however, he is outmanoeuvred regarding his professional aspirations by Perruque. On 12 April, he buys an extra life ticket from an impoverished worker. This act subverts the claim made by the bureaucrat Maleffroi that the decree has had the desired effect of sapping the black market and removing social parasites from the economic cycle. Maleffroi remarks sententiously:

> On se rend compte alors à quel point les riches, les chômeurs, les intellectuels et les catins peuvent être dangereux dans une société où ils n'introduisent que le trouble, l'agitation vaine, le dérèglement et la nostalgie de l'impossible. (p. 75)

This remark invites us to condemn the speaker as a misguided totalitarian apparatchik: not only in his condemnation of troublemakers odiously inhuman, but it also betrays an inability to foresee how in practice such agitators will soon manage to overthrow his system.

Flegmon disappears for the second time between 16 April and 1 May. His return opens the fourth (and final) development of the story, which reveals the unexpected consequences of time-rationing through 'La Carte' and causes its eventual abolition. We are informed that the victims of rationing (whose other privileges have not been curtailed) soon learn how to turn the new régime to their benefit essentially by adapting it to the pre-existing economic system. And conversely, those exempted from rationing (such as the labouring and peasant classes) increasingly envy those who are excluded from existence and its privations: 'La mort relative leur apparaît comme des vacances et ils ont l'impression d'être rivés à leur chaîne' (p. 76). As a result, a new black market in 'life tickets' emerges and thrives. Initially, Flegmon refuses to participate (and notes his loss of Lucette to a rival, 'espèce *swing*' on 10 May [p. 77]). Since in his case principle is invariably outweighed by selfish gratification, his eventual purchase of tickets comes as no surprise, particularly as members of his social circle have decried his short-lived scruples. The bishop, Mgr Delabonne, offers him a parable about a farmer who buys up his neighbour's fallow land and makes it prosper. What happens to the neighbour is not recorded. With its implicit acceptance of an élite exempted from the constraints to which the masses are subjected, the parable evidently also fits the counter-revolutionary ideology of the Vichy régime; for that matter, it would not be hard to see it as a justification of Nazi imperialism.

Jules Flegmon retreats to Normandy to enjoy the extra five days which he has bought and disappears for the third time, with farcical consequences when he reappears on the delayed train returning him to Paris. A corollary of the reduced existence of those subject to rationing turns out to be the extended existence of those who acquire surplus tickets, despite the rise in black-market prices. Thus it transpires that an actress has lived for thirty-six days in May; other individuals manage to live until 66 June or even for an extra five years within the month. Although the hapless cuckold Roquenton attempts to profit from the black market, he dies from grief after discovering Lucette's infidelity. Flegmon, on the other hand, extends his existence in the fourth month until 35 June (whereas he notes, on 32 June, that 'les vivants à part entière n'ont pas la moindre conscience d'une anomalie dans le déroulement du temps' [p. 83]). In effect 'La Carte' has generated two parallel universes (or perhaps a whole succession of them); in his extended, parallel universe, Flegmon meets Élisa on 31 June and they become engaged. On his return to normal time, however, she claims not to know him, so that the diarist suffers a second amorous humiliation. It remains unclear what the ontological status of these extra days is. Why does Élisa not recognize him, since she prolonged her own existence until 60 June? Is this because individuals' universes when extended into extra time no longer overlap or, more banally, because in the intervening three weeks she has simply forgotten him? The text leaves these problems unresolved. The final entries of the diary report that the proliferation of such anomalies, and the practical failure of the plan to economize on food, can only be rectified by the immediate abolition of the decree and the restoration of normal time. The lovelorn Flegmon, smarting after his personal and professional setbacks, consoles himself finally by planning to write a book about his experiences.

In conclusion, we can attribute the success of Aymé's 'La Carte' as a short story to the author's comic elaboration of a fantastic hypothesis which he integrates into a recognizable social reality. Certain problematic areas remain obscure, no doubt for good reasons. For instance, the source of the decree which puts time-rationing into effect is never explained, whether as a scientific phenomenon or in terms of the political mechanisms needed to enact it. There is thus no direct reference either to the Germans or to the Vichy government, or to any equivalent authority. A *fantaisiste* manner, skirting round such issues, was obviously essential to escape censorship. Nevertheless, Aymé's perceptive exploration of the psychological and social effects of the decree patiently reveals a critical view of the injustices created by the Occupation, injustices compounded by the state and the most privileged classes of society. No one, however, attempts to resist the oppressive consequences of the new system, whether individually or collectively, other than in the sense of exploiting it for personal advantage. The critique can thus be seen to reflect a rather cynical view of private and public selfishness, in no serious way threatening to the stability of the Occupation authorities. However, it is certainly surprising that Aymé was able to draw disapproving attention to anti-Semitic persecution in 1942–43, however elliptically (a character remarks with laconic forebearance in 'En attendant', to a group of people complaining about their hardships: '—Moi, dit un Juif, je suis juif' [p. 241]). This disapproval is all very well, courageous even. Unfortunately, it has to be set against the author's willingness to commit his texts to the blatantly anti-Semitic organs *La Gerbe* and *Je suis partout*. Like his character Flegmon, Aymé subverts his moral authority as a dispassionate commentator by what seems to be self-deceiving compromise or downright opportunism.

Such awkward ambiguities do not, however, detract from Marcel Aymé's status or stature as a creator of short stories. As we have seen, the brevity of the genre is ideally suited to his ability to invent and elaborate on a startling situation and to integrate some element of the marvellous into a closely observed social context. In his post-war writing, Aymé attempted to apply his particular blend of comic fantasy and social satire to the theatre; although his plays were commercially successful, it is noticeable that his initial inventiveness is rarely matched by his skill in sustaining plot, drama and characters over the three hours of a theatrical performance. Moreover, Aymé himself was an intensely private individual, who gave away little about his craft as a writer and had no use for autobiographical outpourings. The nearest he came to theoretical reflexions about his own work was in a few articles written about his playwriting, where, somewhat defensively one feels, he attempted to justify his choice of this new genre (a choice motivated partly by commercial reasons, as he admitted). Many critics see the plays as the least successful part of his writing (they have been excluded from the prestigious Pléiade edition of Aymé's works). In a similar fashion, his views on fiction, as he practised it in novel and story, can be gleaned at best from incidental remarks which he makes in the extensive, journalistic articles he devoted to other writers and topics. What he particularly valued about the short story as a literary form, for instance, is implied in the prefaces which he contributed to anthologies of such celebrated practitioners as Perrault, Andersen and Chekhov. While Hitler and academic pedants disapproved of 'Le Chat botté', for Aymé this 'histoire absurde et merveilleusement désinvolte' is 'L'un des sommets de notre littérature', just as Perrault is as deserving of serious study as Boileau or Gide. Recounting at some length Hans Christian Andersen's rise to glory, Aymé again notes how the *conte* was seen by many of his contemporaries as a disrespectable genre, 'le témoignage d'une sorte d'infantilisme'. In Aymé's opinion, Andersen's genius depends on 'Cette indifférence à la morale et à tout ce qui n'est pas l'enchantement de conter'. In the case of Chekhov, Aymé discovers and prizes 'ce don essentiel du conteur, qui est d'entrer en étroite communion avec ses personnages tout en les considérant avec un détachement lucide, comme s'il avait le pouvoir de se dédoubler'.[11] Such observations offer us tantalizing clues to the writer's own estimation of his craft, even if, for Aymé, practice always outweighs theory.

Like his great predecessor, Maupassant, Aymé is sometimes undervalued by literary historians because his work apparently needs little exegesis by such middlemen in order to reach a large public. The suspicion was reciprocated. In the publisher's blurb or 'prière d'insérer' which he supplied for *Le Passe-Muraille* Aymé parodies what he saw as the preciosity and pomposity of some critical discourse (he writes that stories like 'La Carte' reflect research on 'le métachronisme thérapeutique' and a 'voyage à travers les arcanes de la méta-phistophélie').[12] Appropriately enough, in his illuminating account of *La Nouvelle française*, René Godenne categorizes Marcel Aymé as a brilliant practitioner of the 'récit plaisant'.[13] This judgement is complimentary, but in a sense also subtly denigratory, insofar as Aymé is downgraded to the position of mere entertainer, when in fact he can be an extraordinarily perceptive observer of social and psychological foibles. 'La Carte' cannot be expected to demonstrate all his virtues (or defects) within its twenty pages. Moreover, some of his limitations as a storyteller are those of a genre whose very brevity limits its scope. When dealing with analogous subjects elsewhere. Aymé extends his characterization, plot and social observation immeasurably in post-war writing like the extended novella 'Traversée de Paris' and the novels *Le Chemin des écoliers* and *Uranus*. To appreciate 'La Carte' fully, one needs not merely to restore its historical context, as I have attempted to do, but to place it within the collection in which it appeared in 1943. Short stories acquire the substance they may lack individually by contiguity, by being set in a collection or anthology. 'La Carte', for instance, is only one variation in a whole series of plays on time undertaken in stories like 'Le Décret' (*Le Passe-Muraille*), or 'Le Temps mort' (*Derrière chez Martin*, 1938) and 'Rechute' (*En Arrière*, 1950). Taken as a whole, the stories in *Le Passe-Muraille* combine to make the book a thought-provoking and diverting modern classic.

Albert Camus
'La Pierre qui pousse'

David H. Walker

This text was published in 1957, the year Camus won the Nobel Prize for Literature, in a volume of stories entitled *L'Exil et le royaume*.[1] Prior to the appearance of this collection, Camus's work shows little trace of an explicit interest in the short-story form. There exists no discussion of the *nouvelle* among his writings; and yet there are several features of his approach to literary creation that point to an affinity. Firstly, as a news reporter by profession, Camus undoubtedly had an eye for the story that would offer a concise yet revealing insight into human reality. His first novel, *L'Étranger* (1942), bears traces of two so-called *faits divers* culled from newspapers, and his last published novel, *La Chute* (1956), originally intended as one of the texts in *L'Exil et le royaume*, is in essence a collection of savage and sardonic anecdotes many of which might have become short stories in themselves.[2] Secondly, from the early texts of *L'Envers et l'endroit* (1937) through to his last, posthumously-published novel *Le Premier Homme* (1994), Camus is explicitly concerned, as these texts repeatedly make clear, with 'deux ou trois images simples' which sum up the essence of experience:[3] such snapshots of existence crystallize an intuition in a brief, telling episode such as the short story exists to consummate. And thirdly, one must not overlook the great importance in Camus's *œuvre* of the lyrical essay, a prose meditation blending philosophical insights with personal reflection, and frequently incorporating the depiction of events or gestures which are freighted with significance for the observing sensibility. From this perspective, the juvenilia entitled *Intuitions*, pages written around 1932 when the author was a young man of nineteen and unpublished before 1973,[4] already show a propensity for the fragment or short text of uncertain generic character, to which Camus will remain faithful right up to the collection entitled *L'Été* of 1954, and which is not, in fact, unrelated to certain forms of the short story.

The collective title *L'Exil et le royaume* indicates a concern with themes which are both existential and religious. As early as his essay *Le Mythe de Sisyphe* of 1942, Camus had argued that human existence is a form of exile. The universe which humans find themselves in does not correspond to their desires. They cannot understand or explain why things are the way they are: why humans die, why happiness eludes them. The natural world is impervious to human needs: flood, famine, pestilence afflict people for no apparent reason. It is as if we have somehow strayed from where we belonged into this world of what Camus calls the absurd where we can never feel at home: this is how life comes to be seen as exile.

Such themes echo Christian mythology, of course: since Adam and Eve were expelled from the garden of Eden, humankind has been dreaming of a return to Paradise, and that aspiration is what Camus, too, describes as a longing for a kingdom—'thy kingdom come', as the Lord's Prayer has it. However, though Camus concedes that Christian imagery corresponds to the deep-seated human needs he acknowledges in himself, he takes issue with its acceptance of present misfortunes in return for the promise of a solution in a life after death. For Camus, there is no basis to the dream of another existence: 'cet exil est sans recours puisqu'il est privé des souvenirs d'une patrie perdue ou de l'espoir d'une terre promise.'[5] We have to make the best, literally, of the universe we have, for there is nothing outside or beyond it. In fact, as Camus says in a 'prière d'insérer' or publisher's blurb intended to clarify the sense of *L'Exil et le royaume*, the experience of exile shows us what is lacking in existence and points the way to the kingdom, 'une certaine vie libre et nue que nous avons à retrouver, pour renaître enfin' (I, p. 2031). For Camus, Christianity complicates, obscures and diverts from the real issues by directing attention to a purely hypothetical world beyond this one. This is not the least of Christianity's errors, as our consideration of this short story will show.

'La Pierre qui pousse' arose from a visit Camus made to Brazil during a lecture-tour of South America in mid-1949. The trip represented for him a kind of escape from the conflicts and controversies of the Cold War that began to polarize Europe in the late 1940s. As editor of the leading newspaper *Combat*, Camus had been deeply involved in much of this tension, and he sought to put it behind him by gathering together a volume of his selected journalism and other essays, *Actuelles, Chroniques 1944–1948*, before setting out for new horizons and what he hoped would be new beginnings.[6] In Brazil he witnessed the strange dance ceremony that his fictional character attends, and substantial parts of the story can be traced back to Camus's travel diary, published posthumously in 1978.[7] At the time he wrote the story, however (around 1955), he was already looking forward to a great novel he had planned which would trace the history of his own family in the context of the French colonization of Algeria. Still unfinished at his death, the text of this novel, *Le Premier Homme*, was published in 1994. From it we can see that the epic journey d'Arrast has undertaken in search of a new kingdom in a foreign land echoes and prefigures Camus's reconstruction of the journey made by his own ancestors in the nineteenth century. Looked at in another way, the world-weary misfit of 1948–9 had much in common with the rebels and outsiders who fled France exactly a century earlier, in the aftermath of revolutionary upheavals across Europe. In this pre-railway era, they set out from north-east France aboard barges 'dérivant pendant un mois sur les rivières et les fleuves' and crossed vast expanses of water in pursuit of a 'Terre promise',[8] as the novel puts it in terms very reminiscent of 'La Pierre qui pousse'.

Indeed, the importance of the role played in the short story by water imagery is clear from the most superficial reading.[9] Similarly, the general outline of the plot is simple; but if the overall sense of 'La Pierre qui pousse' emerges fairly readily as we read it, what is less clear is the significance of the allusions and symbols which the text throws up. Olivier Todd, Camus's most recent biographer, refers to 'La Pierre qui pousse' as unusually mysterious but unusually saturated with deep-seated unconscious impulses in its deployment of imagery.[10] The interconnections between these images and their relationship to certain mythological figures is a dimension I wish to examine. The problem they present defines the key elements in the story, for the import of 'La Pierre qui pousse' can best be arrived at through a detailed analysis of the interplay of images. The conciseness of the short-story form lends itself particularly well to such dense allusiveness. This text belongs to a particular category of short story, that of the symbolic tale whose narrative content is essentially a pretext for patterns of metaphor which convey an indirect, often archetypal, thematic sense. In fact, 'La Pierre qui pousse' has been summed up as a 'récit-mythe'.[11]

Journeying to Iguape in Brazil, d'Arrast becomes increasingly aware of the all-pervading liquidity of his environment: the sky is 'spongieux', 'humide', and in it, 'les étoiles exténuées . . . nage[nt]' (p. 1658). A thick mist obscures everything, and a persistent drizzle dissolves the beam of the headlights as the travellers skid and bump through the 'forêt humide' (p. 1659). The trip is likened to a 'longue, longue navigation' (p. 1659). The river crossing itself provokes in d'Arrast the feeling that he is heading for an island, cut off from the rest of reality by vast watery expanses:

> L'homme se retourna vers la rive qu'ils venaient de quitter. Elle était à son tour recouverte par la nuit et les eaux, immense et farouche comme le continent d'arbres qui s'étendait au-delà sur des milliers de kilomètres. Entre l'océan tout proche et cette mer végétale, la poignée d'hommes qui dérivait à cette heure sur un fleuve sauvage semblait maintenant perdue. Quand le radeau heurta le nouvel embarcadère ce fut comme si, toutes amarres rompues, ils abordaient une île dans les ténèbres. (p. 1658)

These pages in particular recall the description of the emigrants leaving France for Algeria, in *Le Premier Homme*. But at a level more profound than that, Camus is presenting here a vision which is characteristic of his work: the 'monde clos' in which people are exiled and isolated, beleaguered by the hostile forces of nature. The concept is further elaborated on d'Arrast's arrival at Iguape: the town (particularly the poor quarter) is constantly flooded when the river rises in the incessant rain; the surrounding forest silently absorbs the 'voile d'eau fine' as would 'une énorme éponge' (p. 1661). The entire community is a prey to water: the sky is 'liquide', and the stars are extinguished 'comme si le ciel dégouttait de ses dernières lumières' (p. 1671); the mist, the 'air épais' (p. 1671), 'humide' and 'lourd' (p. 1676), oppresses the people; the dripping wall of vegetation, the

45

swollen river and the ocean hem them in; the ground underfoot is everywhere muddy; and as d'Arrast walks in the 'pluie impalpable', he is continually aware of a 'grand bruit spacieux qu'il n'avait cessé d'entendre depuis son arrivée, et dont on ne pouvait dire s'il était fait du froissement des eaux ou des arbres' (p. 1665). 'A travers les espaces spongieux du ciel, la rumeur du fleuve et des arbres' (p. 1669) serves as an audible reminder of the stifling forces which weigh on Iguape.

The effect of this oppressive atmosphere is spiritual as well as physical. The fluids which afflict this world are not just meteorological phenomena: they are, so to speak, an exudation of the soul as well, and even d'Arrast eventually feels himself being affected by a certain inner deterioration which is associated with images of liquids:

> D'Arrast remontait la pente glissante [. . .] trébuchait comme un homme ivre dans les chemins troués. La forêt grondait un peu, toute proche. Le bruit du fleuve grandissait, le continent tout entier émergeait dans la nuit et l'écœurement envahissait d'Arrast. Il lui semblait qu'il aurait voulu vomir ce pays tout entier, la tristesse de ses grands espaces, la lumière glauque des forêts, et le clapotis nocturne de ses grands fleuves déserts. Cette terre était trop grande, le sang et les saisons s'y confondaient, le temps se liquéfiait. (p. 1676)

It seems clear that Camus has created a variation on the central image of his novel *La Peste* of 1947: in both works, the reader finds a community cut off and threatened by powers inimical to man, representative of aspects of the absurd. In both cases, the 'exile' is portrayed as being, the result of one predominant factor, disease in the one, water in the other, but its significance is broadened by the associated use of other natural imagery. In *La Peste*, the 'soleil de la peste', the wind, and the elements in general propagate the plague;[12] in 'La Pierre qui pousse' water is similarly insidious: it impregnates the air, the trees, the ground, and its ominous presence is felt even in the heat, the 'chaleur humide' which 'écras[e] la ville et la forêt immobile' (p. 1676) and which 'descend [. . .] du ciel en flots presque visibles' (p. 1678).

Thus, what Rieux the doctor is to the plague, d'Arrast the civil engineer is to the water which threatens to engulf Iguape: in seeking

46

to remedy the damage it does he embodies revolt against the imperfections of the human condition. True to Camus's conception of such a stance, his revolt manifests itself in thought as well as deed, through resonant declarations as well as down-to-earth actions, at the metaphysical as well as the practical level. At the outset the engineer, whose task it is to prevent the river from overflowing its banks by building a dam, is greeted as a saviour by the dignitaries: 'Commander aux eaux, dompter les fleuves, ah! le grand métier', cries the judge (p. 1661). But the waters with which d'Arrast has to deal are of a more complex and far-reaching nature than he suspects. For the use of water as a symbol of the absurd which dominates men's lives admits of more subtle developments than the symbol of the plague had made possible. The disease is a straightforward menace to man: but water, though it can be a threat, is none the less necessary for human survival. There is no question of putting the plague to good use; but the hospital at Iguape actually needs water (p. 1660), and in the midst of the rain-soaked, flood-ravaged shacks of the Black community, a woman is seen carrying water for domestic use (p. 1664). The basic problem ceases to be a simple battle between man and the elements: the fundamental division in the earlier novel between 'fléaux' and 'victimes'[13] no longer applies, for man's fate is shown to be more intimately bound up with his universe than had appeared to be the case in *La Peste*. Indeed, the novel was criticized by Camus's political and literary opponents for having oversimplified the problem it set out to treat. In an essay written subsequently, out of the experience of crossing the ocean en route to Brazil, Camus underlines the ambiguity, the ambivalence of his attitude towards the notions of good and evil in the world: 'Je reconnus le monde pour ce qu'il était, je décidai d'accepter que son bien fût en même temps malfaisant et salutaires ses forfaits . . . je compris qu'il y avait deux vérités' (II, p. 883). In 'La Pierre qui pousse', the relationship between humans and the element symbolizing their oppression embraces precisely such areas of ambivalence, which are mediated by several complex patterns of imagery.

But these comments seem to have little to do with the growing stone of the title. How does d'Arrast, at the end of the story, come to be carrying a rock on his head, while his original engineering mission has been forgotten?[14] In fact, the work progresses quite logically to this conclusion: but the logic involved, and the themes it underpins, emerge from the exploration of a series of interrelated images which form the substance of the story.

Though the waterlogged populace of Iguape flounders in the mud and the poor quarter is continually inundated when the river bursts its banks, religion has benefited dramatically from the waters. For the river and the ocean, sources of the greatest threat to the well-being of the townspeople, are also the route by which the statue of 'le bon Jésus' came to Iguape. Socrate relates the story to d'Arrast in his pidgin French:

> Un jour, la bonne statue de Jésus, elle est arrivée de la mer, en remontant le fleuve. Des pêcheurs l'a trouvée. Que belle! Que belle! Alors, ils l'a lavée ici dans la grotte. Et maintenant une pierre a poussé dans la grotte. Chaque année, c'est la fête. Avec le marteau, tu casses, tu casses des morceaux pour le bonheur béni. Et puis quoi, elle pousse toujours, toujours tu casses. C'est le miracle. (p. 1666)

This constitutes the first of a number of links between the waters and the growing stone. The statue of Jesus, the focal point of the inhabitants' religion, is deposited at Iguape by the river which is thus the origin of their cult of Christ as well as of their distress. The people consider that the stone brings good fortune: in reality, the queue of pilgrims waiting meekly in the pouring rain to chip off a piece bears witness to man's submission, through superstition, to his misfortune.[15] When one recalls that the image of water is, at the outset, primarily representative of a hostile environment, one can infer that Camus sees in this legend an expression of what for him is a fundamental aspect of Christianity: it is a religion which has its roots in suffering, and it thrives on human misery. The miraculous stone growing in the waters which have come into contact with the statue of Jesus is therefore a product of man's wretchedness, with religious devotion acting as a catalyst, as it were. Indeed, other associated symbols bring out the fact that the waters, the stone and the Christianity which they perpetuate are all forms of burdens for mankind.

D'Arrast is sick at heart at this spectacle of resigned piety before the grotto; it reminds him of his own desperate and unsatisfied search for something he cannot even define:

Il attendait [. . .] comme si le travail qu'il était venu faire ici n'était qu'un prétexte, l'occasion d'une surprise, ou d'une rencontre qu'il n'imaginait même pas, mais qui l'aurait attendu, patiemment, au bout du monde. (p. 1666)

He leaves the grotto abruptly, but on his way out of the Jardin de la Fontaine he is introduced to 'le coq', the ship's cook who has experienced at first hand the mortal danger that water can represent for man. He tells d'Arrast how his ship caught fire, and how the lifeboat he had escaped in was subsequently capsized by a storm which blew up. In his fear of drowning, he promised to Jesus that if he survived he would carry a hundred-pound rock on his head in the annual religious procession. The sea grew calm, and the cook attributes this to a miracle: in the procession the following day, he will fulfil his promise. D'Arrast finds this promise absurd, though the man's good-natured smile appeals to him; he asks if Jesus always replies to prayers.

'Toujours, non, Capitaine!
Alors?'
Le coq éclata d'un rire frais et enfantin.
'Eh bien, dit-il, il est libre, non?' (p. 1670)

The cook's faith is touching, but d'Arrast's enquiry shows that it is possible to question the arbitrary nature of what the man credulously calls divine. If Jesus saved him, who caused the catastrophe in the first place? The singular succession of chance misfortunes which placed the cook's life in jeopardy—'Pas par ma faute, eh! je sais mon métier!' (p. 1668) he protests—should be eloquent testimony to the hostility of the universe in which man finds himself, but it provokes in 'le coq' the leap of faith which Camus had analysed in his essay Le Mythe de Sisyphe, where he calls it, in fact, 'le suicide philosophique'; mishaps thus serve to reinforce religious beliefs. The cook, typical Christian that he is in this respect, believes that man is incapable of saving himself and that because he escaped drowning he must owe a debt to Christ.[16] Once again the believer is immersed in water and comes out of it carrying a stone.

Hence there appears a clear analogy between the stone which grows in the grotto and the one which the cook carries in the procession.

Both are tokens of the burdens and servitude man accepts as a result of an unenlightened, superstitious attitude to his condition. These two examples carry overtones of religious devotion but the essential link between the two stones is the symbol of water, from which all burdens ultimately derive.[17] The linking image occurs early in the story, for the later descriptions of 'le coq' staggering under his load (pp. 1680–1) and of d'Arrast taking care not to slip with the rock as he carries it along the muddy path to the huts in the Black quarter (p. 1683) are in reality echoes of a brief incident which is alluded to when d'Arrast first visits the poor quarter with the notables of the town:

> Ils croisèrent une femme qui descendait le sentier, glissant parfois sur ses pieds nus, portant haut sur la tête un bidon de fer plein d'eau. (p. 1664)

This fleeting image establishes a connection between the rock on the head of 'le coq' and subsequently on that of d'Arrast, the growing stone in the Jardin de la Fontaine, and water as the *fons et origo* of burdens.

Another crucial example of a burden affords Camus an opportunity to enrich the water symbolism in the story. The religious procession in which the cook participates with his boulder involves an expiation of sins on the part of penitents who in order to purge themselves carry the statue of 'le bon Jésus' through the streets. The description of the procession is revealing:

> à l'autre extremité de la rue [. . .] un tumulte éclata et une foule en ébullition apparut. De loin, on la voyait agglutinée autour de la châsse, pèlerins et pénitents mêlés, et ils avançaient, au milieu des pétards et des hurlements de joie, le long de la rue étroite. En quelques secondes, ils la remplirent jusqu'aux bords [. . .] la foule, sous le balcon, sembla monter le long des parois. (p. 1680)[18]

This torrent of people carrying the holy effigy just as the cook carries his rock, as a token of their submission to Christ, is depicted as a flood of water, a 'marée humaine', bearing 'le bon Jésus' just as the river did when the statue first came from the sea. Camus shows how people become indistinguishable from, in fact contributors to, those forces which threaten human existence,[19] through their adherence to a religion which for two thousand years has sought to make man conform, in Camus's words, to 'une image humiliée de lui-même'.[20] This religion has sought to make humans worship that image in the shape of Christ—whose effigy is pictured here as 'saignant et chancelant au-dessus de la foule' (p. 1679)—through their submission to what Camus calls 'une doctrine de l'injustice'.[21] The author indicates that the elements which menace human beings derive their strength partly from man's inherent habit of servitude and his submissiveness to unjustified burdens.

This point is underlined by a further symbolic association of the river, whose ominous presence dominates the town, with the crowd in the religious procession. As Alexander Fischler has pointed out,[22] an important leitmotif in the story is the legend of Saint George and the dragon: this underlying myth is represented 'en abyme'[23] when d'Arrast sees, on the altar of the natives' church, a picture in which 'saint Georges, avec des airs séducteurs, prenait avantage d'un dragon moustachu' (p. 1672).[24] Thus, the river which d'Arrast crosses on his way to Iguape is described as having 'écailles brillantes' (p. 1655), 'longs muscles liquides' (p. 1656); and its menacing 'souffle' is noticed by the engineer at this point (p. 1656) and when he reaches the town (p. 1661). Small wonder that the populace prays for the arrival of Saint George, with such a monster in the vicinity. But it transpires that this monster has a human counterpart: Fischler argues that the procession bearing 'le bon Jésus' is an incarnation of the 'protean dragon' which holds the town in thrall. The crowd is portrayed as

> une masse bariolée, couverte d'yeux et de bouches vociférantes,
> et d'où sortaient, comme des lances, une armée de cierges dont
> la flamme s'évaporait dans la lumière ardente du jour. (p. 1680)

This roaring, fire-breathing vision makes the point that the community suffers as much from the religious devotion of its inhabitants as from the external elements.

But the oppressive powers which afflict Iguape have other components which also concern d'Arrast personally. We have noted that several symbolic representations reveal Christ coming to the people on the back of what dominates the town—the river-cum-dragon—and perpetuating that domination through the religious ceremonies in which He holds sway, floating on a human river, borne along by a human dragon. Now, strikingly, these evocations recall one of the first descriptions of d'Arrast himself, as the engineer rides across the river when travelling to Iguape. The statue of 'le bon Jésus' in its shrine above the human torrent is a reflection of d'Arrast who is seen to 's'immobiliser sur le bord du radeau, face à l'amont' (p. 1657)—which again calls to mind the holy statue coming to Iguape 'en remontant le fleuve' (p. 1666). The European 'Saint George' actually arrives on the dragon which 's'arc-bout[e] sous le radeau et le soul[ève] sur la surface des eaux' (p. 1657). In some mysterious way, then, d'Arrast, journeying over seas and rivers to reach Iguape, is deriving advantage from the elements which oppress the town, just as 'le bon Jésus' did.

This points to the social and political implications of the story. For as a European with Iberian connections—he speaks Spanish (pp. 1663–4, 1667) and his name has a familiar ring to Portuguese and Spanish ears[25]—d'Arrast finds himself implicated, however unwillingly, in the colonial domination of Brazil by the Portuguese, whose influence is still felt in Iguape. As a representative of 'la Société française de Rio' (pp. 1665, 1670), the engineer is an agent of what was called 'economic colonialism'.[26] D'Arrast, the descendant of an aristocratic family[27] whose origins are in the developed world, has benefited from the domination of the Third World on which Europe has based its wealth and power. The fact that the demeanour of the twentieth-century 'dompteur des eaux' when crossing the river recalls the image of 'le bon Jésus' who calmed Galilee, walked on the water, and allegedley saved the cook from drowning is given its full significance when the reader is informed that the church which dominates the town is 'de style colonial' (p. 1662). The religion which contributes to the towns- people's misery is but one manifestation among many of the colonial background which profoundly affected the life of the community.[28]

These details, which seem to classify d'Arrast as an accessory of colonialism and neocolonialism, constitute a serious obstacle for the engineer, for he hates Europe, ruled as it is by 'des policiers ou des marchands' (p. 1667), and hopes that in Brazil he will find peace of mind and a fulfilment 'qui l'aurait attendu, patiemment, au bout du monde' (p. 1666). He has escaped from the spiritual exile of Europe;

but it becomes evident that he is prevented from finding a new kingdom among the people of Iguape by the uncomfortable historical culpability of which every European bears a trace in regard to the Third World. Camus, born in Algeria of European stock, felt such unease very intimately.

On his arrival, d'Arrast is immediately identified with and absorbed into the class of 'notables'; he is seen by the dignitaries as a member of their set which governs the community. Though it is, in fact, to help the poor quarter that d'Arrast has come, and though he fails to see 'ce qu'un juge pouvait avoir à faire avec une digue' (p. 1661), the specific task which he has come to perform is of less importance in the eyes of the townspeople than what he stands for: European prestige, welcomed by the notables, but dumbly resented by the poor of the shanty town. For there is a distinct class division among the people of Iguape, and Camus underlines this point.[29] Indeed, the river-dragon which periodically exacts its tribute from the town floods only the low-lying poor quarters where the most wretched section of the inhabitants, mainly composed of Blacks, struggles to live. The central image of a community threatened by water is further elaborated to embody the social and political injustice which permits one group of the population to achieve relative immunity from the common misfortune while 'les plus pauvres' (p. 1665) bear the brunt of the universe's hostility.[30] It is with a somewhat critical eye that d'Arrast views the parasitical dignitaries who sport 'fins souliers' (p. 1665) while the Black population goes barefoot, for example. Camus here further refines on *La Peste*, which had been criticized —unjustly—by Sartre for blurring social inequalities. However, the fact that the notables expect d'Arrast to sign 'le livre d'or de la municipalité' as a 'témoignage [. . .] du grand événement que constitu[e] sa venue à Iguape' (p. 1670) shows how far the engineer finds himself annexed by this class and cut off from those whom he most wishes to help.

The same point emerges when d'Arrast visits the poor quarter. He is seen by the Black inhabitants as a representative of the notables, and his request to view the inside of one of the huts meets with mute hostility: it is granted only when the 'commandant du port' makes it into an order (p. 1664).[31] Long years of submission have even bred in the poor community a certain habit of servitude akin to the way in which they consent to the domination of Christianity: 'le coq' spontaneously calls d'Arrast 'Capitaine' and 'seigneur' (pp. 1667, 1682), and once d'Arrast has penetrated one of the huts, on a signal from the harbourmaster he is presented with a drink, the customary token of hospitality (p. 1664). These are factors in the process whereby d'Arrast is forced into the posture of an accessory to oppression, both by virtue of his standing in the eyes of the privileged, and as a result of the role conferred upon him by the attitude of the victims. D'Arrast's task will be to annul the adverse political and social concomitants of those very skills and endowments which put him in a position to bring succour to the destitute population. Having already experienced anguish at the thought that 'quelqu'un allait mourir par [sa] faute' (p. 1670), d'Arrast is clearly a man who knows what it means to bear responsibility for the sufferings of others; he is haunted by the 'honte' of Europe (p. 1676) and seeks to escape it. Here, too, we discern a very personal angst experienced by Camus himself.

The problematic position which d'Arrast occupies with regard to the poor community of Iguape is further illustrated during the macumba or dance ceremony which he is invited to attend. Again, it is the imagery which reveals the significance of this strange ritual. The men and women form two concentric circles and dance around a leader who is costumed in red. The ceremony is an attempt to invoke Saint George, and is explicitly related to other symbols in the story when the leader sticks a lighted candle in the ground and pours water from a bowl in two concentric circles around it. There is an obvious correspondence between the burning candle and the leader, who is described as a 'grand diable rouge' with an 'œil enflammé' (p. 1673). Similarly, the circles of water around the flame are associated with the men and women encircling the dance leader. It is evident that the fire and water here symbolize two opposing spiritual forces.[32] There is a suggestion that the people are contaminated by the forces of the absurd as represented by the water (this is also the case when Camus depicts the procession as a human torrent). The dancers seem, therefore, to be attempting to purge themselves of the powers of oppression which inhabit them. The fire, on the other hand, is evidently the symbol of the spirit which will drive out the water, and each of the participants attempts to 'obtenir la descente du dieu en soi par le moyen de danses et de chants'.[33] Just as water is linked with the dragon, so the opposing role of fire played by the leader relates him to Saint George: his wild flailing with a sword might be seen as an imitation of the saint's gestures as he kills the monster (p. 1673). Therefore, what is being expressed in a primitive form in this rite is the desire of the community to rid itself of water and the many-faceted oppression which it symbolizes; the dancers seek to drive out the dragon which holds them in its power by appealing to Saint George and by allowing themselves to be possessed by him.

However, if, as Camus says in the 'prière d'insérer' for *L'Exil et le royaume*, we must refuse 'la servitude', here represented by water and the dragon, it is equally necessary 'en même temps' to reject 'la possession';[34] and we note that the collective hysteria by which the poor of Iguape are gripped during the dance ceremony merely leads to their being 'possessed', the text says, by 'un être jusque-là absolument silencieux' (p. 1674). Their cries become 'inarticulés' and are described as a 'hurlement collectif' (p. 1673); as the ceremony progresses, 'le cri général faibl[it], s'alt[ère], dégén[ère] en une sorte de rauque aboiement' (p. 1674). If this ceremony expresses the reaction of the people to the oppression, both natural and social, which they suffer from, it has to be said that it brings about a frenzy as far removed from true humanity as is their original degradation.

Thus even the face of the good-natured cook is 'maintenant décomposé', and 'la bonté [a] disparu de ses yeux qui ne re[flètent] qu'une sorte d'avidité inconnue'. He now speaks 'sans bienveillance' and 'd'un air fermé' (p. 1675) as he bids d'Arrast leave the company. Such a transformation justifies the engineer's misgivings about the events he has witnessed: although he is not impervious to the atmosphere—'Il s'aperçut que lui-même, depuis un moment, sans déplacer les pieds pourtant, dansait de tout son poids' (1673)—the brutish abandon and loss of lucidity it gives rise to are quite alien to him. Furthermore, the cook, although he asked d'Arrast to help him resist the temptations of the ritual, has nevertheless succumbed and tomorrow will be exhausted, incapable of carrying the stone: his sense of being beholden to Christ will merely increase as a result of this temporary flight from his condition. Hence d'Arrast's feeling of revulsion as he leaves the gathering:

l'écœurement envahissait d'Arrast. Il lui semblait qu'il aurait voulu vomir ce pays tout entier [. . .]. La vie ici était à ras de terre et, pour s'y intégrer, il fallait se coucher et dormir, pendant des années, à même le sol boueux ou desséché. (p. 1676)

The engineer finds himself truly exiled from the entire population of Iguape. He is considered to be a notable, but is prevented from feeling at ease in the society of the dignitaries by his disgust for the Europe which they prize so highly and by the instinctive irony provoked in him by their bumptious zeal; nevertheless, as a European, a professional and a bourgeois, he is objectively associated with the country's colonial background and with its present ruling élite and is thus isolated from the poor community. He is disheartened by the manner in which the victims consent to their servitude and exacerbate it through their rituals and religion. He is adrift between two poles which apparently admit of no reconciliation:

Là-bas, en Europe, c'était la honte et la colère. Ici, l'exil ou la solitude, au milieu de ces fous languissants et trépidants, qui dansaient pour mourir. (p. 1676)

However, there remains one mysterious bond between d'Arrast and the poor community: he is strangely attracted to the girl who made the gesture of hospitality in the hut he visited. Instinctively, he 'eut soudain envie de la retenir' (p. 1665); but she disappeared into the crowd. It is partly in the hope of seeing her that he accepts the invitation to the macumba on hearing that the women of the shanty town will be there (p. 1669); and indeed, the girl reappears at a significant stage in the proceedings. She seems to be an important participant, dressed as she is in ceremonial robes and feathers, and carrying a bow with an arrow on which is impaled a bird whose multicoloured plumage resembles her own attire. The girl is in a trance, and amidst the throng of people attempting to escape their degradation by working themselves up into a state of frenzy, she takes on the qualities of a sacrificial victim, like the transfixed bird she carries. D'Arrast is fascinated by her dance and her 'étrange cri d'oiseau, perçant et pourtant mélodieux' (p. 1675); and despite his subsequent recoil from what he has seen, 'à travers la nuit humide, [. . .] l'étrange cri d'oiseau blessé, poussé par la belle endormie, lui parv[ient] encore' (p. 1676).

Through the girl cries the wretched community of which she is part: this 'sleeping beauty' personifies the suffering Blacks who know no other escape from their tribulations than to 'se coucher et dormir à même le sol boueux ou desséché' (p. 1676). The enigmatic emotion which the girl awakes in d'Arrast is directed towards all of her people and is a form of compassion for all the burdens they bear: not for nothing did the engineer think, 'sans savoir pourquoi', of the girl at the moment when he agreed to help the cook fulfil his promise to carry the stone (p. 1669). The cry of distressed humanity resounds across all the barriers which separate d'Arrast from those he has come to help. However, until the day of the procession the European does not fully understand what his mission is: even on the morning of that day, he confesses to Socrate that he does not know where he is going, but that since he 'ne sai[t] pas danser' he can find no way of becoming a part of his friend's people. 'Je n'ai pas trouvé ma place', he says ruefully (p. 1677).

As the hour of the procession approaches, d'Arrast finds himself once again taken in hand by the dignitaries. All has been arranged so that he may enjoy the spectacle from a privileged vantage point: first from the judge's balcony, then from that of the town hall, he will be able, in the company of the judge and the chief of police, those two pillars of oppression, to look down on the mass of people atoning for their sins by marching to the church, that further pillar of oppression.

The crowd, bearing aloft the statue of Christ, draws level with the balcony on which d'Arrast is standing with the policeman and the judge: the reader imagines the spectacle of these four figures—the policeman, the judge, Christ, and d'Arrast—tellingly grouped together above the sweating multitude. This is the moment of truth for d'Arrast: noting the absence of 'le coq', he immediately leaves the balcony, 'd'un seul mouvement, sans s'excuser' (p. 1680), and descends to ground level. Now d'Arrast no longer rides on the backs of the people as do the other agents of oppression in the town; now, having given up the privileges of the ruling class, he assumes the role of Saint George and attacks the dragon with which he had formerly been associated and which stands in the way between him and the burdened cook:

> il dut lutter contre la foule joyeuse, les porteurs de cierges, les pénitents offusqués. Mais irrésistiblement, remontant de tout son

> poids la marée humaine, il s'ouvrit un chemin, d'un mouvement
> si emporté, qu'il chancela et faillit tomber lorsqu'il se retrouva
> libre[. . .] Collé contre le mur brûlant, il attendit que la
> respiration lui revînt (p. 1680).

D'Arrast has mastered the dragon and what it stands for—man's
complicity in oppression and his subservience in the face of the
doctrines of culpability which bolster injustice. He must now come
to terms with mankind's burdens, in the shape of the cook's boulder.
It is clear that this rock has many symbolic components. It is the
unavoidable burden resulting from the indifference of the universe
and the absurdity of the human condition—the rock of Sisyphus, in
the essay Camus had published in 1942. It is the necessary burden
of the effort required to extract from a hostile nature those elements
indispensable to man (despite the floods and rain, water still has to
be found for the hospital and the home). It is the burden man carries
when he accepts the doctrine of Original Sin, the Christian view that
men's efforts to improve their lot are futile without the grace of a
God who must be constantly appeased. At the same time, 'le coq''s
stone evokes socioeconomic injustice: like the affluence and power of
the privileged classes, it is supported by the exertions of the poor and
the oppressed. And in a symbolic as well as a literal sense, the stone
is the black man's burden: it recalls the developed countries, those
whom Camus elsewhere calls 'les profiteurs de la colonisation', which
thrive on the misery of the poor in the Third World.[35] These latter
elements are hinted at in the description of the cook:

> Il s'arrêtait, puis, courbé sous l'énorme pierre, il courait un peu,
> du pas pressé des débardeurs et des coolies, le petit trot de la
> misère, rapide, le pied frappant le sol de toute sa plante (p. 1680).

The cook collapses: the engineer picks up the rock to carry it for him.
However, having accomplished this gesture of fundamental solidarity
he proceeds to show that he is actually opposed to those habits of
servitude and resignation which compound the community's misery.
He advances somewhat aggressively on the crowd and 'fend [. . .]
avec décision les premiers rangs' (p. 1682). At this point the church
and the statue of Christ lie before him: but although d'Arrast has
revealed himself ready to share, for the sake of a common humanity,

those burdens which man cannot escape, he affirms through his actions that he will not accept the further oppression of Christianity and the church 'de style colonial' with its suggestion of social and political injustice and exploitation:

> brutalement, sans savoir pourquoi[36] il obliqua vers la gauche, et se détourna du chemin de l'église, obligeant les pèlerins à lui faire face (p. 1682).

This brusque swing to the Left is a challenge to the people who seek their salvation in the bosom of the Church, under the eye of human oppressors. D'Arrast forces the pilgrims to face up to the alternative he proposes as he sets out for the poor quarter, makes his way to the cook's hut and throws down his burden 'au centre de la pièce, sur le feu qui rougeoyait encore' (p. 1683).

In terms of the story's symbolism, this gesture has many ramifications. Considering the watery origins of the stone, depositing it on the hearthfire is an answer to the macumba with its hysterical attempts to overcome the power of water by means of fire. At the same time, d'Arrast has robbed Christ of the irrational tribute He exacts and has returned to his fellow men the rock which thereby becomes the symbol of man's higher aspirations redirected towards the human community itself.

The invitation offered to d'Arrast to sit with the inhabitants of the hut indicates that the engineer has won a place for himself among the people. This 'dompteur des eaux' has successfully struggled with the dragon within and without the human being. The secular saviour accepts his share of the common load. As an individual, throwing in his lot with the oppressed allows him to throw off the burden of guilt engendered by the privileges he has enjoyed at their expense: hence the 'joie obscure et haletante' he now feels (p. 1683); hence also his sense of being reborn to 'la vie qui recommençait' (p. 1683). He and his creator attempt to free men from their habits of servitude by revealing to them that the responsibility for changing their condition rests with them. In such circumstances water brings blessings, as in the 'flot' or floods of joy d'Arrast feels welling up inside him: 'le bruit des eaux l'emplissait d'un bonheur tumultueux' (p. 1683).

4

Marguerite Yourcenar
'Le Lait de la mort'

Sally Wallis

When asked why she wrote fiction rather than historical studies, Marguerite Yourcenar told Matthieu Galey:

> Parce que je voulais offrir un certain angle de vue . . . une certaine peinture de la condition humaine qui ne peut passer qu'à travers un homme, ou des hommes. Je crois à la grande liberté que nous octroie l'Histoire en montrant aux gens de notre temps que ce qu'ils croient unique appartient au rythme de la condition humaine et aux solutions qu'ils superposent . . . on pourrait superposer d'autres solutions, qui ont été essayées ailleurs.[1]

This comment perhaps best encapsulates where Yourcenar saw the value of her work to lie, particularly in relation to her novels and short stories. In them she constantly reworks patterns of events and/or emotions which are repeated through time and which are approached by their protagonists from different angles. 'Le Lait de la mort', as we shall see, draws together common themes found in her work, such as the universality of the human condition and the recurrence of human patterns of behaviour. By drawing on myth, 'une voie d'accès vers différentes grandes images possibles de l'humain',[2] Yourcenar, particularly in her early work, seems to be searching for solutions to the complexities of the human condition. The short story of 'Le Lait de la mort' has an added piquancy because of Yourcenar's own situation.[3] Separated as she was from her real mother by the latter's death following childbirth, one approaches the story with the suspicion that it may be an expiatory piece, the result of a writer whose life has from the very beginning been associated with suffering and death. In various interviews, Yourcenar seems to have protested too much that the absence of her mother never troubled her[4] while at the same time frequently involving the mother-figures to be found in her work in violence or death. Another possibility is that Yourcenar wanted to wipe out any trace of Fernande, her real mother, and replace it with a depiction of the ideal mother. As I have suggested elsewhere,[5] her attempts to alienate herself from her real mother may have been to facilitate her imagined adoption by her mother's best friend and her father's lover, Jeanne de Reval,[6] an altogether worthier mother-figure. Alternatively, the reader can believe that the story articulates the necessary scission from the mother-figure at an early age to avoid an unhealthy mutual dependence between mother and child. Yourcenar was, after all, intelligent enough to realize that her life would have been very different had her mother lived.[7]

'Le Lait de la mort' is also important in the context of Yourcenar's complete œuvre because of frequent criticism that her work has a dearth of substantial female characters.[8] These allegations, while not without foundation, fail to take into account Yourcenar's perception of the female condition. She observes:[9]

> Pour des raisons en partie naturelles et biologiques, en partie sûrement sociales, la femme accepte trop souvent l'image artificielle que la société où elle vit lui renvoie d'elle-même, consent, comme à plaisir, à s'enfermer étroitement dans des intérêts souvent facticement féminins, au lieu d'être en tout, et magnifiquement, un être humain femme.

This acceptance of a socially imposed role is depicted by Yourcenar in her writing. It is in the context of how things are rather than how she would like them to be that she writes. 'Le Lait de la mort', then, is a text which draws together common themes in Yourcenar's œuvre as a whole: it demonstrates Yourcenar's experiments with often cumbersome mythical structures, and it has personal relevance to Yourcenar both as a woman and as an individual left motherless at the age of ten days.

This particular short story is found in her collection entitled *Les Nouvelles orientales*,[10] written in the course of the 1930s and dedicated to André Embiricos, a Greek writer and homosexual with whom she was in love at the time of writing. The stories are nearly all of Eastern origin although 'Le Lait de la mort' is based on a Balkan ballad dating from the Middle Ages. There are really two stories, one set within the other. On a cruise ship one passenger tells another the story surrounding a tower he has visited the previous day. In the story three brothers attempt to build a watchtower by means of which they intend to protect themselves from the pillaging Turks. However, every time they construct the tower, it falls down. The instability is atttibuted not to a lack of construction skills but to the fact that it does not have in its foundations the skeleton of a man or woman to hold it up. The three men agree that one of their wives should be used in the structure to ensure their collective safety from the marauding Turks. The eldest brother no longer loves his wife and would be happy to see her entombed in a wall; the second brother plans to warn his wife to stay away from the site where they are building the tower on the appointed day; and only the youngest brother has misgivings about the plan as he still loves his wife and is too honest to deceive his brothers. Inevitably, it is the latter's wife who brings the men their lunch the next day and is chosen to be encased in the Scutari Tower. On her arrival, her husband protests and is accidently killed by his brothers. When she sees her husband lying dead, the woman protests no further and allows herself to be bricked into the tower. She belatedly remembers her baby and asks that gaps be left for her breasts and her eyes so that her baby may be brought for feeding and she may watch him thrive. The two brothers agree to this and the child is brought three times a day. There is a miraculous and prodigious flow of milk and the baby has ample sustenance until he himself turns away from the breast, at which point the milk gradually dries up. The tourist's tale is interrupted by a gypsy who has a small child with her and is begging. His listener, so inspired by this story of maternal courage and selflessness, offers the woman money, only to be told by his storyteller that the gypsy woman rubs ointment on her child's eyes to make them red and inflamed in order to evoke pity in passers-by. Such treatment will eventually make the child go blind. They conclude that 'il y a mères et mères' (p. 58).

The mother walled up in the Scutari Tower is of particular interest because in her fictional and autobiographical writing, Yourcenar generally creates two sorts of mother. As has been observed, there are those closely associated with death often directly or indirectly through childbirth; for example, Clytemnestre, who is lured to Electre's house by the latter's pretence that she is pregnant and then mercilessly slain by her violent daughter, in Yourcenar's play *Electre ou la chute des masques*; also Yourcenar's own mother who died in childbirth leaving behind her a room that 'avait l'air du lieu d'un crime' (*Souvenirs pieux*, p. 32). In contrast to these women there are others who are depicted as ideal mothers, such as Valentine in *Anna, soror . . .* and Jeanne in *Quoi: L'Éternité*. The resemblance between these two characters is striking: both have beautiful hands and soft voices; both combine Christian ideals with a measure of their own philosophy; both put the people they love before themselves. What is particularly unusual about the mother in 'Le Lait de la mort' is that she combines both types, since she is associated with death but at the same time transforms the violence she suffers into life for her child, much being made of her soft warmth and passive acceptance of her fate. After all, on realizing that her husband is already dead, she allows herself to be bricked up without demur: 'elle se laissa sans cris et sans larmes conduire par les deux frères jusqu'à la niche creusée dans la muraille ronde de la tour' (p. 53). One is reminded of Yourcenar's words in the Postface to *Anna, soror . . .* where she describes Anna's mother Valentine as:

> un premier état de la femme parfaite telle qu'il m'est souvent arrivé de la rêver: à la fois aimante et détachée, passive par sagesse et non par faiblesse. (p. 246)

In some respects the mother of the Scutari Tower seems to reconcile Yourcenar's feelings of anger and idealism towards the mother-figure and embody them in this particular literary creation. This said, there is no doubt that the complex emotions Yourcenar felt towards her dead mother are reflected in different fictional, mythical and real models in her work. This notion of one life being articulated by and through the experiences and emotions of a whole series of real, fictional and mythical people is explored much later in Yourcenar's autobiographical trilogy. It is hinted at here, when, in his introduction to the story of the mother of the Scutari Tower, the narrator alludes to 'un poète qui ne pouvait aimer aucune femme parce qu'il avait dans une autre vie rencontré Antigone' (p. 47). The line recalls a line from one of Yourcenar's favourite poems by Rimbaud, 'Délires II, Alchimie du verbe', in which the poet writes 'A chaque être, plusieurs autres vies me semblaient dues'.[11] Through her writing, Yourcenar is able to explore different mother-figures, all of whom remain separate and distinct. To take this to its logical conclusion, every mother-figure in her fictional and autobiographical narratives, whether associated with death and anguish, or love and forgiveness, or both, is a potential mother-figure for the writer herself.

As 'Le Lait de la mort' was written at a time when, for Yourcenar, the part that myth played in her work was essential,[12] it is within a mythical framework that Yourcenar articulates a sense of Other; a feeling that universal patterns of behaviour are repeated within a series of different contexts. Her early works are characterized by mythical models which she later found to be too inflexible and lacking in credibility or interesting motivation. Like her first version of *Denier du rêve*, 'Le Lait de la mort' is rather clumsily encumbered with too many mythical and cultural references. Whether this is a deliberate attempt to demonstrate her erudition, or a desire to bring another dimension to the text, is hard to say. There is no doubt that in some of her early works the use of several unrelated cultural references, one after another, works quite effectively, notably in *Le Coup de grâce*.[13] The reader can be certain of the worthiness of the protagonist in 'Le Lait de la mort' when on the third page the narrator, in the space of eight lines, puts her on an equal footing with Antigone, Andromaque, Griselda, Isolde and Aude (p. 47). In Greek mythology, Antigone put sisterly duty before everything in order to bury her brother, Polyneices, believing it was a sacred duty, superior to all human laws, to bury one's kin.[14] The story of Andromaque, also based on Greek myth, is retold in Racine's famous French tragedy. Andromaque is held captive by Pyrrhus who is in love with her. To bend Andromaque to his will, Pyrrhus threatens to surrender her son, Astyanax, to the Greeks. Andromaque wishes to remain loyal to her dead husband, Hector, but fears for her son. She finally agrees to marry Pyrrhus, but plans to kill herself thereafter. Not content to limit herself to Greek myth, Yourcenar also draws on Boccaccio's character, patient Griselda, found in the tenth story of his *Decameron*[15], and then jumps to the medieval romances, citing Isolde[16] and Aude.[17] The plight and behaviour of these women underline the extent to which patterns of behaviour are repeated through time. The quiet heroism of these women, their endurance, their love for their men and children, their wisdom, can and have recurred through time. One is reminded of the words of Yourcenar's later protagonist, Emperor Hadrien, when at the end of his life he says:

> quelques hommes penseront, travailleront et sentiront comme nous: j'ose compter sur ces continuateurs placés à intervalles irréguliers le long des siècles, sur cette intermittente immortalité.[18]

The mother of the Scutari Tower is undoubtedly one of these 'continuatrices' on a route peopled with many literary and mythical examples of motherly devotion.

Unusually for Yourcenar, in *Les Nouvelles orientales* there is no long preface or postscript in which she analyses and explains her own writing.[19] It has already been observed, however, that 'Le Lait de la mort' encloses a legend in a contemporary narrative frame that is as significant as the story itself. The narrator of the story is Jules Boutrin, an engineer whose profession leaves us no reason to doubt the precision with which the story will be told, although, significantly, it links him to the brothers in his story. He has come ashore from a cruise ship which has docked at Ragusa and is talking to an acquaintance he has made on board called Philip Mild. The name is not without significance. This is not an interlocutor who will frequently interject or query the narrator. On the first page, Yourcenar artfully sets the scene for both the narration and the story itself (not the only parallel between these two narratives) by emphasizing the heat and the dazzling brightness created by reflections off the bare mountains and the water off the Adriatic. The reader is told:

> Les montagnes pelées de l'Herzégovine maintenaient Raguse sous des feux de miroirs ardents. (p. 45)

Also, that 'des mouettes' are 'presque insupportablement blanches' (p. 45), and that they sit 'à l'ombre d'un parasol couleur feu' (p. 46). The writer emphasizes the stuffiness and lack of air with observations such as 'il faisait chaud comme il ne fait chaud qu'en enfer' (p. 45); 'une demi-obscurité étouffante' (p. 45); 'une puanteur' (p. 45). This is a cruel environment and particularly appropriate for the claustro-phobic tale the reader is about to hear. Philip asks Boutrin to tell

> l'histoire la plus belle et la moins vraie possible, et qui me fasse oublier les mensonges patriotiques et contradictoires des quelques journaux que je viens d'acheter. (p. 46)

Already the reader perceives that there is to be a certain amount of cynicism attached to the telling of the story, for although it will restore the characters' faith in human nature, it cannot possibly be a true reflection of their everyday experience. Furthermore, it is desirable that the story be a far cry from the important and principally male domain of politics and work. They are, after all, on holiday and it is therefore appropriate that the story essentially takes place in the domestic space where people, and principally women, are traditionally honest and unselfish. There is a patronizing tone about their whole discussion. Boutrin asks Mild:

> A propos, Philip, êtes-vous assez chanceux pour avoir ce qu'on appelle une bonne mère?—Quelle question, fit négligemment le jeune Anglais. Ma mère est belle, mince, maquillée, dure comme la glace d'une vitrine. Que voulez-vous encore que je vous dise? Quand nous sortons ensemble, on me prend pour son frère aîné. (pp. 46-7)

In other words, he cynically suggests that although she looks all she should in society's eyes—youthful and beautiful—she, like other mothers of her time, is not as genuine as mothers once were but is rather one of those 'poupées incassables qui passent pour la réalité' (p. 47). The expression 'dure comme la glace d'une vitrine' is striking, firstly because one does not normally expect a son to perceive his mother as hard, lacking in warmth and difficult to reach, and secondly because the emphasis seems to be placed on the reflection of his mother rather than the mother herself. She has less substance than the examples of womanhood that Boutrin goes on to describe, such as Antigone, Andromaque and Griselda. Does their boorish and disrespectful attitude not warn the reader early on in the tale that the narrator and his friend are only able to see things in terms of black and white? They are judgemental and undiscerning.

66

We should be in no doubt that the narrator and his friend share a sexist view of the perfect woman which demands her complete submission, self-sacrifice, and unquestioning devotion to family. They believe that motherhood is the ultimate and indeed only province for women's self-realization. The men observe:

> ce n'est plus que dans les légendes des pays à demi barbares qu'on rencontre encore ces créatures riches de lait et de larmes dont on serait fier d'être l'enfant . . . (p. 47)

As far as Philip and Boutrin are concerned, perfect examples of womanhood only exist in places where women have not learned the rules of a selfish, image-conscious and duplicitous society and where they are governed only by a biological imperative. It is just this sort of text which has earned Yourcenar her bad reputation with the feminist critics, for she seems to be colluding with a patriarchal society which is seen by feminists to impose limiting female stereotypes on women. However, it also seems clear that Yourcenar writes with tongue in cheek when she creates such obviously flawed male perceptions in her characters. It is highly significant that far from colluding with a patriarchal society, she flags up what is wrong with one by choosing the tale within a tale technique to emphasize her point. Her tale, in which motherhood becomes synonymous with sacrifice in the face of male aggression, is recounted by a narrator who is as guilty as his protagonist's male captors. Their guilt lies principally in their decision to force one of the wives to become part of the tower's foundations. What should one make of this decision? On the face of it, the Turks represent the enemy or Other and the brothers and their wives must work together to keep themselves safe from the Turkish threat. However, within their group there are also social divisions in which the women are seen as Other. The eldest brother's wife is only saved because her husband talks in his sleep and she learns in advance the plan to encase one of the wives in the tower. Interestingly, she does not see fit to warn the other wives of the scheme. The women fail to work as a collective body and so more easily become victims. The second is subjugated by her husband to the extent that she cowers at his displeasure and dashes off to clean his clothes, whilst the third and most loved wife falls foul of the plan devised by the brothers. As Joan E. Howard[20] suggests, the social

67

structure within which the group interacts then 'relies upon the sacrifice of women to keep [it] from crumbling. The profoundly phallic image of the tower itself could hardly more vividly suggest just who stands to gain from this state of affairs' (p. 89). As the brothers start to brick her up, the third wife dwells on the pleasures she will no longer enjoy. Emphasis is placed on how she uses her body to nurture, feed, love and serve her husband and child: she will no longer be able to rock her child on her knees; to cook a meal; to be held and admired by her beloved husband.

The mother of the tale is, of course, Madonna-like: 'toute droite au fond de sa niche, elle avait l'air d'une Marie debout derrière son autel' (p. 54). Use of the word 'autel' suggests the sacrificial nature of her actions. She embodies love and transforms the violence inflicted on her into a creative response by continuing to love and nurture her child. Powerful images of the life-giving flow of milk are repeated several times: 'des flots de lait coulèrent de ses seins durs et tièdes' (p. 56); 'ses seins immobiles n'avaient rien perdu de leur douce abondance de sources' (p. 56); 'le jaillissement miraculeux continua' (p. 57). Words like 'flots', 'abondance', 'sources' and 'jaillissement' suggest a plentiful supply of nourishment; others like 'tièdes and 'douce' reinforce the warmth and comfort of the mother's milk. None of these descriptions have associations with the cold sterility of death. The milk seems to flow freely from the wall of the tower, and whereas words like 'jaillissement' and 'flots' suggest a spontaneous gushing, breast milk would normally only come if the breast were stimulated by the child sucking. The milk appears to flow as if from the wall itself, suggesting that the mother has become part of a greater life-cycle.

The mother's love seems to conquer even death but it is not this positive message with which the reader is left. On the contrary, the narrator seeks to undermine the high idealism of his story by observing that his interlocutor is unable to distinguish between a worthy mother and an unworthy one. The beggar woman to whom he gives money puts ointment on her child's eyes. In the long term such applications will turn the child blind. This will assure the woman's financial future and will create a permanent mutual dependence between mother and child. By recounting the rumours surrounding the gypsy woman, the narrator negates the underlying positive message of his story and further emphasizes his own misogynistic position.

Yourcenar thus plays with her readers' expectations and assumptions. The narrator and his interlocutor represent the cynical and chauvinistic view of women's place in society. Their prejudices and preconceptions are frequently seen to be unjustified. They never hesitate to emphasize that they are different from the barbaric men in the story and the wicked gypsy beggar-woman. In fact, they are in a position to offer their protection to the gypsy woman but instead they judge her and indulge in their own unrealistic fantasies of the perfect woman without for a moment stopping to judge themselves. Effectively, they are no better than the three brothers who build the tower. They are guilty of prejudice on the grounds of race and sex. Instead of learning from the tale of the mother of the Scutari Tower, they repeat the act of male aggression by refusing to help the gypsy woman and pass judgement on her instead.

The conduct of the two mothers diverges on another crucial point: the gentle, selfless mother encased in the Scutari Tower nurtures her child until he no longer needs or wants her, 'le jaillissement [. . .] continua, jusqu'à ce que l'enfant sevré se détournât de lui-même du sein' (p. 57); the gypsy woman, by making her child blind, renders him permanently dependent on her for his physical and financial well-being: 'cette femme aura alors son gagne-pain assuré, et pour toute la vie, car le soin d'un infirme est une profession lucrative' (p. 58). This brusque jolt back to reality reminds the men of the high price one can pay for having one's own 'créature riche de lait et de larmes' (p. 47). To remain tied to the maternal figure implies a loss of freedom and a renunciation of any loving bond other than the maternal one. Yourcenar, rather than expiating any guilt she may have felt concerning her mother's death may instead be expressing relief at having escaped her mother's influence. A life dictated by Fernande's religious superstitions and social conventions would have produced a very different Yourcenar. In *Souvenirs pieux*, Yourcenar reflects on how things might have been had Fernande lived[21] And concludes that 'tout porte à croire que je l'aurais d'abord aimée d'un amour égoïste et distrait [. . .] puis d'une affection faite surtout d'habitude, traversée de querelles, de plus en plus mitigée par l'indifférence' (p. 66).

She feels she would have managed to break free from Fernande's influence. Her account of Fernande cannot compare with the heroic ideal mother of the Scutari Tower, a passive, gentle, selfless woman whose whole existence revolves around her husband and child. Although this woman's experience is the literal opposite of liberation, made a prisoner within the walls of the tower as she is, her goodness and creative powers burst forth in the form of the milk. Able as she is to rise above the brothers' brutish behaviour, to turn it into a power for good, the mother of the Scutari Tower is undoubtedly a testimony of both Yourcenar's guilt and desire. She is a 'créature [. . .] dont on serait fier d'être l'enfant' (p. 47) for she embodies the passivity and selflessness which Yourcenar outlines elsewhere in her work as the female ideal.[22] She also represents a darker side of Yourcenar's consciousness, for she is the mother who is conveniently removed from the child's existence and whose influence is cut dramatically short. She is, for Yourcenar, in every sense the ideal mother: heroic but banished.

Simone de Beauvoir
'La Femme rompue'

Ray Davison

La Femme rompue is a collection of three short stories published by Simone de Beauvoir in 1967–8. The volume title, translated into English by Patrick O'Brian as *The Woman Destroyed*,[1] is also the title of the final and easily the longest story.[2] This collection, it should be noted, is Beauvoir's last fictional work and, like *Les Belles Images* of 1966, is sandwiched between the various tomes of the auto-biographical project which carried Beauvoir, to a large extent, away from fiction from 1958 onwards. *La Femme rompue* is not, however, Beauvoir's only collection of short stories, for she published, in 1979, under the revised title *Quand prime le spirituel*, five short stories, originally called *La Primanté du spirituel*, which were written in the 1930s but were rejected for publication at that time.[3]

La Femme rompue is of particular interest because of its power to generate debate. Beauvoir takes a quasi-exhausted and, some would say, totally exhausted thematic—the married woman discovering her husband's infidelity, the triangularity thereby created, the fragmen-tation and near dissolution of the woman under pressure—and manages to reanimate and redynamize it. She manages to do this, at one level, by situating her fiction discreetly at the interface of her philosophical ideas, including her conceptions of independent and complicitous womanhood. In this way, the rather mundane naturalistic cadre is made to flag wide-ranging and important philosophical debates about freedom, fidelity, authenticity, sincerity, inauthenticity and dependency, and to raise the question of power relations between the sexes. At a further level, Beauvoir breathes new life into the thematic by a skilled use of the diary form: Monique Lacombe, the betrayed wife, is both producer and reader of her *Journal* and Beauvoir felicitously uses the optical advantages of the diary form (Monique's self-awareness, self-deception, evasion strategies and so forth) to pose the central question of Monique's agency in her fate as victim of infidelity and eventual abandonment. At this level, as we shall see, Beauvoir is very much concerned with depicting Monique as largely the victim of her own inauthenticity and flight into emotional dependency. However, there is a further and perhaps more important level of meaning to the short story: Beauvoir's description of Monique's fate seems to raise problems beyond Beauvoir's conscious intellectual intentions and designs. The harrowingly painful evocations of Monique's solitude and near disintegration of her sense of self articulate the all too human vulnerabilities and fears which Beauvoir herself had painfully experienced but was not so keen to explore directly in the autobiographical project. My argument here would be that because Beauvoir so resolutely believed that Monique is a victim of herself and of dependency, and that she herself, Simone, has avoided these self-same traps, as an authentic independent woman, this short story enables Beauvoir to talk about herself unconsciously in a manner that autobiography does not. In other words, and paradoxically, because Beauvoir is so distanced in her conscious mind from Monique Lacombe, the victim, precisely because she does not think she is talking about herself, she does manage to talk about herself more interestingly than when she uses the direct autobiographical mode. Such an argument, as we shall see, calls into play the Freudian notion of repression, reverses the claims that Beauvoir herself made about autobiography and fiction, and simultaneously enhances the interpretative possibilities and vitality of this short story.

What follows is structured to focus on four principal areas. First, I want to look at Beauvoir's understanding, at the time of writing 'La Femme rompue', of the relationship between fiction and philosophy and her general view of the purpose of fictional constructs. This will include, by implication at least, the short story, for Beauvoir never discusses the 'genre' as such, even when composing her 'Introduction aux *Contes* de Perrault'.[4] Rather, she uses the generic term 'roman'[5] to cover both long and short works of fiction as though the actual central features of fiction have a generality beyond specific types. Secondly, I shall examine Beauvoir's own declared aims, in 'La Femme rompue', to show how she envisaged the link between the concrete particulars of the story or the naturalistic framework and her own philosophy, particularly her theses concerning the dangers awaiting women who try to avoid the exigencies of authentic freedom and cocoon themselves in false and fragile worlds of emotional security. Thirdly, Beauvoir's comments about the actual reception of her text and the critical responses which it aroused beyond the parameters set by her own subjective intentions will be examined. This will enable us to see both the inadequacy and inanity of some critical discourses and it will also make clear that Beauvoir is a more complex writer than she consciously intended to be in 'La Femme rompue' and that her story creates ambiguities and interpretative possibilities beyond her intentional objectives. This ambiguity will lead us into a fourth and final area: the complexity and variety of philosophical viewpoint articulated by this easily read short story, the expressive capacity of the concrete particulars to explore the ontology of the victim and to open up perspectives on existence and relationships beyond those of an admonitory tale encoded within the narration of a commonplace event. 'La Femme rompue' will thus be seen as providing a far deeper insight into existence (her own and others) than Beauvoir's autobiographical writings of the time.

In 'Mon Expérience d'écrivain', a lecture delivered in Japan in October 1966,[6] Beauvoir declared, echoing Sartre, that the role of the writer in general is to communicate 'le sens vécu de l'être dans le monde'. The writer does this by the creation of an object, a text, which has the power to be a universal singular, that is to say, a concrete particular or set of concrete particulars, a private experience, capable of achieving an expressive generalizability or universality. This universality will create a bridge between individual subjectivities to create what she calls the privileged domain of the intersubjective, the domain of literature in its widest sense. Novelists and philosophers construct this universal singular in discreet and differing but complementary ways. Developing ideas already contained in the 1948 article, 'Littérature et Métaphysique' in *L'Existentialisme et la sagesse des nations*[7] but refining them substantially, she argues that the philosopher produces conceptual systems in an attempt to formulate universal categories capable of synthesizing a multitude of

73

contingent, random particulars resistant to systematic thought. The novelist, however, takes these same particulars but creates 'un objet aux multiples facettes',[8] an object capable of varied interpretation, seizing the experience of existence as ambiguous, complex, unpredictable and resistant to final and definitive enunciation. In fiction, ideas best arise not 'en clair', she says (as tended to be the case in her earlier works, so she thinks),[9] not explicitly but as interpretative superstructures generated by the infrastructure of concrete particulars coming from 'le vécu', the contingencies of lived experience. However, if irreducibility and the avoidance of a definitive viewpoint are generic to fictional constructs, Beauvoir is at pains to distance herself, in 'Mon Expérience d'écrivain', from the *nouveaux romanciers* and the *Tel Quel* Group, those precursors of postmodernism in the France of *l'après-guerre*. Fiction still explores, for Beauvoir, the real world and reveals it in its complexity. Because of this, fiction has heuristic value, helps us to understand experience and retains its powers of exploration and communication of existence. Fiction is not to be solipsized in self-referentiality.[10] We may also note, in passing, that if she has any dissatisfaction to express with fiction, it is because fiction requires structure and choice whereas existence is contingency and profusion. For this reason, she tells us, she is turning to autobiography because its modalities of expression more adequately capture the truth and fluid diversity of life. Finally, two dangers beset the writer of fiction which aspires to philosophical exploration. First, abstraction or over-explicit statement or enunciation of ideas run the risk of producing the impoverished *roman à thèse*, a devitalized and reductionist text devoid of existential ambiguity and variety. Second, if the concrete particulars fail to articulate ideas beyond their referential starting point, if they remain locked in immanence and particularity, the story will fail to achieve the status of a universal singular and simply remain anecdotal and banal.[11]

The starting point, then, of 'La Femme rompue' is 'le sens vécu de l'être dans le monde' of the married woman in her forties who discovers her husband's infidelity. Beauvoir takes a situation which is seemingly so commonplace as to constitute a natural, almost an inevitable, event and to use its concrete particulars for philosophical exploration. In *Tout Compte fait*, she writes:

J'avais récemment reçu les confidences de plusieurs femmes d'une quarantaine d'années que leurs maris venaient de quitter pour une autre. Malgré la diversité de leurs caractères et des circonstances, il y avait dans toutes leurs histoires d'intéressantes similitudes: elles ne comprenaient rien à ce qui leur arrivait, les conduites de leur mari leur paraissaient contradictoires et aberrantes, leur rivale indigne de son amour; leur univers s'écroulait, elles finissaient par ne plus savoir qui elles étaient. D'une autre manière que Laurence [of *Les Belles Images*] elles se débattaient dans l'ignorance et l'idée m'est venue de donner à voir leur nuit.[12]

Thus, we can see that Beauvoir takes a commonplace event but has a clear communicative and, one might say, almost pedagogic purpose: she is going to provide these women with a fictional structure which will express and illuminate their dilemmas 'donner à voir leur nuit', a torch so they can prospect in the dark and understand what is happening to them. However, Beauvoir also makes clear, in conformity with her theory of fiction, that this story is not to be a tract or explicit lesson in the dangers of dependency, phallic complicity or self-victimization articulated through Monique as 'The Little Mermaid' or 'L'Amoureuse'. As in *Les Belles Images*, Beauvoir, despite the dangers that she knows only too well, will ask the public to 'lire entre les lignes'[13] and to work out the meanings for themselves:

Il ne s'agissait pas pour moi de raconter en clair cette banale histoire mais de montrer, à travers son journal intime, comment la victime essayait d'en fuir la vérité. La difficulté était encore plus grande que dans *Les Belles Images* car Laurence cherche timidement la lumière tandis que tout l'effort de Monique tend à l'oblitérer, par des mensonges à soi, des oublis, des erreurs; de page en page le journal se conteste: mais à travers de nouvelles fabulations, de nouvelles omissions. Elle tisse elle-même les ténèbres dans lesquelles elle sombre au point de perdre sa propre image. J'aurais voulu que le lecteur lût ce récit comme un roman policier; j'ai semé de-ci de-là des indices qui permettent de trouver la clé du mystère: mais à condition qu'on dépiste Monique comme on dépiste un coupable. Aucune phrase n'a en soi son sens, aucun détail n'a de valeur sinon replacé dans l'ensemble du journal. La vérité n'est jamais avouée: elle se trahit si on y regarde d'assez près.[14]

The fictional construct created by Beauvoir to explore the paradigm of the married woman betrayed, the generic woman destroyed, is Monique's diary which constitutes the story. Composed over a six and a half month period, with some eighty-five entries, the diary is to be read by us, Beauvoir says, as detectives seeking to track down Monique's culpability for her own fate. The diary form will make the detective work more difficult because Monique will not wish to acknowledge that her own life-choices are the cause of her betrayal. The story is not conceived by Beauvoir as a feminist protest against the way men treat women or husbands treat their wives in marriage, but as a carefully crafted, well-designed lesson to bring into focus and to expose the ploys of evasion and self-deception adopted by Monique to mask her own responsibility and agency for her victimized state. As Beauvoir stated very clearly in the 'Prière d'insérer' of 'La Femme rompue':

> La femme rompue est la victime stupéfaite de la vie qu'elle s'est choisie: une dépendence conjugale qui la laisse dépouillée de tout et de son être même quand l'amour lui est refusé.[15]

Although, in the same preface, Beauvoir disputes the point that she is not creating a fiction 'à thèse' or proposing any lessons, it is clear that she has a well-defined purpose in 'La Femme rompue' when describing Monique's pain. One might be tempted to project whole-sale into those spaces between the lines of which Beauvoir speaks, the theoretical propositions of Le Deuxième Sexe of 1949 which are certainly reaffirmed in their entirety (at roughly the time of the composition of 'La Femme rompue') in the 1966 lecture in Japan, 'Situation de la femme d'aujourd'hui'.[16] In such works, of course, Beauvoir, famously and infamously, describes the woman who devotes her whole life to the dependent loving of a man. Such a woman cocoons herself in his world of male power as an escape from the demanding project to build a sense of independent personhood only to be jettisoned by the male in later life as oppressive immanence on the high seas of emotional contingency. Certainly Monique inhabits this dependecy culture and subscribes to the 'myth' of the ideal couple. She says of her husband, Maurice: 'Il m'a suffi, je n'ai vécu que pour lui' (p. 133) and: 'Nous étions l'un pour l'autre une absolue transparence' (p. 129). She has constructed the protective love-nest of domesticity and children for her and Maurice, and has allowed herself to be removed from the world of productive work, earning power and independent self-definition. She is the loving wife and mother, locked in the prison of the home, Noëllie, the mistress, is the Nemesis figure, the other that Monique might have been, who steals away her husband because of the characteristics Monique has not developed: independence and a professional career. Monique describes Noëllie thus in a moment of telling irony and self-deception: 'Noëllie est une avocate brillante et dévorée d'ambition; c'est une femme seule— divorcée, avec une fille—de moeurs très libres, mondaine, très lancée: juste mon contraire' (p. 136). Noëllie plays the role of 'le tiers', the triangulating third person, slowly decentering Monique's world, destroying its intimate space and her illusions of oneness and permanence with Maurice. The love-nest is torn apart, Monique's identity is shredded and she is thrown back, alone and vulnerable, into the original contingency of being.

It is painful to witness Monique's response to the rivalling mistress. Advised by her well-meaning friend, Isabelle, and constituting herself as 'la championne de l'intégrale fidélité' (p. 164) she chooses 'la tactique du sourire' (p. 137), endeavouring passively and with a loving smile to tolerate Maurice's infidelity. She represents it to herself as 'une histoire de peau', a transient sexual pleasure, devoid of authentic emotional substance. Noëllie is thoroughly demonized by Monique who describes her thus:

> l'arrivisme, le snobisme, le goût de l'argent, la passion de paraître. Elle n'a aucune idée personnelle, elle manque radicalement de sensibilité: elle se plie aux modes. Il y a tant d'impudeur et d'exhibitionnisme dans ses coquetteries que je me demande même si elle n'est pas frigide. (p. 139)

Monique sees herself as authentic, caring, loyal and true but it is one of the cruel ironies of this text, as it progresses, that these conventional notions appear to lose their polar-star clarity and disperse in ambivalence. Monique loses all confidence in herself and in the memory of her past life as loyal wife and loving mother as Noëllie relentlessly establishes an ascendancy in her husband's life: 'Je sais tout mon passé par cœur et soudain je n'en sais plus rien' (pp. 193–4). The flowing language of the early pages of the diary breaks down as

Monique's personality crumbles and her emotional confidence fails. Compare: 'Le soir va tomber, mais il fait encore tiède. C'est un de ces instants émouvants où la terre est si bien accordée aux hommes [sic] qu'il semble impossible que tous ne soient pas heureux' (p. 123) and 'Ma vie derrière moi s'est tout entière effondrée, comme dans ces tremblements de terre où le sol se dévore lui-même' (p. 192). Monique eventually feels that Maurice has murdered language (echoing Macbeth's murder of sleep) and her alienation from her world of conjugal security is total.

The disintegration of Monique's world and sense of self is pursued with a clinical precision by Beauvoir who says of this part of her text:

> je n'ai jamais rien écrit de plus sombre que cette histoire: toute la seconde partie n'est qu'un cri d'angoisse et l'effritement final de l'héroïne est plus lugubre qu'une mort.[17]

Haemorrhaging profusely from irregular periods, losing weight, pathetically seeking comfort in astrology, graphology and the simplistic utterances of her friend, Isabelle, unable any more to wear the necklace that Maurice, in what is now a former life, once bought for her, Monique certainly does not present a pretty picture to the world: she is indeed a broken woman. Naturally, it is possible to argue from all this that Monique pays a very high price indeed for not having, as it were, read Le Deuxième Sexe properly and for not heeding its warnings before she embarked so precipitously and so improvidently on the journey to marriage, children, domesticity, dependency and rejection. However, at the same time, the emotional power of the closing passages suggest also that these spaces between the lines do not necessarily lead us only to Beauvoir's pedagogic project to construct Monique as the self-created victim of her own evasions, inauthenticity and 'mauvaise foi'. In tandem with Monique as the expression of the inauthenticity of the 'amoureuse' is another Monique representing what I like to call the repressed ideal of committed love. Since Beauvoir's own theory of fiction invites us to avoid finality of enunciation and interpretation and thus to go beyond the parameters set by her conscious designs; it is this reading of Monique that I now wish to explore.

In pursuing such an alternative reading of Monique's status as a victim, a useful starting point is Beauvoir's own statement about the reception of her text:

Quand le livre [*La Femme rompue*] sortit la fin de janvier 68, le public lui fit le même succès de vente qu'aux *Belles Images*; j'ai reçu un grand nombre de lettres écrites par des écrivains, des étudiants, des professeurs qui avaient très bien saisi mes intentions et me félicitaient de m'être encore une fois renouvelée. Cependant dans l'ensemble le livre fut encore plus mal compris que le précédent et cette fois la plupart des critiques m'éreintèrent. Depuis longtemps nous souhaitions, ma sœur et moi, qu'elle illustrât un inédit de moi; il ne s'en était jamais trouvé d'assez bref. Le récit qui donne son nom au livre, 'La Femme rompue' avait les dimensions requises et lui inspira de très beaux burins. J'ai voulu faire connaître au public l'existence de ce volume, à tirage restreint, signé de nos deux noms et j'ai accepté que mon texte parût en livraison dans *Elle* accompagné des burins de ma sœur. Aussitôt je fus submergée de lettres émanant de femmes rompues, demi-rompues, ou en instance de rupture. S'identifiant à l'héroïne, elles lui attribuaient toutes les vertus et elles s'étonnaient qu'elle restât attachée à un homme indigne; leur partialité indiquait qu'à l'égard de leur mari, de leur rivale, et d'elles-mêmes, elles partageaient l'aveuglement de Monique. Leurs réactions reposaient sur un énorme contresens.
Beaucoup d'autres lecteurs, donnant de ce récit la même interprétation simpliste, l'ont déclaré insignifiant. La plupart des critiques ont prouvé par leurs comptes-rendus qu'ils l'avaient très mal lu. Ayant seulement pris connaissance de la première livraison d'*Elle*, M. Bernard Pivot s'est hâté de déclarer dans *Le Figaro littéraire* que puisque *La Femme rompue* paraissait dans un journal féminin, c'était un roman pour midinettes, un roman à l'eau de rose . . . L'étourderie de mes censeurs ne m'a pas étonnée. Ce que je n'ai pas compris, c'est pourquoi ce petit livre a déchaîné tant de haine . . . A de rares exceptions près, le jugement des critiques m'indiffère: je me fie à celui de quelques amis exigeants. Mais j'ai regretté qu'à cause de leur malveillance une partie du public n'ait pas eu envie de me lire et qu'une autre ait abordé mon roman avec un esprit prévenu. Il y a des femmes que mes idées dérangent: elles se sont empressées de croire ce qu'ils disaient de moi et elles en ont profité pour prendre des supériorités. 'Elle attend d'avoir soixante ans pour découvrir ce que sait n'importe quelle petite bonne femme', a dit l'une d'elles;

je n'ai pas su à quelle découverte elle faisait allusion. J'ai été plus touchée par la réaction de certaines femmes qui luttent pour la cause des femmes et que mes récits ont déçues parce qu'ils n'avaient rien de militant. 'Elle nous a trahies!' ont-elles dit et elles m'ont envoyé des lettres de reproche. Rien n'interdit de tirer une conclusion féministe de *La Femme rompue*: son malheur vient de la dépendance à laquelle elle a consenti. Mais surtout je ne me sens pas astreinte à choisir des héroïnes exemplaires. Décrire l'échec, l'erreur, la mauvaise foi, ce n'est, me semble-t-il, trahir personne.[18]

Clearly, Beauvoir's reactions to the critical reception of her text is quite an interesting story in its own right. However, what I find of primary importance here is Beauvoir's total confidence about her own reading of the text. As we can see, many readers, no doubt encountering this text serialized in *Elle*, empathized with Monique and saw her not so much as a victim of herself but as a victim of a cruel and unworthy husband and a ruthless, usurping, unsisterly sister, Noëllie, herself a divorcee and unable to leave alone another woman's husband. Beauvoir has no hesitation in dismissing such an interpretation as simplistic and rooted in 'un énorme contresens', that is to say that the women and readers who see themselves and Monique as victim suffer primarily from the same 'aveuglement' as Monique herself. Whilst one can certainly invoke the intentional fallacy and see Beauvoir's wish to predetermine the parameters of interpretation of her own work as sheer authorial vanity, I think that psycho-biographically something much more interesting is going on between Monique and Beauvoir and this in turn provides the story with an ambiguity and complexity in its concrete particulars beyond Beauvoir's own viewpoint. Needless to say, this ambiguity and complexity fully conform to Beauvoir's own theory of fiction as anti-reductionist and touch also upon the question raised earlier of her view of the superiority of autobiography over fiction as nearer to the truth of existence.

The first point to be made in this argument is linked to Monique's power to arouse sympathy. Fallaize has argued that whatever severity of judgement Beauvoir and her readers may reserve for Monique, this does not mean that an unsympathetic attitude underpins our responses.[19] She may well be an accomplice in her fate but her situation, as Keefe also points out, is very sad indeed and we share her pain and confusion, whatever way we apportion the blame.[20] No doubt, Monique can be seen as both agent and victim, 'à moitié victime[s], à moitié complice[s], comme tout le monde', as Sartre graphically put it.[21] However, it seems precisely as an embodiment in the text of ideal love and the myth of the couple that Monique's fate seems so sad and possibly unfair. In one sense, Monique is to lose her illusions of oneness and permanence; she discovers the truth of change and that emotions are in time and transitory. The fragmentation of her sense of the past and of the meaning of her emotional life with Maurice destroys the security of her emotional responses. Closeness to and intimacy with Maurice is lost and she enters into a cold and lonely world. Betrayal ruptures her sense of plenitude and she is on the receiving end of a very nasty experience —rejection. No great sense of freedom and possibility in the future emanates from the abandoned state—Camus once observed, through one of his characters: 'On croit mourir pour punir sa femme, et on lui rend la liberté'[22]—but rather Monique is hurt at the centre of her being and arouses our compassion. The power of emotional ties, notwithstanding economic circumstances, the reality of emotional surrender to the other, the all too human proclivity to invest heavily in a partner, these all form part of Monique's make-up and help to prevent her from being seen as simply culpable and pathetic. Beauvoir arguably has fed into Monique's portrait her own anguished pre-occupation with the myth of the couple and oneness, and the pain she herself experienced in her triangular dealings with Sartre. Toril Moi has lucidly charted the expressions of lost oneness in Beauvoir, paying particular attention to their ramifications in *L'Invitée* and, more significantly for our purposes, in those diary entries made by Beauvoir after Sartre's revelations about his attachment to Dolorès which made Beauvoir feel that she had been eclipsed by her rival and produced the famous ultimatum: 'She or I?'[23] We may well not wish to follow Moi when she invites us to view these expressions in psychoanalytic terms as exemplifications of 'an imaginary fantasy of unity with the other' and attempts to chronicle Beauvoir's 'difficult separation from the imaginary matrix and her painful entry into the symbolic order'.[24] Yet whatever view one takes of this thematic of lost oneness in Beauvoir, there is no denying its relevance and its power, and it underpins what Moi calls 'the harrowing descriptions of depressive passivity'[25] which accompany the references to 'The Little Mermaid', 'amoureuse' and 'tête de mort' dimensions of Beauvoir's work, of which 'La Femme rompue' is such an excellent example.

A further point which can be made to underline the curious relationship between Beauvoir and Monique in this story is related to the use of the diary form. Fallaize has rightly pointed out that Monique uses the diary form to confirm her own self-image under pressure[26] but she does not discuss this fact with reference to Beauvoir's *own* use of the diary when the author herself is under pressure. Conversely, Moi makes this point very effectively—that Beauvoir's 'personal writing'[27] (Moi's term for Beauvoir's letters and diaries, including fragments of diaries used in her autobiographical works) are undertaken 'to help and sustain the writer in all but the most extreme distress'.[28] She also argues that Beauvoir uses diary excerpts in her memoirs precisely during 1939–40, 1947 and 1958, the periods of great emotional turmoil and unrest. However, Moi, in her study of 'La Femme rompue', does not link these observations about Beauvoir and her use of the diary form under emotional pressure to Monique's use of the same form when under similar emotional pressure. It is not just a question of pointing out that Beauvoir attributes to one of her characters a habit of her own. One might argue, to borrow an idea from the SNCF, that 'un journal peut en cacher un autre' and that Monique's diary could easily be mistaken for Beauvoir's own and vice versa. For example, here is an extract from Beauvoir's *Journal de guerre* from February 1940, at a time when she has been separated from Sartre:

> Journée dure à passer—beaucoup de fatigue par manque de sommeil, en vain au matin j'essaie de dormir un peu longtemps, je suis réveillée à 8 h. 1/2, je m'ennuie au lit et quand le réveil sonne à 9 h. je me lève. Tout de suite le cœur serré, je l'ai eu d'ailleurs comme ça pendant le sommeil. Rien de passionnel, ce n'est pas que Sartre soit avec Wanda qui me pèse, ça serait tout pareil s'il était dans sa famille—une souffrance pleine de ne pas le voir. Et ce n'est pas seulement le vide d'aujourd'hui que je vis, c'est déjà son départ, ce sont tous ces jours où je n'aurai plus à me dire: dans deux jours. Je comprends mal comment je pouvais m'accommoder si bien de son absence, je me sens délaissée dans

un monde indifférent, hostile; peut-être est-ce ainsi parce que je sens si peu la conscience des autres gens, que sa conscience est tellement un absolu pour moi et que ce matin le monde me semble absolument vide, comme si j'étais jetée dans une solitude minérale. Quand je pense aux succédanés: Kos, Védrine, c'est avec écœurement, j'aimerais mieux (en cet instant) me penser absolument isolée, ça me fait pesant d'avoir à les voir aujourd'hui.[29]

One could illustrate these points of similarity at some length but it is unnecessary to do so for the purposes of this argument.[30] Beauvoir's depiction of Monique owes some of its evocative power and ambiguity to her own conflicts and ambivalence on the subject of the ideal couple and committed love. Beauvoir's feelings come through in Monique's voice precisely because she does not think that she is talking about herself through Monique. What Moi, following Freud, calls Beauvoir's tendency to 'disavowal' or not to recognize and admit to her own sorrow is very much in evidence in what Beauvoir writes about Monique in *Tout Compte fait*.[31] For example, Moi makes the general and cogent point that *Tout Compte fait* is a 'lifeless ghost of an autobiography'[32] precisely because Beauvoir is 'disavowing' or repressing the loneliness and anxiety of these years and the pain caused by Sartre's lack of loyalty to both their common ideas and to her as a person.[33] I would underline the corollary: 'La Femme rompue' has vitality, power and complexity precisely because it embodies these disavowed dimensions, including Beauvoir's own proclivities for emotional dependency, whatever her notion of herself as an independent person may have been. Beauvoir is able to express herself fully in the text and come better to grips with her own emotional realities because she does not consciously identify with Monique but rather sees her as the victim that she herself is not. I leave to others the possible Freudian and psychoanalytical explanations of such procesures of disavowal and distancing since it is more my purpose to illustrate the philosophical complexity of the story and the ambivalent ontology of the victim, as well as to demonstrate that Beauvoir's view of autobiography as somehow superior to fiction in the quest for the truth of existence is very much open to question. Additionally, if this view of Beauvoir as an example of dependency is considered far-fetched, a perusal of her letters to Nelson Algren, recently published, could be a useful antidote to her standard public persona.[34]

This double-sided optic in the text allows us to see Monique both as self-victim of improvident thought about marriage, nest-building and emotional change, and as victim of betrayal by, and loss of, a committed partner. This duality of emotional response in the reader gives Beauvoir's text a certain gravitational pull beyond the common-places of the love triangle. Take the following entry in Monique's diary for Lundi 22 novembre:

> Non, je ne dois pas essayer de suivre Noëllie sur son propre terrain, mais me battre sur le mien. Maurice était sensible à tous les soins dont je l'entourais, et je le néglige. J'ai passé la journée à mettre de l'ordre dans nos armoires. J'ai définitivement rangé les affaires d'été, sorti de la naphtaline et aéré les vêtements d'hiver, dressé un inventaire. Demain j'irais lui acheter les chaussettes, les pull-overs, les pyjamas dont il a besoin. Il lui faudrait aussi deux bonnes paires de souliers: nous les choisirons ensemble dès qu'il aura un moment libre. C'est réconfortant, des placards bien remplis où chaque chose est à sa place. Abondance, sécurité . . . Les piles de fins mouchoirs, de bas, de tricots m'ont donné l'impression que l'avenir ne pouvait pas me faire défaut.
> (p. 178)

Here, Monique self-evidently incarnates the heavily domesticated woman, pathetically tidying up her cupboards and thinking about her husband's socks and so forth. Yet she also comes over as a traumatized individual, terrified of losing her partner to an unintelligible rival and seeking some kind of psychotherapy in domestic trivia or comfort in the established routines of her relationship—and who is to say what they would not do under the impact of rejection and pain within the infernal triangle? Her suffering and fears are well-captured and capable of arousing empathy as she copes as best she can with the seismic disturbances in her life.

So far, I have concentrated on underlining the philosophical expressivity of the concrete particulars of the story in terms of the ontology of Monique as victim. I wish, finally, to touch upon some of the other questions embodied in the text to demonstrate further Beauvoir's art as a writer of philosophical fiction.

Although Beauvoir claimed of 'La Femme rompue' in general that it was a book about women and not men ('je n'ai guère cherché à élucider le rôle des hommes'),[35] she was able to acknowledge, in her preface to Anne Ophir's *Regards féminins*,[36] that her stories did, in fact, give rise to a multiplicity of questions concerning male behaviour. This is very much the case for 'La Femme rompue' which poses directly and indirectly the problem of male sexual behaviour in marriage. Couturier, Maurice's partner, tells Monique that fidelity in marriage after a fourteen-year period is 'rare' and her second daughter, Lucienne, goes further and says that it is 'naturel', after fifteen years of marriage to stop loving your wife and that it would be a real surprise if the opposite were true. The ever-helpful best friend, Isabelle, also tells Monique that it is normal for men to have affairs, particularly after twenty-two years of marriage. Such expressions of opinion from her friends conspire to give Monique the sense that what is happening to her is simply part of the natural order of things: the male of the species is physiologically constituted in this way, infidelity is natural to men, and questions of will, accountability and trust are just inapplicable as soon as testicles are involved.

Maurice actually fits well into such a frame of interpretation for the reader discovers eventually that the affair with Noëllie is his fourth infidelity, so his behaviour is very much determined by physiology. Whilst it is not possible to claim that the story *debates* this issue of male self-control, it certainly raises it and generates debate about it in the reader's mind. The text itself almost takes for granted that men cannot be faithful to one partner and this might well express a typically French cultural view of mistresses that is embodied in Beauvoir's own assumptions about male behaviour and sexuality (certainly Sartre had told her that it was impossible for a man to sleep with only one woman for all his belief that we are 'libres par-delà la nature'). If the question of the relationship between physiology and the will is raised in relation to Maurice's behaviour, so readers' responses to Maurice will vary in accordance with how one thinks about this issue. Maurice will be seen simply as unable to help himself because this is the way men are: his deceptions, his duplicity his convoluted half-truths, total lies and strategic confusions all arise from the physiological necessity of sexual variety. He will not be classed as a 'salaud' or as a patriarchal primate, as Monique, in her extreme moments of pain, might be tempted (legitimately) to describe him, but as a victim himself of the natural order, and possibly even to be pitied.

Our reaction, then, to Maurice's behaviour, also participates in the general ambivalence of the text. The same can be said of our reactions to Noëllie. Indeed, one might argue that our responses to the story are 'triangulated' and that we read it according to where we have been in the triangle, betrayer, betrayed, the third person, or possibly all three, or any combination of them, and this in itself enhances the interpretative possibilities of the text. Many mistresses might well find themselves identifying positively with Noëllie, many betrayed wives with Monique against her, many unfaithful husbands with Maurice. The wide-ranging moral implications of fidelity and commitment, the central issues of freedom and commitment, all work their way into the body of the story. If only poor Monique had realized that men cannot be faithful, she would not have trusted Maurice or invested so much of herself in him; she would not be the victim of the blindness, complacency and stupidity of the cocooned, loving wife.

A further problem raised by the text centres on children and parental responsibility for how they grow up and develop. Contemplating her two daughters, Colette and Lucienne, wondering about Noëllie's relationship with her own child, Monique asks herself whether she has been a good mother or failed her children in some way (p. 248). Monique's children are very different people. Colette is described as having the 'vocation du foyer' and is conventionally married with children. Lucienne is a New York feminist, fiercely independent, who appears to suffer from emotional bulimia: she tells her mother that she drops her lovers as soon as she becomes too emotionally attached to them in order to preserve her independence. Monique wonders whether either of her children are particularly happy with their situations and she is particularly suspicious of Lucienne's notion of independence purchased through rejection of deep emotional ties and childbearing. Once again, the text doesn't debate the question of parental agency in child development but it raises it to provoke responses. We have to do the detective work. Lucienne tells her mother: 'Tu as toujours eu un sens très exagéré de tes responsabilités' (p. 248). This remark further erodes Monique's belief in herself and her past conviction that being a devoted mother and wife was an all-important element in creating a successful family. She finally asks herself:

Je réalise seulement maintenant quelle estime au fond j'avais pour moi. Mais tous les mots par lesquels j'essaierais de la justifier, Maurice les a assassinés; le code d'après lequel je jugeais autrui et moi-même, il l'a renié. Je n'avais jamais songé à le contester —c'est-à-dire à me contester. Et je me demande à présent: au nom de quoi préférer la vie intérieure à la vie mondaine, la contemplation aux frivolités, le dévouement à l'ambition? Je n'en avais pas d'autre que de créer du bonheur autour de moi. Je n'ai pas rendu Maurice heureux. Et mes filles ne le sont pas non plus. Alors? Je ne sais plus rien. Non seulement pas qui je suis mais comment il faudrait être. Le noir et le blanc se confondent, le monde est un magma et je n'ai plus de contours. Comment vivre sans croire à rien ni à moi-même? (p. 249)

The collapse of Monique's affective world does not only leave her in a mess, it raises in the reader's mind the whole question of children, marriage, the committed love relationship, the social cost of freedom, solitude in old age and so on. At this level, the story makes the ideal of the committed relationship look like something worth fighting for rather than avoiding with providence, since the alternative perspectives look so dejecting and alienating. Beauvoir was surely right when she claimed to have written nothing bleaker than the ending of this story but the bleakness does not simply relate to the break-up of Monique's cocooned world but opens up perspectives on the loss of the ideals of trust, security and durable love.

There is also one final point: could Monique have done anything to save her relationship with Maurice or was it doomed by a process of 'inevitabilism' linked to male physiology and time? Beauvoir herself is acutely aware at the time of writing the story of the effects of time and change upon emotional realities and confidence in the self for she has little security with Sartre. In choosing, somewhat like her creator in relation to Sartre, to adopt the 'tactique du sourire', indulging Maurice's behaviour and interpreting his liaison with Noëllie as a transient 'histoire de peau', Monique defines the parameters of her agency in this situation in a particularly restricted way. This is not to say that she should leap with joy at Maurice's infidelity and seize her new independence with fervour (nothing in the text would appear to make such an emotional discontinuity likely or even possible),[37] but a less passive reaction to her situation may well have forced Maurice into a more considered response about his own 'choices'.

No doubt there are many other issues raised by the story including the importance of the impact on the body of emotional trauma, the related questions of anorexia and bulimia and so forth, but I hope that my central objective has at least partly been realized: namely to demonstrate how a banal set of concrete particulars can achieve philosophical expressivity of a dense and interesting kind.

Michel Tournier
'Les Suaires de Véronique'

Rachel Edwards

Michel Tournier has produced two collections of short stories for an adult audience—*Le Coq de bruyère* (1978) and *Le Médianoche amoureux* (1989). However, many of the stories in these works have also been published for children, which allows Tournier to reach as wide an audience as possible and suggests the widespread appeal of his narratives. Indeed, he is as well known for his children's literature as he is for his adult fiction. In terms of their form, the two collections are quite different. The first consists of 13 unrelated narratives and one play,[1] whilst in the second the stories are framed by the meal of the title and the plight of a married couple, Nadège and Yves, who are about to separate but who become reconciled at the end having listened to the stories told by the guests. Both collections consist of a mixture of *contes* and *nouvelles*, although many of the stories would be more accurately described as a mixture of both.

In *Le Vol du vampire* Tournier draws the distinction between three different types of short story: the *nouvelle*, the *fable* and the *conte*.[2] He sees the *nouvelle* as being characterized by 'sa fidélité au réel' (p. 36); the *fable* is recognizable by its obvious message, whereas the *conte* is situated 'à mi-chemin de l'opacité brutale de la nouvelle et de la transparence cristalline de la fable' (p. 37). The *conte* is 'translucide mais non transparent, comme une épaisseur glauque dans laquelle le lecteur voit se dessiner des figures qu'il ne parvient jamais à saisir tout à fait' (p. 37). What is more, the 'conte est une nouvelle hantée. Hantée par une signification fantomatique qui nous touche, nous enrichit, mais ne nous éclaire pas' (p. 37). If we take this as a guide, then many of Tournier's stories fall somewhere between the *nouvelle* and the *conte*. Often set in contemporary time with clearly recognizable places and characters, they nevertheless go beyond what is truly credible in a *nouvelle*. Michel Mansuy has perhaps found the best definition for stories like this when he refers to those in *Le Coq de bruyère* as 'contes d'enfants pour adultes'.[3] Like all *contes* they clothe in symbolic terms essential issues which concern us all and with which we are wittingly or unwittingly preoccupied throughout our lives. They also explore, on a smaller scale, those issues with which Tournier is concerned in his novels as a whole.

One of the reasons for choosing to write about 'Les Suaires de Véronique'[4] is that the short story highlights many of Tournier's preoccupations, not least his obsession with photography which is often ambivalent in nature: on the one hand, he is fascinated by photography and the image in general, on the other, there is a genuine fear of taking pictures and of the resulting image, the latter often being seen as a malevolent force to be reckoned with. Indeed, Tournier's fiction often concentrates on the triumph of the sign (in terms of the written word) over the image, the most developed example of this being found in his exploration of photography in the novel *La Goutte d'or*, which, Tournier admitted when he was a guest on Pivot's *Apostrophes* in 1992, could have been called 'La Photographie'. Furthermore, 'Les Suaires de Véronique', like much of Tournier's fiction, highlights his preoccupation with rewriting. From the title we immediately recognize St Veronica who wiped Christ's face with a kerchief or veil upon which His image became miraculously imprinted. In *Le Crépuscule des masques* Tournier points to the meaning of the name Véronique: 'Le nom de cette femme pieuse de Jérusalem veut dire: *image vraie*. Véronique a essuyé avec son voile le visage ruisselant de sang, de larmes et de sueur du Sauveur. Et le miracle s'est produit: le visage de Jésus imprima son image sur le voile de Véronique'.[5]

Véronique is therefore heralded by Tournier as the inventor of photography (this being all the more striking given the fact that she is a woman). However, in substituting 'voile' for 'suaire' in the title of his story, Tournier also refers us to the Shroud of Turin which is said to be the cloth in which Christ's body was wrapped when he was taken from the cross and which bears the image of His crucified body. (At the time of publication of 'Les Suaires de Véronique' the mystery of the shroud was still intact given that it was not until 1988 that the cloth was proven to have been made somewhere between 1260 and 1390.) Calvin, in his *Traité des reliques*, of which Tournier is more than likely aware, considers, in the same passage, both Veronica's cloth and the various shrouds in which Christ's body was supposedly wrapped. Of the latter there were said to be at least six, accounting perhaps for the plural in Tournier's title. What is also worthy of note is that in the ancient scriptures the word 'suaire' meant 'un mouchoir, ou couvrechef', and not 'un grand linceul qui serve à envelopper le corps',[6] which justifies Véronique's cloth being referred to as a 'suaire' in Calvin's text. The old meaning of 'suaire' and its modern sense both come together in Tournier's title. Right from the outset, therefore, we know that Tournier intends to use the story of Veronica for his own purposes (just as the title of *Vendredi ou les limbes du Pacifique* prepares us for a different type of Robinson Crusoe story). It is also clear from the beginning that photography and death are closely allied.

Tournier is not only using ancient texts as intertexts for this story but he also adapts elements from his own fiction—most notably from *Le Roi des aulnes* (1970) in which the main character, Abel Tiffauges, is an ogre who hunts down children and shoots them with his camera. In fictional terms Dunblane[7] had already taken place in this novel when Tiffauges takes pictures of schoolchildren through the railings of the playground fence and shoots them down as easily as if they were animals in a cage at the zoo. Véronique is also established as an ogre-figure who systematically destroys her prey with an 'amour dévorant' which clearly mirrors Tiffauges's love of the children whom he photographs. Tournier is also playing with traditional gender roles here; the domain of the predatory ogre is no longer solely that of the male.

The process of borrowing, or even of copying, as it appears in Tournier's work (he has announced in an article: 'Je copie et j'en suis fier'),[8] can be likened to what Lévi-Strauss refers to as *bricolage* when he examines the way in which myths are constructed in primitive societies.[9] In intertextual terms, and for our purposes, odds and ends are pasted together from previous texts in order to construct a new version of a narrative. Roberts has coined the term 'autobricolage' when referring to Tournier's use of his own works in such a way.[10]

Other examples of 'autobricolage' will become apparent when we look at 'Les Suaires de Véronique' in more detail.

Although clearly written for adults, 'Les Suaires de Véronique' it has much in common with children's *contes*. It aims to awaken primary fears within us and does so by using symbolic language. The epigraph at the beginning of *Le Coq de bruyère*, by Lanza del Vasto, makes this quite clear: 'Au fond de chaque chose, un poisson nage/Poisson de peur que tu n'en sortes nu/Je te jetterai mon manteau d'images' (p. 7). The 'manteau d'images' in 'Les Suaires de Véronique' clothes basic unconscious fears which make up part of our collective and individual psyche. It draws on primeval fears of being eaten alive or swallowed up in both literal and figurative terms. In the story, these fears find their concretization in the tiger's tooth which is initially seen around Hector's neck and last perceived around Véronique's. On the one hand, Hector is devoured by this ogress-cum-tigress, referring us back to primitive fears relevant at the beginning of our collective history; on the other, he has been swallowed up by this woman who steals the tooth, making her, as Redfern would have it, a kind of symbolic 'vagina dentata' which equally awakens unconscious fears within us.[11]

Photography itself seems to kindle similarly irrational fears. Many peoples, especially in parts of China and Africa, believe that being photographed is tantamount to having one's soul stolen. Balzac dreaded having his photograph taken believing that he lost a layer of himself each time. Debray has termed this fear 'le complexe de l'oignon'.[12] In *Le Roi des aulnes* Tiffauges asserts that 'quiconque craint d'être "pris" en photographie fait preuve du plus élémentaire bon sens',[13] and Tournier points to the fact that there are very few self-portraits in photography, unlike painting, probably because people do not want to do to themselves that which they take great pleasure in doing to others. Tournier, however, has braved his own camera as his self-portrait in *Des Clefs et des serrures* indicates. It provides a striking contrast to Debray's favourite picture of himself in *L'Oeil naïf*, which is simply a blank page with a rectangle drawn on it to imitate the frame. Fear of being photographed therefore presents itself as a modern manifestation of the primary fears of being eaten up, swallowed or devoured.

There is also an initiatory aspect to the *conte*: initiation rites all follow a similar pattern—that of a preparatory period, followed by either a symbolic death or a return to the womb, and finally a rebirth. In 'Les Suaires de Véronique', Hector is firstly seduced by Véronique, then returns to a symbolic womb in the house in the Camargue and is finally reborn as the main exhibit in Véronique's exhibition. Most of Tournier's narratives do indeed deal with some aspect of initiation.[14] For example, Crusoé is initiated into a new way of life by Vendredi in *Vendredi ou les limbes du Pacifique*. Likewise, Tiffauges undertakes an initiatory voyage in *Le Roi des aulnes* as does Paul in *Les Météores*.

It is bearing all the above factors in mind that we can now consider 'Les Suaires de Véronique' in some detail. When we initially start reading the story we seem to be situated in the realms of the *nouvelle* rather than the *conte*. The setting is a realistic one—we are in Arles at the Rencontres Internationales de Photographie, which Tournier himself founded. The place is littered with well-known photographers, amongst them 'Ansel Adams et Ernst Haas, Jacques Lartigues et Fulvio Foitier, Robert Doisneau et Arthur Tress, Eva Rubinstein et Gisèle Freund' (p. 153) to name some of them, and we could indeed be reading the *nouvelles*. When we turn the page we realize that the narrative is being written in the first person which seems to lend added authenticity to what is being recounted.[15] However, it is also now that we are paradoxically entering the world of the *conte* where we meet Hector and Véronique, who are simply referred to by their first names unlike the famous photographers who are given both a first name and a surname. They do not need surnames—we know who they are, for they come straight out of our literary and cultural tradition: Veronica wiped the face of Christ and Hector is one of the heroes of the *Iliad*, son of Priam and husband of Andromache, who is eventually killed by Achilles and whose body is then dragged around the walls of Troy. It is this which casts the spell of the *conte* over the narrative. Furthermore, if we suppose that the narrator is actually Tournier—there is no reason why it should not be, given his passion for and involvement with photography —then this would explain why we are plunged into a world which is bordering on the fantastic.

In encountering Hector and Véronique we come across the first of many dichotomies which are inherent in the text: that between Ancient Greece, on the one hand, and the Christian tradition, on the other. Further dualities which arise as a direct consequence of

93

Hector and Véronique are Nature versus Culture, Antiquity versus the Renaissance, 'le pris-sur-le-vif' versus 'le pris-sur-la-mort', and eventually life and death. The setting up of various dichotomies is very important in Tournier's fiction and this is one of the reasons why it is considered to be mythological in nature. Lévi-Strauss, whose courses Tournier followed at the Sorbonne, sees myth as an attempt to resolve certain cultural contradictions. It is precisely the resolution of such opposites that comes about at the end of this story, as we shall see.

The first meeting with Hector and Véronique occurs in the Camargue where the narrator has gone with a group of people to take 'des photos de nu' (p. 154). What is immediately apparent from the outset of the session is that the narrator only notices the model, Hector, as he moves across the landscape assuming different postures. His nudity is described as 'superbe et généreuse' and he is endowed with 'chair splendide' (p. 154). He resembles a Greek god and we remember also that the ancient Greeks worshipped male as opposed to female beauty. On the other hand, he is like an animal—he has a 'front de taurillon' and we are told that he 'jouait pleinement de son animalité naturelle'. He is therefore reminiscent of 'le premier homme', from what Lévi-Strauss terms 'le temps mythique', a time when human beings, animals and gods were indistinguishable. He is at home in the essentially female elements of a mixture of land and sea, and gender distinctions are blurred in that he is like a type of Venus rising out of the waters.

Véronique provides a sharp contrast. She is 'une petite femme mince et vive' (pp. 154–5), which reads pejoratively beside Hector's 'chair splendide'. However, she is endowed with something which is clearly missing from the narrator's description of Hector: 'l'intelligence'. In what is a surprising reversal of stereotypical gender roles, Véronique can be seen in terms of mind to Hector's body. Hector is the body-object, traditionally a female role, whilst Véronique is one of the people exploiting this object, traditionally therefore in the male role. She is also armed with a surrogate penis—her camera and lenses—which she uses to exploit Hector. The camera as penis and as an instrument of violation is also explored in *Le Roi des aulnes* in which Tiffauges travels around with his camera between his thighs.

Véronique is in a bad mood and as such she seems to be a negative version, or as Robert's asserts, an 'inversion maligne', of her namesake.

Hector is also the exact opposite of Christ. Whereas Christ is weak and suffering, carrying the burden of the cross when he meets Veronica, Hector is the picture of health and has no burdens. The only thing he carries or wears (*porter*) is a tiger's tooth on a leather thong around his neck, which simply adds to his nudity. And in this, too, he is diametrically opposed to Véronique who travels encumbered with all sorts of photographic paraphernalia. A further duality is therefore set up between Hector/Nature and Véronique/Culture.

Véronique is concerned with the fabricated rather than the given, which is made clear by her condemnation of the initial photographic session, its setting and Hector. The only joy she managed to get from the session was in using a wide-angled lens which enabled her to distort his body: 'Pour peu qu'Hector tende la main vers l'objectif, il aura une main géante avec derrière un petit corps et une tête de moineau. Amusant' (p. 155). He is therefore reduced in stature: from being 'lourdement musclé; with 'un front de taurillon' he becomes 'un petit corps' with 'une tête de moineau'. He is already a diminutive figure for Véronique, and her admission rings out ominously: 'On aimerait en faire quelque chose. Seulement, ça demanderait du travail. Du travail et des sacrifices . . .' (p. 155). But on whose part one wonders? Redfern pertinently points out that *travail* also means ordeal and comes from the Latin *tripalium* meaning an instrument of torture (p. 63). This is exactly what the physical-training equipment used to get Hector into shape becomes.

It is here for the first time that the opposites of good photography and evil photography come into being. This is, indeed, unusual in Tournier's fiction where photography is usually solely aligned with malignant forces. In this narrative, good photography does not harm its victim, it is, as Hector calls it, 'pas sérieuse'; in contrast, evil photography, or that which is 'sérieuse', is harmful. This is further explored in the rest of the narrative.

The first stage of the story ends with the narrator, and hence the reader, overhearing Hector tell Véronique about the tiger's tooth which is hanging around his neck: it is a charm which is supposed to keep him from being devoured by tigers. Significantly, this is the one and only time that we actually hear Hector speak. At this point, therefore, he still has a voice of his own. But in telling Véronique about his tiger's tooth, Hector, as Françoise Kaye points out, is like Sampson revealing the secret of his strength to Delilah.[16]

Véronique's seduction of Hector has therefore been successful and the first part of his initiation has begun.

The second stage of the narrative begins the following summer, again at the Rencontres Internationales de Photographie. Whilst Véronique is 'inchangée', Hector is 'méconnaissable'. We are told: 'De sa patauderie un peu enfantine, de sa jactance de bel animal, de son épanouissement optimiste et solaire, il ne restait rien' (p. 156). Ironically, he has become more like Véronique: he has grown much thinner and has acquired her feverish energy. Later we realize why. The narrator is invited to the house which Véronique is renting in the Camargue, a house which blends in so well with its surroundings that it remains camouflaged to the point of being undetectable until one is almost upon it. This, added to the fact that behind closed doors anything but the natural life-style suggested by the exterior is taking place, lends sinister overtones to the narrative. One is reminded of the concentration camps which were kept out of sight or, when visible, masqueraded as work-camps rather than death-camps.

In this farmhouse Véronique is hatching Hector in 'une coquille d'œuf' (p. 164). The description of the room in which he is sleeping is like that of a womb. Its milky whiteness recalls the womb/tomb cave into which Crusoé slips in *Vendredi ou les limbes du Pacifique* and from which he eventually emerges like a newborn infant. The second phase of Hector's initiation is clearly underway here in this symbolic womb. However, Véronique is not just a simple matrix. She challenges the idea of the non-biological creative process being essentially a male domain, for she is the creator/artist. But her only means of creation is through destruction: Hector, rather than assuming the foetal position, is 'écrasé à plat ventre' in this womb-cum-tomb (p. 164). Paradoxically, it is also the case that in order to become, in photographic terms, more than he was, Hector has to become less than he is. This is a typical instance of Tournierian logic which is particularly evident in *Le Roi des aulnes* where it often seems that less becomes more and more becomes less.

Despite the somewhat sinister ambience of the farmhouse, the narrator has to admit that Hector has indeed become a 'beau spectacle' (p. 164). But the 'beau spectacle' has come about by the fact that Culture has worked on Nature. If Hector was 'le premier homme', Véronique is playing God, indeed more than God: not only is she creating man in her image (he has become like her) but she is transforming him beyond her image. The copy is becoming not a mere reflection of the original, but a superior creation. This is something which is also reflected in Véronique's musing on what it means to be 'beau' rather that 'photogénique'. Hector began as the former and is now the latter: from a natural being ('beau') he has been transformed into a cultural artefact ('photogénique'). Whereas his photographs were once inferior copies of himself, they are now superior. The idea of the copy being the original's superior is also a theme which is common in Tournier's work, the most striking discussion of this taking place in *Les Météores*.[17]

The natural as opposed to the created is further explored through the idea of the two schools of photography: that which practises 'le pris-sur-le-vif' as opposed to 'la nature morte' (p. 160). Tournier plays with the meanings here and inverts the terms. The narrator comments: 'J'ai presque envie de jouer sur ces mots et de dire: d'un côté la nature vive, de l'autre le pris-sur-le-mort' (p. 161). 'La nature vive' is allied to the type of photography in the initial photo session. It is synonymous with the study of the human anatomy as undertaken by the likes of Praxiteles in antiquity. Antiquity here stands in contrast to the Renaissance, which saw the birth of anatomy and which is described as 'l'ère du morbide' (p. 162), when Vesalius, in his quest for knowledge, began dissecting bodies both dead and alive. The dissection and vivisection undertaken during this era is synonymous in the *conte* with Véronique cutting up Hector with her photography. Photography literally means writing with light, and there is a sense in which Véronique's use of light acts upon Hector's body like a laser. Whereas before we are told that 'la lumière glissait sans accrocher ni jouer' on Hector's body (p. 158), now we see that his body, 'découpé par les ombres et les plages de lumière d'une source lumineuse unique et violente, paraît figé, fouillé jusqu'à l'os, disséqué comme par un simulacre d'autopsie ou de démonstration anatomique' (p. 160). This gives new meaning to Valéry's words: 'La vérité est nue, mais sous le nu il y a l'écorché' (p. 160). Metaphor becomes concrete. She is literally beginning to flay him alive.

Writing on the body here strongly evokes Kafka's 'In the Penal Settlement' in which prisoners have the lessons to be learnt from their crimes written on their bodies by the harrow, a torture machine made up of tiny needles. The salutary statement is inscribed into their skin at an ever-increasing depth until death occurs after twelve hours by which time the prisoner has fully understood his crime. Enlightenment, however, occurs around the sixth hour which is the turning-point for the prisoner. He now has no more strength and waits to die. For Hector, enlightenment seems to come just prior to his writing the letter to Véronique. He has the strength to escape, but he is caught again, and as surely as the prisoners in Kafka's tale, he too succumbs to his fate. More recently, in his film *The Pillow Book*, Peter Greenaway has explored the erotic side to writing on the body. In Tournier's story, torture and eroticism come together in Véronique's treatment of Hector.

The textualization of the body is also relevant in the discussion that Véronique and the narrator have about the 'nu' and the importance of the 'visage'. Véronique asserts that the face is the key to the body: 'Le visage est le chiffre du corps. Je veux dire: le corps même traduit dans un autre système de signes. Et en même temps, la clé du corps' (p. 159). She complains that many photographs are spoilt by a face that is out of harmony with the body. Lucien Clergue has solved this problem 'en coupant la tête de ses nus' which is referred to as 'un procédé radical' (p. 158). According to Véronique, this only works for women and not for men. Men must keep their heads because 'l'homme sans tête devient indéchiffrable' (p. 159). Men emerge as essentially mind, whereas women are essentially body: 'La statue de la femme s'épanouit d'autant plus dans sa plénitude charnelle qu'elle a perdu la tête' (p. 159). The man/mind, woman/ body dichotomy is a typical theme in Tournier's writing and one is reminded of the island Spermanza in *Vendredi ou les limbes du Pacifique* which is described as looking like 'un corps féminin sans tête'.[18] The idea that woman is in essence a body reveals a certain misogyny on the part of Tournier which is recurrent throughout his work. It is ironic, however, that in this story it is Hector who loses not only his head but also his entire body, and in this way Tournier is characteristically able to avoid being pinned down as a total misogynist. Paradoxically, therefore, for every example of misogyny in his work there seem to be others which prove just the opposite.

In this particular story, Tournier also redeems himself somewhat by the fact that he is the inventor of the 'portrait nu'. The anecdote surrounding this invention is recounted in *Des Clefs et des serrures* and is worth briefly repeating here. He tells us of a nineteen-year-old female student who was preparing a maîtrise on the ogre and who visited his home in order to interview him. She was impressed by all his photographs and agreed to let Tournier take her picture. He then set up his equipment whilst she prepared herself in the next room. When she reappeared she was 'nue comme Eve au Paradis'.[19] Tournier continues: 'En disant "photo", j'avais pensé "portrait". Elle avait compris "nu". Mais il y avait une autre surprise: ce corps n'était pas—tant s'en faut—celui qu'annonçait son visage: un corps plein de douceurs et de rondeurs, avenant, presque douillet, aussi féminin que possible.' (pp. 112–13). Her face on the contrary was 'aigu, presque coupant, sommaire, trop grave' (p. 111). Tournier, however, adhered to his original project and simply photographed her face. The result was that the body became reflected in the face. He comments: 'Il s'agit d'une sorte de rayonnement venu d'en bas, d'une émanation corporelle agissant comme une sorte de filtre, comme si la chair dénudée faisait monter vers le visage une buée de chaleur et de couleur' (p. 114). In a sense, Tournier's procedure is no less radical than Lucien Clergue's in that he cuts off the body from the head, rather than the inverse. In preserving the head rather than the body he cannot be accused of treating the student as a simple body-object.

Hector, on the other hand, up until this point in the narrative has been merely seen in terms of a body-object. When he is encountered as a thinking subject it is, interestingly enough, not through his images but in a letter which he writes to Véronique when he leaves her. The letter gives us an insight into Hector's mind and his feelings for the first time. Three days after his visit to the farmhouse, the narrator finds Véronique in an insalubrious bar drowning her sorrows because Hector has left her. His disappearance recalls Christ vanishing from the tomb and, indeed, Hector is not seen in the same form by the narrator or the reader again. In his letter we are shown that Hector can indeed think and is not merely a body. This is largely thanks to Véronique, for as Hector says: 'La photographie sérieuse instaure un échange perpétuel entre le modèle et le photographe. Il y a un système de vases communicants. Je vous dois beaucoup, Véronique chérie. Vous avez fait de moi un autre homme' (p. 165). We remember that the aim of all types of initiation is to enable one to 'devenir autre'. From a rustic person at one with nature, Hector has become a thinking being whose spiritual side is mirrored in the fact that he can now write with elegance and grace. In return, Hector

trophées barbares' (p. 171). One is instantly reminded again of Nazi experiments and the trophies which were made out of the human body. This scene also recalls *Le Roi des aulnes* and the Nazi doctor Blättchen's experiments on the children of the Napola, as well as Göring's emasculation of the stags and his subsequent displaying of their antlers. What also clearly comes to mind are Tiffauges's experiments with the negatives of photographs of children which he projects through an enlarger in his dark room.

As far as Hector is concerned, Véronique has indeed ended up by having 'sa peau'. Metaphor has indeed become concrete as is so often the case in Tournier's fiction. Hector's initiation is now over. He has become like Christ: all that is left of him is the image of his body on the shrouds.

Véronique is able to get away with what she has done because she has become an exhibitor at the Rencontres Internationales. She is up there now with the rest of the great photographers. She has found a way to avoid being punished and we recall what she says to the narrator when he tells her that during the Renaissance she would have been burnt at the stake: 'Il y avait alors un moyen bien simple de baigner dans la sorcellerie sans courir aucun risque . . . En faisant partie du tribunal de la Sainte Inquisition!' (p. 163). She, too, like the great names in the beginning, now forms part of the 'Gotha de la photographie' and is therefore safe.

The ending of the story succeeds in resolving certain contradictions which arise throughout the narrative. Ancient Greece and the Christian tradition come together in the Hector/Christ figure represented on Véronique's shrouds. Nature and Culture also merge in the 'suaires' in that they are fabricated using the human body. Body and soul become one in that Hector is both present and absent; he is there and yet elsewhere. Finally, life and death, creation and destruction are cancelled out: in creating/killing off Hector, Véronique has succeeded in destroying/preserving him for all time.

Marguerite Duras
'La Mort du jeune aviateur anglais'

James Williams

'La Mort du jeune aviateur anglais' (henceforth 'Aviateur') is one of
Duras's last works, published in 1993 by Gallimard as part of a small
collection entitled *Ecrire*. The five texts featured there are all too
individual to be considered together, although each raises important
questions about the creative process, whether in the areas of language
and writing ('Aviateur', the title-text, and 'Le nombre pur') or of
film-making 'Roma') and painting ('L'exposition de la peinture').
'Aviateur' itself originated as the soundtrack of a short film of the
same name made in 1993 by Benoît Jacquot, which features Duras
reciting directly to camera the story of an English pilot. Duras gives
no indication in her brief preface to *Ecrire* of how much the published
text of 'Aviateur' is a modification or reinvention of her original
spoken text, and since the film is currently unavailable (it was shown
once on French television but never distributed), it is impossible to
trace the process of transformation from the oral into the written. It
should be observed, however, that 'Aviateur' is not presented as a
nouvelle. Indeed, it is ascribed no specific genre, even though its
length—thirty-one pages in the original Gallimard edition—is of
fine short-story proportions. Nor did Duras specialize particularly in
the short-story form. While she adapted for the stage a couple of
short stories by Henry James, namely *The Aspern Papers* in 1961 and
The Beast in the Jungle in 1962, those of her own works which could
qualify for the title of short story (a string of short texts from the
mid-1950s including 'Le boa' and 'Madame Dodin')[1] are classified

in the official bibliography simply as *récits*. Hence, to establish definitively whether 'Aviateur' conforms or not to the conventions of the modern short story would constitute a limited and unrealistic response, especially in view of the range of conflicting descriptions and theoretical accounts of the genre.

A far more appropriate approach in the circumstances would be to take 'Aviateur' as a case study of narrative in Duras, for the core-story could not be more compact or powerful, and it exhibits some of Duras's major preoccupations, including her obsession with death, the value and painful necessity of memory, and the pre-eminence of the body. Of course, Duras, who was an early, if always marginal, exponent of the *nouveau roman*, is well known for her profound mistrust of the assumptions on which traditional forms of narrative are based. Her corpus is littered with unreliable narrators, such as Jacques Hold in the 1964 novel *Le Ravissement de Lol V. Stein*, who is progressively 'unmade' as he tries to tell the story of his lover, the apparently 'mad' Lol V. Stein. This process is extended in Duras's film-work. In *Le Navire Night* (1978), for example, the indirectly acquired story of an anonymous relationship conducted over the phone between a man and woman is framed and reframed by the dialogue on the soundtrack between Duras and Jacquot, set against assorted visual images of Paris which have no obvious connection with the story. Further examples of Duras's naturally deconstructing approach to narrative could be provided, but it is enough to say that part of the excitement of reading 'Aviateur' lies precisely in anticipating for how long Duras can remain faithful to her chosen story; how long, that is, before she refuses to conform to the usual obligations of storytelling. After all, would these not run directly counter to her literary style, in particular the techniques she developed during the 1980s in texts such as *L'Amant* (1984) and *Emily L.* (1987), where she refined what she termed an *écriture courante*, a cursive, poetic form of writing designed to record anything personal, social or political that 'passes' during the Scene of Writing, and which, she claimed, transports all that it encounters, without discrimination, almost without choice.[2] *Ecriture courante* is characterized on a formal level by parataxis and metonyms and by the use to varying degrees of the vocative address. In most cases a female first-person narrator actively propels the reader (*toi/vous*) into an aggressive, transferential and counter-transferential relationship, which Duras once referred to as a 'private affair' between text and reader. Can, therefore, a fluid, potentially all-encompassing *ecriture courante* be sustained in the face of the pilot's appalling, lonely death in 'Aviateur'? Or would the desire for textual openness be ultimately denied by the sheer force of historical fact?

Crucial to any discussion of these questions is the fact that 'Aviateur' recounts the process whereby Duras hears the story of the English pilot for the first time. We might perhaps expect the smooth transformation of the news (*nouvelles*) into one perfect short story (*nouvelle*). It will be the contention of this study, however, that what 'Aviateur' presents is rather the fascinating case of a text that generates itself through its very impossibility to identify—and account formally for—its status as writing. Far from being the story of one English pilot's death, the real subject and concern of 'Aviateur' becomes the success, or otherwise, of the writing process, and of Duras's ability to position herself first as witness and finally as author. The text proceeds via a series of stages, each constituting a different formal approach. It is proposed to examine each of these in turn in order to determine the changing nature and ambition of 'Aviateur'. By comparing the text with other parts of the Duras corpus it will then be possible to assess its full implications for an understanding of the literary process in her work, in particular the workings of literary sublimation.

The opening pages of 'Aviateur' (pp. 69–74) contain the story proper, and Duras's first move is to set up a discursive relationship between narrator, text, and reader. She states:

> Le début, le commencement d'une histoire.
> C'est l'histoire que je vais raconter, pour la première fois. Celle de ce livre ici.
> Je crois que c'est une direction de l'écrit. C'est ça, l'écrit adressé, par exemple, à toi, dont je ne sais encore rien.
> A toi, lecteur: (p. 69)

This hyper-deliberate framing of the story in the form of an address to a reader about whom Duras claims as yet to know nothing is really a staging of narrative to the point of parody. For the next three pages the narrative could not be more linear, brief or economical, and it moves along almost classic short-story lines. It is written in the past tense and presents the story of a lone, anonymous character in a fixed, closed space. The narrator relates how she had gone in the summertime to the church at Vauville in the Calvados region of Normandy, and had seen the grave of a young English airman shot down during the last days of the Second World War in his single-seater Meteor plane. Again and again she returned to the grave and discovered that the village people had kept watch over the body for a day and a night before extracting it from the plane and immediately burying it. Having fulfilled the promise of the title, 'La mort du jeune aviateur anglais', this ultra short story appears to be already complete.

Duras's approach has effectively outplayed the narrative by voiding it of any suspense or mystique. She has stripped the story down to its literal bare bones and removed the merely anecdotal in order to prioritize the narrative core of the airman's death and burial. The latter is dispatched in cursory fashion, yet paradoxically nothing is left unsaid; everything, to use a current critical cliché, is always already dead. It is as though Duras were negating the short-story form at the very moment of invoking it. Any of the power that Edgar Allan Poe once proposed as the desired 'unique or single effect' of the short story has been deflated,[3] and in the various typologies of the modern French short story offered by such critics as Michel Viegnes and René Godenne (they include the historical short story, the biographical short story and the short-story portrait), perhaps the only one that could really be applied to this mini-account of the pilot is *la nouvelle-instant*. One of the variants outlined by Godenne, with reference to the writer Marcel Arland, is the *instant-constellation*, which, like a prism, becomes the subjective mirror for a plurality of sensations, thoughts and memories.[4] The difference, of course, is that the decisive moment in 'Aviateur' is the protracted agony of one man's dying and is thus hardly a liminal or formative experience. It is, if anything, an *'instant-mort'*. Duras may provide further details about the elderly English gentleman who, every year for seven years (perhaps eight, it is unclear), came to pay his respects to the pilot; she may even provide the name of the English pilot, W. J. Cliffe, and reveal that he was originally an orphan; yet the story really advances to no further than a literal dead-end. There is even a sense of Biblical doom: of the English gentleman we are told: 'Jamais plus il n'est revenu' (p. 74). The story is stillborn, as stark and as deadly simple as the clear granite slab of the erected tombstone.

What Duras has done here, with almost brutal ease, is to turn the narrative itself of the airman's death into a textual grave. This approach contrasts dramatically with that taken by another contemporary short story on a similar theme, Julian Barnes's 'Evermore' (1996), where a third-person narrator gently and patiently details the elaborate series of rituals established by an Englishwoman as her way of honouring the memory of her brother, who perished fighting in the Normandy trenches during the First World War.[5] Barnes uses his story to ask profound questions about the fragility of human memory, which is shown to be threatened not only by a universal wish to do away with history but also by the work of archivists merely processing information. Yet it is important to note that from the very beginning of 'Aviateur' Duras directs our attention not so much to the fact of the pilot's death as to his dead body, thus essentially separating it from its final resting place. The pilot, whether or not eternal as she claims ('sous la dalle de granit, la mort a continué de s'éterniser' [p. 73]), becomes in the process a potentially free and totally concrete textual entity. As such, he could perhaps be made to function as the real of the text itself, that is to say, as the future ground of—and grounds for—more writing. The first section of 'Aviateur' ends with this possible hope of a new—and by implication non-narrative—form of textual activity.

When Duras starts up again, however, she does so in a totally different vein. She suddenly invokes the personal memory of her 'small brother' Paulo, a figure familiar from previous works like *L'Amant* where he is actually revealed to be two years her senior. This switch to the brother sets in motion an expanding cycle of pain and loss that links the death of the young pilot first to that of Paulo, who died at the age of twenty-seven from broncho-pneumonia in Japanese-occupied Saigon and whose body was thrown into a mass, unmarked grave, and then to that of a small child of six months, whose age and name are inscribed on a gravestone nearby. The details of the latter are left deliberately vague. If the baby was Duras's, she is being economical with the truth here, since her first child died stillborn. In fact, Duras had already compared in *L'Amant* the loss of her baby in 1942 with that of her brother some months later, making the explicit point that losing a baby in this way was nothing like as traumatic as losing her beloved brother, an immortal soul who, in dying, caused the death of immortality itself.[6] Yet whatever the exact truth and status of this third child in 'Aviateur', a chain of love and death proliferates, and the author is at a loss to explain why since the three 'children' suffered a very different fate. She remains fixated on a remembered vision of the frozen smile lurking in the hollows of her brother's eyes, and she confesses to an almost necrophiliac wish to see for herself whether the destroyed body of the English pilot had a similar deathly blank expression.

This lack of a clear elaboration of parallels is very different from Duras's usual technique of underscoring connections and staging absolute, symbolic links. One recalls, again in *L'Amant*, the stunning inclusion of the six-page Paris episode, where the narrator suddenly digresses with a discussion of two American women living in Paris during the war who collaborated with the Nazis. What unified this episode with the rest of the text was the narrator's statement that, although a communist herself at the time, she shared with these two women the wish to find a political solution to personal problems. 'L'équivalence est absolue, définitive', she proclaimed.[7] Yet if, in 'Aviateur', Duras seems to be at the mercy of the personal elements she has introduced, on one level they do at least constitute a fluid triangle of textual relations: the female narrator assumes the role of a *passante*, the dead body of the pilot is *lui*, and Paulo is designated as the text's intended reader, *toi*. In this new collectivity—a general baptism in death, as she puts it (p. 77)—identity and gender are rendered temporarily indeterminate. The narrator states: 'Ici, on est très loin de l'identité. C'est un mort, une mort de vingt ans qui ira jusqu'à la fin des temps. C'est tout. Le nom, ce n'est plus la peine: c'est un enfant' (p. 78). The growing confusion even affects the grammatical use of the impersonal *on*, which for no obvious reason takes now a masculine plural agreement in the phrase: 'On est devenus amis . . .' (p. 79). There is even the gesture towards a larger intertextual family in the reference to the song of the beggar-woman (p. 80), an echo of Duras's series of texts and films commonly referred to as the India Cycle, which began in 1965 with her novel, *Le Vice-Consul*. In this extended family of pain, the English pilot, once firmly installed as the figure of childhood ('l'Enfant même'), eventually assumes the position of *toi* (p. 82).

What we are really witnessing at this juncture in 'Aviateur' is the transformation of the initial *récit* into a personal lament. Intense feelings of inconsolable grief have been triggered by the narrator hearing and relaying the facts of the pilot's story, and the text becomes a record of these emotions. The mood of loss encompasses even the local trees which, having been scorched anthropomorphically with the blood of wartime fire, stand now mutilated and martyred, frozen in fixed disorder. In the process, the short-story form has completely broken down and decomposed. We are given atomized blocks of description followed by fragments of narrative (the known and presumed history of the airman). Ideas and phrases are repeated in an incantatory manner, with certain refrains acquiring the rhyming, biblical tone of the absolute. One example will suffice: 'Et après, j'ai vu autre chose. Toujours, après, on voit des choses' (p. 77). The narrator is physically overwhelmed by the fact of death, paralyzed even ('engluée'), a feeling exacerbated by her sense that she is also completely alone in her pain. There seems no obvious way of stemming the tide of emotion. One might suppose that Duras, having made the link between the pilot and her brother's ignominious death, would wish to resort to myth—for example the myth of Antigone performing forbidden funeral rites over Polynices—and in so doing produce an allegorical reading of the event. (Interestingly, one possible model, or rather anti-model, here, Jean Anouilh's play *Antigone*, where legend intersects with the contemporary world, opened in Paris in February 1944, just three months before the pilot's death.)[8]. Yet after allowing for a few odd, wonderfully compressed flights of fantasy (the church, for instance, is described as a momentarily abandoned bedroom waiting for lovers held up by inclement weather), Duras insists that nothing should be invented, that the agony must not be cushioned, that the story is 'un fait brutal, isolé, sans aucun écho' (p. 81), and that the meagre details should not be embellished, even (we have to infer) with familial or intertextual references. The narrator commands: 'N'inventer rien, aucun détail. Ne pas inventer du tout. Rien comme tout. Ne pas accompagner la mort' (p. 84). Duras thus rules out any possibility of turning the lament into a formal elegy, in the style, say, of the great medieval elegies like *Pearl*, the late fourteeth-century English poem, where the lost secret pearl that represents the pearl-maiden is eventually discovered by its narrator to be part of a timeless and unchanging divine order of 'flawless, fine' celestial bodies.[9] She may feel instinctively drawn to using vocabulary such as *sacré* and *éternel* (as in the phrase: 'C'était devenu sacré pour moi' [p. 79], and: 'Mort éternelle' [p. 82]), yet she knows as a convinced atheist living in a secular age that these words no longer carry the religious and redemptive meaning they held in the medieval period, when Christ's body was believed to be the incarnation of God's Word. Without faith in a transcendental referent, all we have at our disposal to explain the mystery of life and elevate death is language.

The wholesale injunction in 'Aviateur' against the fictional, mythological, allegorical, theological and even intertextual, would seem to be an impossible wager, and it provokes from Duras a double statement of defeat: 'Je ne peux rien dire. Je ne peux rien écrire' (p. 86). Barely airborne, the text appears completely blocked, offering up only the odd embers of description or the remainders of narration. Vauville is described as 'cette marelle' (p. 85), but this refers only to the sad decipherment of the village's name on the cemetery headstones. The signs of death and doubt are everywhere, and nothing has an affirmative ring to it. It is even suggested that the dead pilot could have been French or American. Duras is emphatic about one thing, however: if the facts of the pilot's death were merely recounted, the text would quickly terminate. How, then, can the story be reactivated in such a way that it breaks free from the purely descriptive lock of its title, 'La mort du jeune aviateur anglais'? Or, to pose the question slightly differently, how can the text proceed to the open regions of writing without in the process diminishing the memory of the English pilot whose life, cut so tragically short, remains in the recurring, originary scene a living, hanging death? That is to say, how can the loose body in the core-story be reached without purifying it away as the ineffable, or re-entombing it under new layers of narrative or symbolism? How, in short, can one remain absolutely committed to the real and honour the memory of the dead, yet still derive some necessary personal relief and consolation?

In the absence of a ready answer, Duras suddenly presents a new theory of writing. She posits the abstract notion of 'une écriture du non-écrit' (p. 86), which she immediately qualifies as 'une écriture brève' (ibid). This is not at all to be taken in the generic sense of the short story but rather as a form of writing 'sans grammaire, une écriture de mots seuls' (ibid). How this might be achieved if the text is not to become free-form poetry is not explained, but it constitutes at least a formal impossibility around which and through which the text can now proceed, that is to say, a new, third direction. Duras returns to the originary scene of death and focuses this time in close-up on the ceremony performed by the villagers for the dead pilot. In this new version, they watched all night over the body imprisoned in the wreckage before retrieving it in the atmosphere of a 'fête funèbre' (p. 87). It was left to the 'discrétion sublime' of the women in the village to clean the body and bury it on the other side of the church. Of this last detail, the narrator admits to being a little unsure, and in fact Duras often has recourse to the adjective *sublime* whenever she is unable to describe people, objects or events that move her beyond words. Details seem less crucial now, and words used before such as *adoration* acquire a new charge: the village-women worshipped literally and celebrated the dead child-pilot.

The exact nature and cause of the narrator's emotions is now, I think, becoming fully clear. They stem from the fact that she did not participate herself in the ritual around the pilot's body. If she had, she admits she may not have felt the 'fantastically strong' emotions that she currently does for the English pilot, presented in unequivocal terms as 'cet enfant devenu le dernier mort de la guerre' (p. 88). For she has, in fact, come to bear witness almost fifty years too late. This position of being on the outside of a sublime event recalls Duras's early text 'Le Boa' alluded to above, where an adult female narrator describes how, as a young girl, she thrilled at the regular spectacle of a boa swallowing a chicken at the zoo. This became a sublime experience of pure violence and silent horror, an impeccable crime of transubstantiation accomplished in 'sacred tranquillity'.[10] For the narrator of 'Aviateur', the real dilemma now is less how to perform a suitable act of memorialization than how to find a way of herself taking part *après coup* in the sublime event of the burial. Alone in intense, inconsolable grief, powerless, lost for words, and orphaned, as it were, by the facts, how can she regain control of her emotion and exercise her own will and 'sublime discretion'? The more Duras insists on the immensity of the wound opened up by the pilot's death (an 'opening' ['brèche'] in the universe [p. 89]), and the more she refers in sheer awe to the 'fait inépuisable' (p. 88) of his age, the less likely would seem to be any hope of a resolution to her mourning. The text's status is again plunged into crisis, almost fatalistically, by Duras. It is nothing, neither a book, nor a song, nor a poem, nor reflections; nothing except uncontrollable tears, pain, and despair, stronger even than faith in God because limitless, and thus more dangerous. With this last point, Duras again stresses that a theological framework to her story is impossible, despite the fact that Cliffe's 'Eternal body' was 'crucified' by the wreckage and that he has the stature of 'le roi de la mort par la guerre' (p. 93). There is no mystery to the pilot's death: everything was seen. The 'event' of the grave (p. 92) continues to exist but only because one can touch, caress and cry over the headstone.

By returning once again in morbid, helpless fascination to the graveyard writing of the name, W. J. Cliffe, Duras reveals the extent of her impasse. There is no chance to proceed if the main options (narrative, descriptive, mythological, etc) are either foreclosed or exhausted. Poetic references to the evening sun or the two mad, twin rivers of the area are as unhelpful as Duras's ironic statement that the new cemetery at Vauville is like one vast Prisunic, or her throwaway reference to 'les Nord-men' of Normandy (p. 95)! Moreover, the textual freedoms afforded by *écriture courante* are flatly refused in the form of a statement that reverses the definition of this style given in *L'Amant*. The original passage in *L'Amant* reads:

> Quelquefois je sais cela: que du moment que ce n'est pas, toutes choses confondues, aller à la vanité et au vent, écrire ce n'est rien. Que du moment que ce n'est pas, chaque fois, toutes choses confondues en une seule par essence inqualifiable, écrire ce n'est rien que publicité.[11]

Here is the corresponding passage in 'Aviateur':

> Ecrire sur tout, tout à la fois, c'est ne pas écrire. C'est rien. Et c'est une lecture intenable, de la même façon qu'une publicité. (p. 91)

We have clearly reached an apex in the later Duras corpus. In the absence of an ideal form or 'écriture du non-écrit' (Duras is still writing prose, after all), the only recourse, paradoxically, is for the text to turn in on itself completely, that is, to take itself as its own, textual body and pursue ever more intensively a metatextual and metacritical approach. In other words, to reverse priorities and make the issue of the pilot's dead body one of secondary importance. Duras maps out this new direction, the text's fourth, with the uncompromising force of a literary manifesto:

> Il faut commencer à l'envers. Je ne parle pas d'écrire. Je parle du livre une fois écrit. Partir de la source et la suivre jusqu'à la réserve de son eau. Partir de la tombe et aller jusqu'à lui, le jeune aviateur anglais. (p. 96)

But what does Duras mean here exactly? She continues to negate fixed literary forms in statements such as: 'Il y a souvent des récits et très peu souvent de l'écriture' (p. 96), and: 'Il n'y a qu'un poème peut-être et encore, pour essayer . . . quoi?' (ibid). But these proclamations merely underscore the enormity of the problem facing the narrator, and they distinctly fail to advance the aims of inversion and reversal which have just been called for. The problem would seem to have been merely displaced: it is now the fragmented textual body of 'Aviateur' that constitutes the open wound and which demands to be covered up and sealed. Yet how?

Duras starts to incorporate elements of inversion within her description of the area by creating a series of oxymorons. The forest, for example, has a 'banalité grandiose', and the cats, carnivorous like dogs, are now both red and black (p. 96). These elements, however, still remain at the descriptive level. Two short paragraphs follow. The first reads: 'L'innocence de la vie, oui, c'est vrai, elle est là, de même que ces rondes chantées par les enfants de l'école'. The second, just one line, is: 'C'est vrai il y a l'innocence de la vie' (p. 96). If we leave aside, as we are clearly invited to, the casual reference to the children and the circularity of the *ronde*, what we see operating between the key elements of these paragraphs, and for the first time in the text, is a motivated chiastic formation: 'L'innocence de la vie . . . /c'est vrai . . . /[c]'est vrai/ . . . l'innocence de la vie'. This chiasmus achieves even greater, poetic force if we bear in mind how Duras delivered her texts orally as if she were scanning verse, a technique that involved the pronunciation of usually silent vowels. This would make the second paragraph a twelve-syllable line of verse: 'C'est vrai il y a l'innocence de la vie'. By cutting into the textual body and in the same moment stitching it up on an internal, structural level, Duras has mounted a cross in her text that is purely rhetorical. This move is almost a basic reflex-action on her part since the trope of inversion often occurs in her work, notably in the cinematic relationship between text and image.[12]

The benefits of such a manoeuvre are not immediately apparent, however. The next paragraph begins: 'Une innocence à pleurer' (p. 97), and Duras consolidates the emotion relating to the trees martyred by German fire by remarking that their bodies of soot had been 'murdered'. But just when it seems that the association between past and present is irredeemable and doomed to eternal repetition, Duras engineers a sudden halt to the downward spiral, so quickly, in fact, that it is easy to miss it on a first reading. She states:

> Non. Il n'y a plus de guerre. L'enfant, de la guerre, il a tout remplacé. L'enfant de vingt ans: toute la forêt, toute la terre, il a remplacé, et aussi l'avenir de la guerre. La guerre, elle est enfermée dans le tombeau avec les os du corps de cet enfant. (p. 97)

The decisive 'Non' directly contradicts the previous statement about the permanence of the 'old war' and in so doing projects 'Aviateur' into a wholly new, fifth gear. The text is no longer locked in repetition but wilfully refuting and inverting itself. The phrase: 'L'enfant de vingt ans: toute la forêt, toute la terre, il a remplacé', extends and develops the preceding chiasmus and its central idea of innocence. For if the airman, as the child of war, stands symbolically for the entire Second World War, the fact of his dying effectively caused the death of that war ('La guerre . . . est enfermée dans le tombeau avec les os du corps de cet enfant' [p. 97]). At the same time, Duras appears to be burying the very idea of war since she is restaging for herself on a higher, conceptual level, a second burial of the airman's bones which she had already 'disinterred' with her earlier obsessive focus on his dead body. I would claim that these imaginary moves of replacement, extension and engulfment have all been provoked by that one event of chiastic reversal which neatly stitched up, and, as it were, discreetly laid to rest the open, wounded textual body of 'Aviateur'.

Of course, on one level, the process of exhumation and inhumation corresponds to the general process of storytelling. Roland Barthes demonstrates in *S/Z* that telling a story means exhuming a body and perversely remarking it for the observer to read as the story is told.[13] Here, however, that process is played out almost literally, and the result is the strange creation of a new peace. Duras writes: 'C'est tranquille maintenant. Ce qui est la splendeur centrale, c'est l'idée, l'idée des vingt ans, l'idée du jeu à la guerre, devenue resplendissante. Un cristal' (p. 97). By representing and replacing 'everything', the body of W. J. Cliffe has transformed itself on an abstract level into an idea, a transparent idea of impudent play, rendered triumphant by Duras in the expanding form of a tricolon ('l'idee/l'idée des vingt ans/l'idée du jeu à la guerre, devenue resplendissante'). We note that for Christians, crystal, composed of matter yet appearing immaterial, is a traditional image of the Immaculate Conception: Mary is crystal and her son heavenly light which passes through. The image of crystal is also present in one of the enlightening visions of paradise in the medieval elegy *Pearl*, mentioned earlier. To quote in modern English: 'a cliff of crystal [*crystal clyffe*] bright/With resplendent rays all aureoled'.[14] Yet in 'Aviateur' Duras demands that we view the metamorphosis of the pilot Cliffe as a totally natural process: the dead bones which were buried deep under a slab of solid, clear granite have simply risen up again in a different form. In structural terms, the story of the pilot, embedded and engraved in the opening *récit*, has been recast as an 'idea' and mounted textually like a jewel. The purely physical has been transformed into the metaphysical.

What is this transformation if not a sublimation of both the real and the textual body? To sublimate chemically is to purify a solid, for example iodine, first by heating it under such a pressure that it sublimes, then by cooling the vapour until it passes directly into a solid state. Yet sublimation in 'Aviateur' can be understood in other ways too, notably in the Freudian sense, since the idea of the pilot's pure play ironically serves a higher social purpose: that of *replacing* all the signs of war. A strong case could also be made, I think, for seeing this as an instance of the poetic process of sublime transcendence. While there are many different representations of the sublime in literary practice and philosophical theory, they usually conform to a sequence of three movements: (i) the normative or conventional stage before otherness has been apprehended; (ii) the traumatic phase, or the apprehension of a tremendous object which entices the subject, disrupts his/her usual modes of consciousness, and challenges the subject's dignity by means of the drastic contrast opened up between its apparently insurmountable powers and his/her own disorientation; (iii) the reactive phase, or the moment of poetic sublimation, when the subject experiences elevation and empowerment through the restoration of blocked or occluded power.[15] Duras, having been held captive in the imaginary by a scene of 'sublime discretion', has managed to reimpose herself authorially with a display of her own rhetorical and authorial power, one that allows her to contain and channel the flow of overwhelming pain and ultimately transcend it. She has, in a word, played God with her material, reinventing the body of the pilot as a textual body and then crossing over it rhetorically.

The paragraphs that follow all bear witness to, and celebrate, this 'sublime' textual event of elevated play. Duras first asserts self-reflexively: 'S'il n'y avait pas des choses comme ça, l'écriture n'aurait pas lieu' (p. 97), before then meditating on the idea of process. Emotions may lie dormant in the body, subtle, deep, and essential, but they are already part of the bodily process of writing. Hence, the issue of the body no longer concerns just one dead English body, or even one textual body; it is the universal idea of writing as a living body that is important, with, at its centre, the writing subject. Duras has now reached a point where everything can be positively reinvested. Even the forest can be described as 'si belle . . . si ancienne, séculaire, même adorable' (p. 99), an idea presented as pure wordplay ('oui, c'est ça, adorable c'est le mot'). The text has thus become an object of narcissistic contemplation, and Duras accounts for her accession to a fully active role with a magisterial one-sentence paragraph, a veritable apotheosis which repeats *dans* five times as it tries to cover all the major aspects of the text's production:

> J'écris à cause de cette chance que j'ai de me mêler de tout, à tout, cette chance d'être dans ce champ de la guerre, dans ce théâtre vidé de la guerre, dans l'élargissement de cette réflexion, et là dans l'élargissement qui gagne le terrain de la guerre, très lentement, le cauchemar en cours de cette mort du jeune enfant de vingt ans, dans ce corps mort de l'enfant anglais de vingt ans d'âge, mort avec les arbres de la forêt normande, de la même mort, illimitée. (p. 98)

In claiming in this way her right to lose herself in, and interfere with, everything ('me mêler de tout, à tout'), Duras is replaying in the real time of the text the extended process of the chiasmus—itself a staging of the long agony of the pilot—as an extension, or *élargissement*, of her own imaginary powers. The insistence on 'ce corps mort' reminds us that if the text is to talk about itself as writing, then it must reconceive of itself as a material process, 'le train de l'écrit qui passe par votre corps' (p. 98), i.e. as a living textual body which can eventually be received and shared by the reader. Out of this may arise a new understanding, even love: 'Et puis un jour—sur toute la terre on comprendra quelque chose comme l'amour' (p. 98).

What we see, therefore, as we approach the end of 'Aviateur', is an ironic play with words and origins, and this, too, is part of the continuing process of abstraction and sublimation. Duras even poses self-consciously the notion of a film about the unknown that would ideally stage its own abandonment, a film that would be about 'la littérature de la mort vivante' (p. 99). This idea is immediately passed off as a cinematic impossibility, although in fact many of Duras's own films, notably *Le Navire Night*, which records the after-effects of an aborted film of the same name, might be considered possible approximations. Certainly 'Aviateur', with its different stages, emphases, rewindings, circularities and reprises, and which at one point cultivates the idea of an 'écriture du non-écrit', is the exact textual equivalent. To appreciate the full sense of the phrase 'la littérature de la mort vivante', and thus the scale of Duras's achievement in 'Aviateur', it is necessary to understand what the term *littérature* actually means for her. It stands not simply for institutionalized writing or the literary canon, but more generally for the weight of the 'already written', or what she calls elsewhere 'l'envahissement de l'écriture',[16] a movement so overwhelming that it exemplifies the force of the real against which, and over which, Duras as a writer must prevail. The drama of much of her later work derives precisely from this almost visceral need to counter the force of the already-read, the already-said or the already-written, often through recourse to intertextual others such as Proust, Robert Musil, and Henry James, whom she calls her 'Great Men', and with whom she engages in various kinds of intertextual erotics.[17] The title text of *Écrire* states simply: 'On ne peut pas écrire sans la force du corps. Il faut être plus fort que soi pour aborder l'écriture, il faut être plus fort que ce qu'on écrit' (p. 29). Hence, what Duras formalizes in 'Aviateur' as the problem of the writing of literature, a problem affecting every serious literary production, should be viewed as a precise concept of literary struggle, of writing produced over and against the general flow of textuality and literary form.

But 'Aviateur' cannot be brought to a final close until Duras has reprised ironically the entire text. The penultimate paragraph is a sweeping restatement of the various episodes of 'Aviateur', complete with oxymorons and inversions. It begins with the death of the pilot in 'the sky of the Normandy forest' and ends with a personal reordering of historical time. Duras insists, if ever we were in doubt, that her text did not become a short story. The news of the pilot's death, 'cette nouvelle, ce seul fait' (p. 100), the day when the world silently caved in like a point of no-return and inserted itself for ever in people's consciousness—this *nouvelle* never lost its original, emotive and mysterious power. Yet ironically, as a direct result of Duras's textual strategies, the young pilot is now dismissed as a pure 'object' ('ce seul objet d'un enfant de vingt ans' [p. 100]) and neatly categorized as 'l'oublié de la dernière guerre du premier âge' (p. 100). The last brief paragraph underlines the authorial distance Duras has carved for herself in the text. One day, she remarks, there will be nothing left to read or write. All that remains will be untranslatable, i.e. the inexpressible and unrepresentable aspects of the 'life of this dead man'. What Duras is celebrating here, at the end of a long and involved textual ritual, is the fact that 'Aviateur' represents a successful 'translation' of the real, and in the most literal, secular sense possible: the idea of the body has been transported to a superior textual level.

Thus 'Aviateur' has undergone a series of aborted stages or textual directions, including a *récit* and a lament, before eventually crystalliz-ing in a transumptive act of textual mourning as a metatextual and philosophical discourse on writing. In the modern-day absence of any divine continuity between the word and the body, Duras is compelled to play God by writing over the body and by discoursing on writing, that is to say, by approaching the text itself as a body and transforming it into a sublime space of play and textual inversion. I have tried to show that 'Aviateur' refuses many of the textual features of Duras's later literary work, such as its strategies of symbolic equivalence, its aggressive 'private' engagement with either the reader or an intertextual other, and its usual staging of a dynamic scene of naming or renaming (the names of Vauville and Cliffe are never played around with or disfigured). What distinguishes 'Aviateur' is precisely the intensity with which Duras gives herself over to the Other, or rather to the extreme emotions involved in remembering the Other, by entering into the human pain and horror of real events. Compare this approach with another example of Duras sublimating a 'fait brutal, isolé, sans aucun écho' (p. 81), this time a contemporary *fait divers* which similarly involves a male body and death. Her intervention in the long-running 'Petit Grégory' affair of the 1980s, with her highly controversial article for *Libération* (17 July 1985), presumed from the outset that the four-year-old Gregory, whose body was found washed up along the banks of the river Vologne in the Vosges region of France, was killed by his mother, Christine Villemin, incarcerated at the time on charges of infanticide.[18] According to Duras, Villemin was not a criminal and could not therefore be 'guilty', except in the eyes of the male judiciary. Instead, she was one of the many innocent female victims of 'la loi du couple faite par l'homme'. Despite Duras's explicit and rather obscene wish to identify with Villemin (she talks at one point of Christine V. 'qui peut-être a tué sans savoir comme moi j'écris sans savoir'),[19] the overall effect of her rhetorical logic, based on the opposition between *nous* (all women) and *vous* (all men, the judiciary), is actually to isolate Villemin as an untouchable and relegate her to the 'materiality of matter'. In a phrase that quickly became notorious, Duras concluded her article thus: 'Christine V. est sublime. Forcément sublime'. If the real is self-consciously 'betrayed' by Duras here in the interests of transgression (the case was still *sub judice*), by contrast her desire in 'Aviateur' to stage a dramatic act of textual sublimation as a result of feeling excluded from an original scene of 'sublime discretion' seems eminently reasonable.

There is one major direction, however, in which 'Aviateur' could have taken its reader but did not; one, in fact, that seems to have been completely elided. Let us return to the very beginning of the text where Duras formally addressed the reader as *toi* in order to provide her story with a necessary discursive frame. Her words, we recall, were: 'Je crois que c'est une direction de l'écrit. C'est ça, l'écrit adressé, par exemple, à toi, dont je ne sais encore rien. A toi, lecteur:' (p. 69). To be sure, the absence of an empathetic listener or addressable Other, an Other who might hear the anguish of one's memories and thus affirm and recognize their reality, can risk jeopardizing the success of one's story. Yet in 'Aviateur', once a basic rapport with the reader has been formally established, Duras never returns explicitly to the reader as *toi* or even *vous*, least of all at the end where one might initially have expected some kind of formal closure to the textual frame. As we have seen, Duras's emotional commitment to the facts of the story outstrips any attempt to contain them in the form of a *récit* or *nouvelle*. If history is loosely defined as the establishment of the facts of the past through their narrativization, then the exploding of narrative in 'Aviateur' clearly makes it impossible for the text to be judged in such terms. It operates, rather, according to the logic of the emotions until it resolves itself through rhetorical manoeuvres. Nevertheless, Duras consistently skirts and invokes historical reality through her mention of the war with Japan and D-Day, along with her vague reference to the 'dispersion' of the dead, whether in the plains of northern Germany or in what she calls the 'hecatombs' of the Atlantic coast ('le nombre a été dispersé ailleurs' [p. 93]). She also uses provocatively charged terms such as *innocence* to describe the heroic English pilot, and in the absence of any proper reference to the historical and political context in France at the end of the war, a dark period of social reckoning that sought to identify and punish those guilty of collaboration. If Duras had provided such a context, it would perhaps be easier to understand why she should make a foreign pilot so fundamentally innocent. It would not, however, account for her far from naïve wish not simply to accept the doubts and lack of accuracy affecting her story but actively to encourage them, when claiming, for example, that the English pilot may even have been French or American. Nor would it explain Duras's personal reorganization of history through her romantic notion that the pilot was the 'forgotten soldier of the last war in the first age' (p. 98). Such ideas are, as we have seen, part of Duras's way of gaining a complete, ironic distance from her text by turning the pilot into a textual object.

The dangers inherent in abstracting historical reality can be further grasped if we turn finally to another personal, 'sacred' account by Duras of the war, this time from her 1985 collection of wartime memoirs, *La Douleur*. In the chapter entitled 'Albert des Capitales', set in the early days of the Liberation of Paris, a member of the

Resistance called Thérèse (acknowledged by Duras to be herself) subjected a Nazi informer to physical torture in order to extract information. The critic Ann Smock has justifiably claimed that the intense use here of such terms as *le donneur d'hommes*, which gradually assume the mystical and philosophical weight of Maurice Blanchot's notions of *le don* and *l'inavouable*, allows the thought that the determination to expose a human being as not human actually lies deeper than the history of racism and oppression to which it is absolutely central.[20] The question of whether Duras has the right to indulge in this kind of vocabulary is a crucial one, especially since what is at stake in *La Douleur* is not merely the supposed purity of the Resistance but the suffering of another human being. Yet Duras never makes this an issue, just as in 'Aviateur' she never puts into question her absolute need to eternalize and 'sacralize' the English pilot, and ultimately the text itself.[21] In both cases she goes far beyond a simple wish to bear witness. Indeed, her work flies in the face of other contemporary artistic attempts to provide testimony of a still largely unspeakable historical period, such as, for example, Claude Lanzmann's 1985 film *Shoah*, a landmark work composed of interviews with survivors of the Holocaust as well as ex-Nazis and bystanders. What this film, subtitled 'An Oral History of the Holocaust', does is to burst open the shared cultural secret of the Holocaust precisely by decanonizing the silence borne by survivors and by desacralizing the witnesses, with the result that their testimony is liberated. Where Duras stages the hard-won, personal triumph of writing, Lanzmann records a triumphant repossession of the collective human voice.[22]

For Duras, human agony always comes down eventually to the agony of writing. So much of her later work is an ever more profound thematization of the pain and danger of writing and of impossibility overcome. This often leads, as in 'Aviateur', to idealistic statements and impromptu manifestos on the correct nature, method and aims of writing. What the reader is faced with at the end is the need to re-enter the Duras text from the beginning and search out other paths which were not considered or taken, and which remain unexplored. This means, fundamentally, desublimating the sublimating turns of Duras's work by opening up the traces of the real before they are textually stitched up or rhetorically inverted. Of course, the constant risk of such a project would be that the reader rise to perform sublime critical manœuvres on a now essentially closed, discrete—sublimely discrete—*œuvre*. But the risk needs to be taken if the Duras corpus is not simply to become a sublime object of awe and fascination, and if Duras criticism is not in the process to become a living corpse. This chapter is intended as a small contribution to that general project.

From the *Nouvelle* to the *Nouvellistique*

Johnnie Gratton

The difficulties involved in the attempt to map any contemporary literature are obvious enough. Individual authors can easily be identified as promising, individual works as interesting or important, though even at this atomistic level it will take a modicum of consensus to allay suspicions that the individual critic has been guilty of misjudgement, indiscrimination, or hype. It is at the level of general overview, however, that the most serious problems arise. How, for example, with barely any of the hindsight usually available to the literary historian, is one to detect the key trends within a given contemporary literature? How is one to sort out and characterize the energies that make up the force-field of a particular cultural moment when that moment has not yet elapsed, not yet lapsed into a state of pastness amenable to narrative manipulation? Throughout the 1980s and 90s the framework most commonly invoked in response to such a question has been that associated with the term 'postmodernism'. Over the years this has become a term meaning different—often opposing—things to different—often opposed—people, so much so that the confusion surrounding it has left it as open-ended as the contemporary phenomena it is used to make sense of. Despite such fuzziness, and partly perhaps because of it, the notion of a postmodern sensibility embodied in a relatively distinct aesthetic remains both valid and attractive, as I attempt to show in the course of this essay.

The mapping of contemporary French literature happens to be particularly difficult for a number of reasons. Most obvious among these is the fact that, since the demise of the avant-gardist mentality over the course of the 1970s, no major grouping, no distinct 'school' of literary thought—among novelists, for example, no influential 'theory' of fiction—has been discernible. One can look back over earlier periods and characterize them in terms of key points of reference: surrealism before the Second World War, existentialism immediately after the war, the *nouveau roman* in the 1950s and 60s, and *Tel Quel* in the 1960s and 70s. Each of these avant-garde movements drew its strength less from its dominant personalities than from its being a site of convergence between literature and ideas, aesthetics and ethics, art and politics. The *nouveau roman*, for example, was the literary face of structuralism, while *Tel Quel* went on to revamp literary theory and practice in terms of what we have now come to think of as a *post*structuralist idiom. The days of the *nouveau roman* and *Tel Quel* are remembered by most contemporary French writers, however, as a time of intellectual terrorism. A new spirit of individualism, underpinned by a growing shift towards liberalism, has taken root. As a result, French writers today—and this is a point nowhere more visible than across the range of contemporary women's writing—are far more reluctant than their predecessors to allow their identities as writers to be defined in terms of extrinsic or collective labels.

The situation just described can easily be construed as anaemic. In the words of John Taylor, an American writer who lives in France and regularly reports on the contemporary scene:

> Contemporary French literature, especially as it is perceived abroad, provokes bewilderment and pity, as if the thematic boldness and stylistic experimentation expected of French novelists and poets, ever since the days of Flaubert and Baudelaire, were now provided exclusively by a handful of structuralist or poststructuralist philosophers, critics, and psychoanalysts.[1]

Things are probably not as bad as Taylor suggests here. While a whole generation has certainly grown up with far more interest in French critical theory than in recent French literature, the latter has not been completely forsaken. In the Anglo-American world, for example, critical theory has been instrumental in fostering new approaches to, and fresh perspectives on, the study of literature, with the contemporary period high on the list of beneficiaries. I am thinking in particular of the contemporary orientations found within research areas such as women's studies, gay studies, cultural studies and francophone studies. Without these, numerous up-and-coming authors of demonstrable talent would have continued to go un-heralded, especially in the non-francophone world where translations of recent literary writing in French are deplorably thin on the ground. On the other hand, the mixture of research specialization and course modularization in tertiary education today inevitably narrows the range of texts and authors in which one is invited to take an interest. Thus, while the new approaches set up new ways of awakening curiosity about the contemporary, they might also be said to result in a selective, even sectarian curiosity. In this respect the 'interpretive communities' behind some of the research areas currently in favour may well be part of the problem indicated by Taylor when he argues that the 'perception of moribundity' in contemporary French culture 'describes less a factual situation than incurious ways of thinking about French writing'.[2]

This is not to say that criticism in France does not have its own 'incurious ways of thinking'. For example, with a few brave exceptions, French academics remain far more cautious and canonical than their anglophone counterparts when it comes to the authors they are likely to regard as teachable and researchable. According to an intellectual attitude still prevalent in France, the contemporary is a matter for literary journalism rather than literary criticism. In the universities it is common for individual authors to be considered off limits because their work has not yet been the object of a completed doctoral thesis. Unconsecrated, the contemporary remains institutionally untreatable and intellectually unprofitable.

If there is one particular sphere of French literature which has suffered from a lack of interest on the part of French critics, publishers, and readers, it is of course that of short fiction. It is a remarkable fact that in the post-war period only one French author, Daniel Boulanger, has achieved popular and critical acclaim specifically on the basis of his identity as a writer of short fiction. And while one can occasionally point to signs of heightened interest in the genre, the fact remains that over the last few decades very few of France's accomplished short-story writers, and equally very few of its prize-winning short-story collections, have made it into Folio, Livre de poche, or any other of France's major paperback collections —unless, of course, the writer in question also happened to be a successful novelist: a Tournier or a Le Clézio, for example. Indeed, as has been noted with dismay by a number of regular commentators on the genre, the alternative key to success these days would seem to be to write short stories in English, preferably American English, and wait to be translated.

One is tempted to deduce from the indifference or resistance apparent here that it must in the end reflect an objective lack of quality among the practitioners of modern and contemporary short fiction in France. But that would be to embrace once more the self-justifying logic of those who are wedded to 'incurious ways of thinking', this time as encouraged by a history of devaluation of the short story within the French literary institution in modern times. One only has to 'read around' the canon (an expression which implies an exploratory approach to texts by writers within as well as outside the canon) to see the situation differently. For example, in one of the few wide-ranging surveys of contemporary French literature to appear in the 1990s, Pierre Brunel concludes by fastening onto two positive features, two qualities which he sees as offering a way forward for French literature as it moves into the twenty-first century. The first is located in the shift from a modernist logic of rupture and renewal to the postmodern desire for a more conciliatory relationship with the past, one in which the possibilities of the present are explored in part through a return to the past. This for Brunel is a welcome development: 'Où va donc la littérature française aujourd'hui? Moins, me semble-t-il, vers le néant dans une course folle à la modernité que vers une post-modernité où le nouveau se conquiert à partir du donné culturel.'[3] So saying, Brunel makes a relatively predictable point in so far as the recycling of the past, or the envisioning of the present via the past, has formed a widely recognized facet of recent French fiction ever since writers such as Modiano, Tournier, and Yourcenar began during the 1960s to challenge (each in their own way) the aesthetic hegemony of the *nouveau roman*.

However, the second quality highlighted by Brunel comes as something of a surprise, for he detects in contemporary French literature a 'freshness' that is nowhere better exemplified than in *short* literary forms: 'Je dirais aussi que la littérature française de la fin du

XXe siècle n'est pas une littérature fin-de-siècle prise dans le vertige de la décadence. Elle a bien souvent de la fraîcheur, du brillant, surtout peut-être quand elle adopte la forme brève, laissant à des consommateurs plus qu'à des lecteurs les romans-fleuves, les fausses sagas familiales ou les fresques historiques en technicolor.'[4] Given the focus of this chapter, Brunel's evaluation is clearly most encouraging. I shall return in due course to the implications of his reference to a general rather than generic configuration, to the *forme brève* rather than the *nouvelle* as such. First of all, however, I wish to suggest that one the main reasons for the 'freshness' of contemporary French short fiction lies in the significant contribution currently being made to that form by women writers.

Established in 1974, the annual Bourse Goncourt de la Nouvelle is the most important French literary prize awarded in the area of short fiction. Over the first twenty years of its existence, the prize was awarded eight times to women writers—in percentage terms, a rarely equalled achievement. Highlights include Christiane Baroche's *Chambres, avec vue sur le passé* (1978), a collection organized around the theme of nostalgia; Pierrette Fleutiaux's *Les Métamorphoses de la reine* (1985), upbeat rewritings of traditional fairy tales along feminist lines; Noëlle Châtelet's *Histoires de bouches* (1986), a set of stories based on the theme of eating and inspired by the author's own academic thesis on culinary aesthetics; and Catherine Lépont's *Trois gardiennes* (1991), three stories of women who are keepers of secrets, all set in places outside of France and written in a narrative idiom which opens itself up to linguistic, poetic, and cultural otherness. There are no loose strands in any of these volumes. On the contrary, each confirms in its own way the strong value placed during the modern period on the poetics of the collection or *recueil* as a coherent structure housing diversity within unity. Just as significantly, each of these works confirms the centrality of narrative writing to the art of short fiction, not just as a traditional or obligatory ingredient but as a vital, supremely flexible resource, ever capable of shedding new light on human predicaments both great and small.

Nowhere is the sense of a specifically narrative renewal of the art of short fiction more evident than in the work of Annie Saumont, herself a winner of the Bourse Goncourt de la Nouvelle in 1981 for her collection *Quelquefois dans les cérémonies*. Alongside Christiane Baroche and Georges-Olivier Châteaureynaud, Saumont, with some sixteen volumes of short stories to her name between 1968 and 1996, is probably the most highly regarded practitioner of short fiction in France today. And yet, to echo a point made earlier, only one of those collections, *Les voilà quel bonheur*, has made it into a mainstream paperback series: this despite the contemporary setting of most of her stories, their sharp topical edge, and their appeal to a young readership through their author's recurrent concern with the everyday experience of children and adolescents in an increasingly hostile urban culture. For the purposes of the present brief introduction to Saumont's work, I shall focus on the stories contained in two of her more recent collections: *Les voilà quel bonheur* (1993) and *Après* (1996).

Following the tradition of the 'lonely voice', as Frank O'Connor put it in a formulation which has proved remarkably durable, Saumont focuses attention on a variety of isolated, marginalized, and deviant figures, many of whom have been subjected to some form of violence, and most of whom have experienced loss and abandonment. The single most striking instance of this thematic configuration is the story entitled 'Sarah',[5] in which a middle-aged narrator reflects back on his life. Abandoned in a chapel soon after his birth, then taken on by a foster mother, he finds himself at age eleven caught up in the chaos set off by the German invasion of France at the beginning of the Second World War. Having fled south from Paris with his foster mother, he is then abandoned for a second time before finding work and shelter on a farm. There he meets another homeless person, a girl known alternatively as Sarah and Henriette, who also works on the farm. Her job is to force-feed the geese, and it is this activity, rather than the surrounding circumstances of the war, that continues to haunt the narrator as a consummate image of shameful human cruelty. The point of the title, and the sting in the tail of the story, is not, however, revealed until the end, where it turns out that, by calling the girl Sarah rather than Henriette, the narrator gave away her Jewish identity to some German soldiers visiting the farm, which led to her being taken away, never to be seen again. Thus the shame that he, a committed vegetarian, continues to locate in her deeds as a force-feeder of geese is the shame that has warped and withered his own life ever since that fatal day.

From one Saumont story to another, victims of social injustice living in squats ('Taggers taggez'), shanty towns ('La Bâche'), and squalid suburban housing developments ('Les Enfants s'ennuient le dimanche'), rub shoulders with those who are primarily victims of their own obsessions: in 'Un Régime pour Régine' and 'Une Semaine comme les autres', for instance, adult males who are so hung up on their mothers that they are unable to relate successfully to other women.[6] More often than not, Saumont allows her characters to speak for themselves, to express, or to betray their inability to express, the anger and frustration which are consuming them. Indeed, her interest in the rough end of the contemporary everyday is demonstrated most directly in her willingness to espouse the slang-ridden idiom of disaffected youth, a language at once degraded and vibrant, a token of defeat yet an instrument of resistance.

In formal terms, Saumont's texts retain strong links with the tradition of short-story writing. As opposed to those who have sought for various reasons to denarrativize short fiction, Saumont continues to practise the art of the surprise effect associated with the nineteenth-century short story, and in particular to favour the familiar device of the final 'catch' or 'twist'. Just as writers like Pierrette Fleutiaux and Angela Carter rewrite fairy tales in a feminist spirit, so Saumont recycles the device of the surprise ending to make a point against the male of the species. In the curt and chilling 'Il revenait de Chicago, Papa', a series of snapshot-like scenes shows a father deviously coaxing his daughter towards incest over a period of years. By the time she is twenty, the daughter is a secretary having an affair with her boss. Finding herself in a situation which echoes those routinely passed through with her father, she suddenly turns on the man:

> Elle se penche vers la table, elle saisit à deux mains la lampe au pied de marbre. Elle s'approche du lit. Elle frappe.
> Il saigne. Il ne prononce pas un mot. Son regard chavire et se fixe comme s'il contemplait le plafond. Le sang jaillit plus fort et par saccades.
> Elle dit, Oh je ne voulais pas. Elle dit, Ce n'est rien. Je te demande pardon.[7]

Previously it was she who bled and, more pointedly still, it was the father who asked too late for forgiveness, using the very same words now uttered by the daughter. In such a short story, a postmodern *conte cruel* unburdened by a single narratorial comment, it is of course impossible for the reader not to hear these echoes, not to get the final point in all its sharpness. In other stories, the surprise ending tends to be a function of repression on the part of a male narrator or protagonist. The narrator of 'Sarah', for instance, cannot give away his guilt until he has exhausted his already frayed narrative of innocence. Similarly, in 'Rencontre', a male narrator paints a highly negative portrait of the woman he once loved and is about to meet again. An ex-tennis champion who no longer plays sport, she appears to have turned bitter with age. The narrator seems to consider that he will be doing this woman a favour by meeting her. Only at the end of the story does he reveal that the woman is wheelchair-bound because of a car accident for which he himself was responsible. Once more, with obvious encouragement from the author, a male character ends up blowing his own cover. Finally, in 'Une Semaine comme les autres', a male narrator returns home every day from work to be greeted and fed by his mother. Together they watch the television news every night, following certain items as they unfold through the week, notably a police investigation into the murder of a local girl. In this case the 'twist' in the story takes the form of a gradual dawning rather than a final surprise, as bit by bit the narrator gives away his pathological contempt for women. When it eventually comes, his admission of guilt, but not of regret, strikes the reader as perversely logical, as does his final unruffled expression of concern for the safety of his mother now that he will no longer be there to protect her:

> J'ai conservé le prospectus sur le Brésil; je dirai à mère, ne gémis pas, tu viendras me voir là-bas, un fils doit finir par quitter la maison. Je lui recommanderai de bien se nourrir et d'être prudente. En ces temps troublés une femme seule devrait toujours demeurer sur ses gardes (se reporter aux faits divers de cette dernière semaine—pourtant à peu près comme les autres dans l'ensemble). Mieux vaut ne pas courir de risques, prendre les précautions d'usage. Elle trouvera un grand couteau —nouvellement affûté, du Nogent premier choix, modèle professionnel—sous l'album des photos d'autrefois, dans ma commode, dernier tiroir.[8]

Like most successful short-story writers, Saumont treats the brevity and artificiality of the *nouvelle* less as hindrances than as creative assets, thereby constantly reopening the genre to stylization and experimentation. Her inclination to evoke unsettling situations and unsettled states of mind has led her to try out a variety of registers, from the detached and dispassionate narrative filters associated with the *conte cruel* to the bristling syntactic compression she uses to dramatize more hysterical cases of pathological behaviour, as in the following example where a couple pressed for time suddenly find themselves drawn into a domestic crisis:

> Vont arriver. Rien n'est prêt.
> Aurait dû y penser (elle). Depuis longtemps. Aurait dû préparer.
> Pas eu le temps.
> Court ici et là (elle). Regrette. Eparpille. Choisis. S'efforce. Décide. Rassemble. Entasse. S'essuie les mains sur sa robe.[9]

The model for this clipped narrative idiom is soon revealed to be the language of the menu or instruction manual:

> *Balayer*
> *Ouvrir la fenêtre*
> *Eplucher les oignons*
> *Cueillir trois roses rouges au jardin*[10]

Here Saumont falls back on one of her favourite and most effective devices, the imported quotation, sometimes real (as when she quotes elsewhere from the lyrics of a Charles Trenet song), and sometimes —as here—invented for the occasion. Such inserts tend to recur as intermittent leitmotifs, adding a peculiarly rhythmic quality to the narrative structure of Saumont's texts. Repetition, in fact, is the dominant formal characteristic of her writing, so much so that her stories, without ever sacrificing narrativity as such, often seem to have commandeered the structural energies of the *poème en prose*. Indeed, at an abstract level her texts often approach the condition of poetry in verse, attaining a stanzaic rather than merely episodic quality. For, in Saumont's case, repetition is more frequently enabled by the way the author divides her stories into typographically distinct blocks or sections, often headed by subtitles, often corresponding to the separate times and places, the different fragments and threads, making up the mosaic of a given narrative world.

A writer open to experimentation, Saumont never works to a strict generic formula: 'Ce que doit être la nouvelle, après en avoir publié plus d'une centaine, je ne le sais toujours pas.'[11] Indeed, for Saumont, writing an individual short story is always tantamount to reinventing an entire genre: 'à chaque fois la tâche est double: écrire une nouvelle nouvelle et réinventer un genre littéraire.'[12] In all other respects, however, she seems quite content to assume the label *nouvelle* and to accept the identity of *nouvelliste*. As such, Saumont moves only half-way towards the position hinted at by Pierre Brunel when, rounding off his essay on contemporary French writing, he attributes a quality of freshness not to a genre, the *nouvelle*, but to a generality, the *forme brève*. Brunel's move chimes with my own conviction that no account of the contemporary short story can be valid unless it admits the indeterminate nature of its object. This indeterminacy has only partly to do with the perennial problems involved in defining the short story (or any other form) as a genre. In fact, what I wish to argue now is that indeterminacy as a contemporary phenomenon comes about through the marked shift which has taken place over recent decades from a modernist concern with the specificity of individual genres to a more evidently postmodern focus on borderline, hybrid and unclassifiable forms of writing: in a word, if such a word be needed, on transgenericity.

Needless to say, commitment among writers to the idea of the *nouvelle* as a distinct form or genre has not suddenly evaporated. But it has begun to slip. This point emerges clearly in the work which constitutes the most illuminating survey currently available of the state of contemporary French short fiction, the invaluable *131 Nouvellistes par eux-mêmes* (1993), edited by Claude Pujade-Renaud and Daniel Zimmermann. The editors contacted a wide range of writers associated with short fiction and asked them to respond to questions mainly about their views on the theory and practice of the *nouvelle*. A fairly clear split emerges at the level of self-image between those, such as Annie Saumont, who are content to see themselves as writers of *nouvelles* and those who are reluctant to think of their work as fitting neatly into any single genre. Thus a significant number of the writers represented in this survey choose to identify their practice in terms of broad transgeneric categories such as *le récit bref*, or, looser still and even more frequently, *le texte court*: a preference echoed by the growing tendency among anglophone writers and critics over the last few decades to speak about 'short fiction' rather than 'the short story'. As expressed in French, this preference tends to signal some kind of reservation, resistance, or even hostility over the term *nouvelle*, now seen as the repository of a classical form, as a fixed form, or as an unnecessary generic label; for the rhetoric of self-image leads many of these authors into making the now familiar move of seeing themselves primarily as *écrivains*. 'J'ose me prétendre un écrivain,' writes Henri Raczymow, '. . . j'écris pour tenter de trouver du nouveau, non pour restituer une forme préconçue.'[13] Similarly, Jacques Fulgence complains that it is his publisher, not he, who puts the word *Nouvelles* on the cover of his books; what he *writes*, he insists, are 'des choses comme elles me viennent, rebelles à l'étiquetage'.[14]

This general resistance to being pigeonholed clearly manifests the same attitude of cultural sensibility which opens up the space of contemporary short fiction to adjacent forms and modes of writing. One might say that, while there are some who form the core of the literary space mapped out by the book in question, there are others who feel more comfortable (or more creatively *un*comfortable) occupying the outlying areas of that space. The striking thing about this particular book being that, on the evidence provided by the writers themselves, the margins are now exercising a far more powerful attraction than the core. Both the theory and the practice of the *nouvelle* have of course long been marked by a strong awareness of the overlaps and affinities of short fiction with adjacent short forms such as the *conte*, the *fait divers*, the *essai*, the autobiographical fragment and, at the limit of compression or denarrativization, the *poème en prose*. To a critic such as René Godenne, who over many years has devoted his energies to promoting the cause of the francophone short story, this crowded situation has provided all the more reason to insist on the distinct identity of the *nouvelle*. Always a separatist on the question of genre, Godenne can only react with dismay at the results of the survey carried out by Pujade-Renaud and Zimmermann:

Laisser la parole aux nouvellistes dans des ouvrages collectifs qui
se voudraient comme les manifestes de la nouvelle de la fin du
siècle est une bonne chose . . . mais quand on s'aperçoit—avec
effarement —que plusieurs des *131 nouvellistes contemporains par
eux-mêmes* déclarent n'être pas nouvelliste, écrire plutôt des
'petits romans', etc, on s'interrogera sur le mauvais service que
rendent de tels livres à la nouvelle, si ce n'est de reprendre l'idée
commune, déjà si répandue, que la nouvelle est un genre
mineur.[15]

In contrast to Godenne, I believe not only that we must accept the
existence of crossover and borderline *formes brèves* as an integral part
of the new literary landscape, but that we should be willing to take
this fact on board as a welcome and interesting phenomenon in its
own right.

One of the standard moves, perhaps *the* standard move, in the
definitional rhetoric deployed by both writers and critics of short
fiction is to posit a strong, often colourfully metaphoric contrast
between *nouvelle* and *roman*. This is understandable enough in so far
as both are perceived as belonging to the same family of narrative
forms, making it all the more necessary for the *nouvelle* to stand its
ground and assert its specificity over and against its 'big brother'. The
rhetoric seems to be changing, however, as more and more writers
abandon this protectionist standpoint and consider the virtues of
crossover between these two narrative forms. At once dislocated and
reinvigorated by the example of magic realism, the novel, after all,
has sought increasingly since the 1970s to embrace the pluralities,
brevities and intensities of short fiction, with the figure of the narrator
either giving way to a growing pluralization of narrative voice or being
maintained in order to function as a relay station to others and others'
stories. Such a narrator is as much a cipher as it is a centre.

There exist in French literature numerous examples of fictions
anticipating this area of crossover between novel and short story. One
thinks in particular of the use of specially configured spaces, such as
the single building occupied by numerous persons, to generate
multiple-strand fictions. Hence the structure of novels such as Marcel
Aymé's *Maison basse* (1935) and Michel Butor's *Passage de Milan*
(1954). These novels turn out to have been the forerunners of a
work now generally regarded as one of the great achievements of

twentieth-century French fiction, Georges Perec's *La Vie mode d'emploi* (1978). Written over a nine-year period, this novel sets out to describe in detail what would be revealed to the eye if a Parisian apartment block suddenly had its façade peeled away. Whence the novel's brilliantly realized merger of temporal and spatial coordinates into a 'chronotope', an overall unit of representation, a particular kind of narrative 'world', consisting here of a group of apartments, along with the various animate and inanimate objects visible inside them, all frozen in a single present moment, set just before 8.00 p.m. on 23 June 1975.

The stark immobility inherent in Perec's initial idea for the novel is reflected in the determining role played by description throughout the text. At the same time, virtually every chapter of the book finds a way of breaking into the narrative mode and generating an *histoire* (the term used by Perec in his own index of the stories contained in the book), which may be the story of a past or present occupant of the room in question, but might equally be inspired by an object such as a painting on a wall. This is the profusion of micro-narratives signalled by Perec when, to the title of his work, he adds the pluralized subtitle, *romans*. In other words, this famous 'novel' is also a collection of short stories of the kind often described as a 'framed miscellany', with the apartment block providing the frame. As Claude Burgelin suggests, Perec's models in this respect are the *Thousand and One Nights* and the *Decameron*, whose enclosed settings provide the ideal launching pad for the narrative excursions of the story-teller.[16]

Modern short fiction has tended to invest more and more in a chronotope characterized by reduced time-spans, delimited spaces, and the attenuated narrativity of a single incident or moment of experience: in short, the form which has come to be known in the francophone world as the *nouvelle-instant*.[17] In contrast, Perec's *histoires* recycle a more old-fashioned poetics based on the compressed life-story. Individual stories are recounted rapidly, with little concern for plausibility, in a zany picaresque style which brings their protagonists through successive episodes and identities until inevitably they meet their death, often a violent one. Little concern is shown for subjective realism or psychological complexity. Most of the huge cast of characters put on display by Perec demonstrate the same core feature. Obsessively bent on having or knowing something, they dedicate their lives to an intense yet methodical and, for most, ultimately futile quest. As such, these protagonists hail less from the world of the modern novel than from that of the classical short story, where characterization tends to be based on the exaggeration or magnification of a single defining feature. As a narrative fiction, then, this is a work which shows distinctly postmodern qualities, firstly by virtue of the way it refunctions past narrative styles in order to produce splendidly inventive stories, and secondly by taking the form of a multiplicity of little stories rather than one continuous narrative.

Amongst contemporary writers working in the area of crossover between novel and short fiction, I have singled out five names worthy of mention. Jean-Noël Blanc has written a number of texts which he describes as 'des romans-par-nouvelles', in which each text is relatively autonomous, but where common themes, settings, and characters produce a non-synthetic unity which Blanc describes as a form of *collage*: 'Si l'on veut que la nouvelle appartienne profondément à notre époque,' he writes, 'je crois que c'est surtout par ce travail de collage qu'on peut y parvenir. C'est du moins ce que j'essaie de faire.'[18]

Paul Fournel, a member of the Oulipo group of writers, like Perec before him, has written several volumes of short stories composed as thematic series, with *Les grosses rêveuses* (1982) coming closest to a 'roman-par-nouvelles'. In this collection, Fournel deals with the dreams, desires and disillusionments of a number of female characters, one per story, who all live in the same village. Thus the collection progresses towards a novel-like status as it inscribes more and more of the interactions and overlappings of its characters within the common setting of a small rural community.

The title of Gilles Leroy's collection *Les derniers seront les premiers* (1991) indicates its close thematic connection not only with Annie Saumont's short fiction but with a long tradition of short-story writing in which lives which would not otherwise have been told, voices which would not otherwise have been heard, are brought to our attention. Leroy's own commentary on his book is enlightening:

> Ces neuf nouvelles ont été écrites en un an, dans l'ordre où elles sont publiées et qui suit une chronologie: des années 1910 à aujourd'hui, les destins de certains personnages s'étalant sur presque un siècle. Bien sûr, chaque nouvelle se lit de façon autonome, mais une unité de lieu les relie (le décor des Faubourgs

devenus plus tard la proche banlieue), ainsi qu'une continuité de temps qui permet de retrouver certains personnages d'un récit à l'autre, à quinze ou quarante années d'écart. Le projet, c'était une traversée de personnages d'apparence très modeste—des gens de rien comme on dirait, à qui je voulais offrir, l'espace d'un livre, la parole que la vie leur avait refusée.[19]

In describing the dynamics of his own 'roman-par-nouvelles', Leroy subscribes to the general idea, all the more powerful for being largely implicit, that short fiction is a modest form which lends itself particularly well to dramatizing the lives overlooked or marginalized by History ('l'Histoire avec sa grande hache', as Georges Perec once put it). The most pointed theoretical formulation of this idea remains Jean-François Lyotard's definition of the postmodern as a condition of 'incrédulité à l'égard des métarécits', otherwise known as 'les grands récits': a state of incredulity whereby 'la fonction narrative perd ses foncteurs, le grand héros, les grands périls, les grands périples et le grand but'.[20] The loss of the big, the great, the grand, the grandiose leads to the configuration of postmodernity as the era of the *petit récit*. And while it would be unwise to suggest that there is any simple or direct connection between the general politics of the *petit récit* and the more specific poetics of the contemporary *récit bref*, there is clearly a strong case to be made on behalf of that connection as something felt, as a correspondence assumed and explored by many contemporary writers.

The theme of 'ordinary people' reappears in the title of an even more recent 'roman-par-nouvelles', Gilbert Lascault's *Gens ordinaires de Sore-les-Sept-Jardins* (1994), though this text and the cast of village inhabitants whose stories are recorded in it turn out to be distinctly *extra*ordinary. This is a village whose past history is accessed through strange and wondrous legends: legends whose basis, however, is visibly ludic, arising through the play of the signifier rather than through any attempt to apply a realist agenda. The narrator, moreover, presents himself somewhat fantastically as an 'ethnologue anonyme' who has bugged every house in the village; he hears and knows everything that is going on, and thus is 'partout et nulle part', so much so that he conceives of himself as a pagan god, 'un petit dieu modeste', 'une minuscule divinité de forme monstrueuse'.[21] Lascault here employs the postmodern tactic of simultaneously inscribing and subverting certain narrative conventions. This is a tactic of oblique critique. In other words, rather than overtly attack the convention of narratorial omniscience, the author chooses to literalize it. Thus he lays bare the informing fantasies of this convention by giving rein to omniscience, and ironizes omniscience precisely to the *extent* that he gives rein to it. This in fact is the enabling condition, or figure, of Lascault's text; this is what generates its very vivacity and productivity as a text.

My final example of a contemporary 'roman-par-nouvelles' is the work which won the 1994 Bourse Goncourt de la Nouvelle, *Les Lettres du Baron* by Jean-Christophe Duchon-Doris. In his contribution to the book *131 Nouvellistes*, at which time he had not yet completed *Les Lettres du Baron*, Duchon-Doris argued that 'en complément des tentatives de "roman par nouvelles" (J.–N. Blanc), il faudrait parvenir à des "nouvelles par roman", c'est-à-dire des nouvelles qui profiteraient du cadre d'un roman pour naître et s'épanouir, des nouvelles squattant la structure d'un roman.'[22] And this is more or less what he has achieved in *Les Lettres du Baron*, a text remarkable for both its conception and its execution. The *Baron* in question here is Haussmann, close associate of Napoléon III and prefect of the Seine from 1853 to 1870, while the *lettres* of the title refer to the countless items of correspondence which failed ever to reach their destination because, due to the *grands travaux* effected under Haussmann's direction, whole streets, indeed whole *quartiers*, suddenly ceased to exist. Accordingly, the framing device invented by Duchon-Doris, and textualized in a short preface, is the figure of a humble postman, Octave, for whom 'le rôle d'un postier . . . est non seulement de porter les nouvelles [obviously a very resonant expression in context], mais aussi de vérifier l'ordonnancement des maisons, de confirmer le tracé des rues, d'être dépositaire des beautés de la ville.'[23] Scandalized by Haussmann's demolitions, and finding himself the trustee of a growing number of 'lettres orphelines . . . incapables d'aller au bout de leur destin', the postman assumes a mission: 'il fallait qu'il les aide à retrouver la paix de l'âme, en leur donnant un sens' (LB, p. 13).

Only a few of the stories which follow correspond to the actual or imagined texts of opened letters. More often the stories are about the person who wrote or the person who was due to receive a given letter. All these persons and their stories seem even within the fiction to be invented. They are invented, of course, by the author, but always via the intermediary of Octave, who doubles as a kind of 'narrative postman', ensuring the safe delivery of the author's imagination to a particular historical past. In so far as it is Octave who delivers these *nouvelles* (this news, these tidings, these stories), it is entirely appropriate that they should be so steeped in the ambience of the *merveilleux*, so emboldened by the resources of the *fantastique*, so in tune with the poetics of the classical nineteenth-century short story. As Duchon-Doris puts it in *131 Nouvellistes*, 'il s'agit de soigner la chute, d'écrire, comme le demandait Poe, l'histoire en fonction de la dernière ligne'.[24]

The sense of a novelistic configuration is further enhanced by the fact that each of the three sections into which the author groups his stories brings us closer and closer to the figure of the *Baron* himself. We begin with a sequence of letters sent from the far-flung corners of the French empire: Central America, Algeria, Egypt, China. In each case, the sender of the letter turns out to have perished, with the surprise element of the story hinging on how or why they came to die. The second section brings us to Paris. Dealing mainly with people disorientated or uprooted by the *grands travaux*, it also introduces us to agents of Haussmann's administration and to fleeting images of the Baron himself. In an unexpected *tour de force*, the third section transmutes the word *lettres* to mean now the raw material of an act of writing through which Octave the postman will seek his imaginary revenge over the Baron. 'Voici venu le temps des cauchemars d'Haussmann', reads the last line of the preface to this last section (LB, p. 147), in a clear allusion to the famous last line from Rimbaud's 'Matinée d'ivresse': 'Voici le temps des *Assassins*'. Accordingly, the last stories, often very short, and in their evocations of urban landscapes often reminiscent of Rimbaud's prose poems in the *Illuminations*, dish up nightmarish visions of hordes of sewer-rats hunting down the unfortunate baron, of primal hordes of past generations literally rising up from the holes dug into the earth by Haussmann's workforce and swamping the city. In the final tale, 'Le Maître de la ville', Haussmann and the emperor are imagined returning to a city transformed, an extravagant teeming labyrinth where new wonders and horrors await them at every turn. Hearing of the existence of a new 'seigneur de la ville', they embark on an epic urban quest which finally delivers them to the master's door:

'L'homme se retourna. C'était un jeune homme d'une vingtaine d'années en uniforme de la Poste. Il tenait à la main une plume et, devant lui, posé sur son bureau, il y avait un tas impressionnant de lettres' (LB, p. 180).

In the French generic system, *roman* and *nouvelle* are both understood to be fictional narrative forms. However, when writers start to describe their work in terms of categories such as the *récit bref* or the *texte court*, they have moved on to a level of generality which no longer recognizes the distinction between fiction and non-fiction. Writers who pitch their literary voices at this level are likely to end up exploring one of the border zones which has proved most attractive to the postmodern sensibility, the area where autobiography and fiction, including short fiction, begin to overlap.

Short fiction and autobiography can be said to have been gradually converging upon one another ever since the mid-1970s. In the case of the *nouvelle*, we have already seen evidence of a significant loss of interest in generic specificity. As Daniel Grojnowski explains:

> La nouvelle s'est de maintes manières libérée d'une conception conventionnelle de l'action . . . au profit des éléments qui ne procèdent pas de l'histoire proprement dite. D'où le caractère protéiforme d'un genre qui fait la part belle à l'essai, au poème, au dialogue, en reléguant au besoin l'action à l'arrière-plan. Cette déperdition tend à devenir monnaie courante dans la littérature contemporaine, si on excepte les nouvelles destinées au grand public.[25]

Grojnowski singles out the overlapping of short fiction with essay-writing, poetry, and dialogue because he is thinking mainly of Borges and Kafkà. Had he dwelt a little longer on what is going on in his own cultural backyard, he would have been forced to recognize that one of the strongest factors enhancing the 'proteiform' condition of short fiction today is autobiography.

As short fiction has opened up to autobiography, so the discourse of autobiography has shifted closer to that of short fiction. Two main reasons can be adduced for this. The first has to do with a general weakening of the frontier between autobiography and fiction, and the second with the increasing fragmentation of autobiographical dis-course over the 1970s and 80s. These factors began to make an impact in France after the demise of structuralism in the mid-1970s. Strongly foregrounded in the writing of Roland Barthes's self-portrait, *Roland Barthes par Roland Barthes* (1975), fictionality and fragmentation soon went on to become key principles in the 'new autobiography' practised by the likes of Nathalie Sarraute, Marguerite Duras, Alain Robbe-Grillet and Claude Simon, and in the 'autofiction' of Serge Doubrovsky. It is the poetics of fragmentation which has done most to make autobiography take on the look and feel of short fiction. The motivations behind fragmentary writing are diverse, ranging from the belief that memory itself yields only bits and pieces of the past, to the more aggressive or interventionist desire on the part of the autobiographer to deconstruct the reassuring narrative armature of the traditional life-story, based as it is on the continuities of chronology and teleology. Whatever the writer's motivation, the result is more often than not the same, in that elements situated at the micronarrative level—incidents, episodes, one-off experiences—tend to resist integration into the macronarrative level, the level at which the text shapes up into a continuous, followable story. One might say that the growing autonomy of these *petits récits* necessarily suggests a conjunction of the autobiographical fragment with the *nouvelle*, and hence of the poetics of the fragment with the dynamics of the volume, or short-story collection. Indeed, the writer and critic Philippe Chardin goes so far as to suggest that:

> renouveler l'investigation autobiographique est une des possibilités relativement négligées du livre de nouvelles, pour autant surtout que le perspectivisme et la fragmentation in-hérents au recueil semblent de nature à contrecarrer les effets bien connus de cohérence artificielle et rétrospective qui, dans l'autobiographie continue, transform toujours plus on moins l'auteur-narrateur-personnage en homme à qualités, à l'identité finalement peu problématique.[26]

Since the early 1980s, more and more writers have produced works which are either volumes of autobiographical short stories or works which in various ways mix autobiography and fiction within a structure of short texts. As with the roman-par-nouvelles, it is possible to find predecessors earlier in the century. One thinks, for example, of certain volumes of short stories by Colette, Paul Morand, and

Drieu la Rochelle that are autobiographical not just by virtue of their narrative material but because they appear designed to enforce a serious autobiographical effect on the reader. In the post-war period, a highly respected writer such as Jean-Loup Trassard, often associated with the *nouvelle* but in his own terms a practitioner of the 'prose brève', has since his very first collection, *L'Amitié des abeilles* (1961), quite casually mixed texts which can by definition only be fictional with texts that give off a strong sense of autobiographical plausibility. Louis Calaferte is another post-war writer whose work has always deserved a wider reading public and who in various ways throughout his writing career has moved restlessly between fiction and auto-biography in a string of volumes of short texts. The blurb on the back of *Ébauche d'un autoportrait* (1983) sets out very clearly the field of play in which these short texts of Calaferte, written in the first person, require to be read:

> Peut-on appeler 'Nouvelles' ces 200 pages de courts textes? Il vaut mieux dire, comme l'auteur, *Autoportrait* à travers le récit, toujours renouvelé, de ses angoisses et obsessions. Pourtant, chaque texte forme un petit monde particulier avec décor, circonstances, personnages. Romans miniatures donc, dont la fin est toujours terrible de cruauté et de pessimisme.[27]

On the one hand, the term *nouvelle* is cast aside here in favour of the notion of a self-portrait, while on the other, the apparent preference for an autobiographical paradigm can only be followed up, and, in the name of aesthetic honesty, be offset, by a return to even more overt fictionality in the form of *romans miniatures*. It is perhaps fitting that the slippages encouraged by this peripheral text should be compounded by our sense of uncertainty as to its authorship.

One point I wish to underline by referring to writers such as Trassard and Calaferte is that the phenomenon of genre-crossing between fiction and autobiography covers a far wider spectrum than that associated with self-consciously avant-garde or postmodernist schools of thought. Patrick Modiano has always maintained a critical and aesthetic distance from literary groupings such as those around the *nouveau roman* and *Tel Quel*. The kind of writer who would feel distinctly uncomfortable at seeing his work described as an example of postmodern genre-hopping, he has nevertheless engaged several times over in a practice assimilable to such categorization. On two of the occasions when this has happened, moreover, in *Livret de famille* (1977) and *De si braves garçons* (1982), the result has been a work more closely resembling a volume of short stories than a novel or autobiographical life-story. Of the first of these works, the back-cover blurb of the Folio paperback edition tells us that it consists of 'quatorze récits où l'autobiographie se mêle aux souvenirs imaginaires'. Repeating almost the same words, the inside blurb then goes on to add: 'Mais l'auteur apporte aux souvenirs imaginaires un caractère de vérité quelquefois plus convaincante que celle de la réalité.'[28] As with the Calaferte text, systematic slippage is the order of the day, with the relatively straightforward assertion of a mixture of the autobiographical and the imaginary giving way to a more challenging paradox whereby a truth effect is said to emerge more strongly from the latter than from the former. *Livret de famille* is indeed a hybrid work in which the reader constantly picks up signs of fictionality alongside signs of a more plausible, autobiographical complexion. As a result, despite Modiano's use of his own name, and despite numerous references to actual members of his family and to certain well-known if rather general circumstances of his life, the reader can never be sure quite who or what is meant to count as 'real'. Not that 'reality' as it is constructed in these stories harbours any virtues of solidity. On the contrary, what we find in *Livret de famille* is a world constantly infused and unsettled by fictionality: a world peopled by actors and actresses, ghosts and doubles; a world obscured by pseudonyms, smokescreens, and layers of fog; a world of strange coincidences, forever provoking questions and uncertainties. Indeed, if there is a transgeneric category that aptly describes Modiano's achievement in these stories, it is surely that, coined by the writer Jean-Claude Pirotte, of the *récit incertain*.[29] The *récit incertain* is shot through with a thematics of uncertainty. It is also generically uncertain and, beyond genre, narratively uncertain. It does not tell a story so much as try to tell—or in some cases to un-tell—a story. The resistance of certain kinds of experience to narrative representation, the faltering of narrative intelligence, and the frequent failure of storytelling as narrative performance are qualities central to both the ethics and aesthetics of the *récit incertain*. Such qualities determine that, as a form, the *récit incertain* will gravitate strongly towards the general domain of the *récit court*, if not towards the classic, narratively confident *nouvelle*. Modernism may well have accustomed us to open-endedness in short fiction, but the abortive, fizzle-out endings of many of Modiano's prose pieces in *Livret de famille* appear to break all the rules of the short text as 'story'.

The growing number of works of a generically indeterminate order now being produced in the territory traditionally allotted to the *nouvelle* is impressive not just for its quantity and variety but for its general quality. Few works have been as exemplary in this respect as Pierre Michon's *Vies minuscules* (1984). Using a blend of family archive, personal memory, and imaginative projection, the first-person narrator of Michon's text homes in on a number of individuals he has known or met in the past, beginning with a man from his native village, one André Dufourneau, who emigrated to French colonial Africa while still a young man, and whom he himself only ever 'met' while still a baby in his mother's pram. One by one, over the course of eight stories, the narrator transforms the humble existences of these individuals into 'lives', a term which remobilizes an entire literary tradition. For the title of Michon's book makes double reference to the 'life' as genre by invoking two of its main historical attributes. The first is the sense of consecration established by the classical tradition of 'lives' of 'great men' as written by Plutarch, Suetonius and Diogenes Laertius, then confirmed by the various medieval collections of *Lives of the Saints* and subsequently by Vasari's *Lives* of Renaissance artists (1550). Michon himself has noted that Flaubert's story *Un Cœur simple* owes much to this tradition, whilst also marking a key moment in its secularization. As he observes of the modern version of such lives, including those recounted in his own work: 'Ces vies sont tangentes à l'absence de Dieu comme les hagiographies l'étaient à sa toute-présence; elles expérimentent le drame de la créature déchue en individu.'[30] The second attribute invoked by Michon is the formal compactness most famously associated with Aubrey's *Brief Lives* (written over the last decades of the seventeenth century but not published until 1813), which then became the model for later works such as Marcel Schwob's *Vies imaginaires* (1896). These resonances are complemented by the allusion in the title *Vies minuscules* to a far more contemporary text by Michel Foucault, a point clarified by Michon himself in an interview:

La vie des hommes infâmes, lu en 1977 ou 78 dans la NRF ou dans les *Cahiers du chemin*, a eu sur moi une influence directe. D'abord c'est, je pense, là que j'ai pêché mon titre. Je ne pouvais pas choisir 'les vies infimes' puisque c'était trop proche d'infâmes, mais l'adjectif minuscule m'a été en quelque sorte soufflé par Foucault qui l'emploie sans arrêt. C'est un adjectif qu'il adore. J'ai donc pensé que ce serait bien.[31]

Using archives in which are recorded the encounters of obscure, illiterate 'gens de peu' with the power of the law, Foucault creates a series of what he calls 'existences éclairs' or 'poèmes-vie', a new order of brief lives which he hopes will cut through the staid aesthetics of the poignant historical anecdote and produce in the contemporary reader 'un certain effet mêlé de beauté et d'effroi'.[32] Michon too is interested in the bruising and often humiliating encounters of his 'petits personnages' with power, especially as embodied in the realm of discourse, and more especially still—from the point of view of those brought up in rural France right up to the early 1960s—as embodied in the finery and nobility of the official French language. Taught to read and write by the narrator's grandmother, but otherwise surrounded by 'les palabres patoises', the orphan André Dufourneau in 1910 is a village boy '[qui] ne sait pas encore qu'à ceux de sa classe ou de son espèce, nés plus près de la terre et plus prompts à y basculer derechef, la Belle Langue ne donne pas la grandeur, mais la nostalgie et le désir de la grandeur'.[33] What drove him to Africa, the narrator surmises, was the prospect of becoming a White Man rather than a peasant, the prospect of finally cementing his relationship with his mother tongue, since there in the colonies he would be unquestionably 'plus près de ses jupes', closer to *her* skirts, than any native; so close, in fact, that the grandeur long withheld would finally be conferred upon him by the mother tongue herself: 'elle lui donnerait, avec tous les pouvoirs, le seul pouvoir qui vaille: celui qui noue toutes les voix quand s'élève la voix du Beau Parleur' (VM, pp. 13–14).

In this opening story of *Vies minuscules*, it is clear that the narrator is projecting onto the figure of André Dufourneau his own self-image as an aspiring writer, in so far as his sense of literary vocation can never be divorced from his situation as a kind of cultural outsider. Michon himself has explained this situation in very blunt terms:

J'ai l'impression parfois que beaucoup d'écrivains de notre génération, ceux . . . de trous perdus dans la campagne et en banlieue, sont tout dans ce cas: comme des métèques, des immigrés de l'intérieur. On est peut-être les derniers rejetons pauvres de l'école laïque: ceux qui apprenaient en classe Racine et Hugo comme une langue étrangère. Cette littérature, cette belle chose qui n'était pas à nous, nous avons voulu violemment nous l'approprier.[34]

The desire to 'appropriate' this foreign language helps explain why Michon, unlike Annie Saumont, has never sought to assume any form of regional or working-class idiom as his own stylistic model. Instead, in *Vies minuscules*, he gives vent to a strongly rhetorical, self-consciously literary, often violently sumptuous style through which he simultaneously redeems and betrays his biographical subjects. Resuscitated in the form of a series of brief lives, those subjects, 'ceux qui furent à peine et redeviennent si peu', can only die once more, each time taking the narrator down with them, each time leaving him hoping that some kind of miracle, some minor reversal of the relentless chrono-logic of disappearance, will have taken place: 'Et que peut-être ils soient apparus, étonnament' (VM, pp. 205–6).

As he transforms these existences into 'lives', so Michon's narrator gradually brings into focus the contours of his own unredeemed subjectivity. At the same time, it should by now have become clear that 'Michon's narrator' is so strongly identifiable with Michon the author that we can quite legitimately think of this text as an autobiographical work. In clarifying the identity between author and narrator in various interviews, Michon merely confirms the strong autobiographical effect inherent in the text itself, as when, on the very first page, the paragraph beginning 'Un jour de l'été 1947, ma mère me porte dans ses bras, sous le grand marronnier des Cards . . .' (VM, p. 9), chimes perfectly with one of only two short sentences on the back cover of the book which divulge anything about the author: 'Pierre Michon est né en 1945 aux Cards, près de Châtelus-le-Marcheix, dans la Creuse.' Thus, straddling numerous borderlines, the book can be read as a novel, a collection of short stories, a work of biography, and a work of autobiography. Its mixed generic economy directly anticipates the creation in 1989 of the Gallimard series 'L'un et l'autre', whose programme, printed inside the back page of all texts in the series, and constituting nothing less than an agenda for postmodern biography, begins as follows: 'Des vies, mais telles que la mémoire les invente, que notre imagination les recrée, qu'une passion les anime. Des récits subjectifs, à mille lieues de la biographie traditionnelle.' Not only that, Michon's 1984 text inspired a renewal of interest in the 'brief life' as a genre in its own right, with recent highlights including Gérard Macé's *Vies antérieures* (1991) and Jacques Roubaud's *L'abominable Tisonnier de John McTaggart Ellis McTaggart et autres Vies plus ou moins brèves* (1997). Finally, Michon's example in *Vies minuscules* and other texts appears to have been a key factor in the emergence of what Jean-Pierre Richard, in an essay first published in 1992, calls 'ce goût de la petitesse qui anime tant d'œuvres littéraires aujourd'hui'.[35] Richard remains one of France's very finest critics, and one of the few French critical essayists, moreover, to have demonstrated on a regular basis his understanding and appreciation of genuinely contemporary writing. In this context it is no accident that to date Michon should be the only contemporary writer to whom Richard has devoted more than one critical essay. The comment just quoted is prompted by his reading of Christian Bobin, in whose work he finds 'une euphorie du minuscule, un goût même de la multiplication et de l'accumulation des petits riens' (p. 47). The theme of the minuscule as a key 'euphoric' value is also to be found in Richard's studies of the work of Eugène Savitskaya (pp. 101–5) and Patrick Drevet (pp. 127–30), while shades of Michon recur most evidently in his analysis of the work of Michel Orcel, a writer of poetry and—to use Orcel's own hybrid label—'romans minuscules'. In one such mini-novel, there occurs a moment when the heroine whispers to her lover that she would like him to write her 'un roman, un petit roman, un tout petit roman'. Richard amplifies the seductive resonance of this request not only by echoing the link drawn by Michon between the short, the small-scale, and the humble, but by asserting once more the special status of that bundle of values in contemporary literature at large: 'Comprenons qu'à l'option de la distance puisse répondre celle de l'humble, du minime . . . ; que la solution du minuscule soit en somme, comme si souvent aujourd'hui, l'une des seules à garantir une fertilité, sexuelle et littéraire' (p. 65).

As characterized by Richard, the poetics of the minuscule stems from an appreciation—ranging in kind from the fetishistic to the deeply moral—of details, particles, nuances, diminutive objects, symptoms, singularities. Such a poetics is in no way excluded from longer forms of writing. After all, one need only think back to Proust to realize how strongly one of the longest and greatest of French novels, *A la recherche du temps perdu*, is marked by a prizing of the diminutive, and specifically of the *petit* (as in the key episodes revolving around 'la petite madeleine', 'la petite phrase', 'le petit pan de mur jaune', and so on). That said, it is equally clear that many contemporary writers impassioned or motivated by the minuscule do feel drawn to the range of *formes brèves* as the forms most commensurate, or likely to prove most commensurate, with their passion. Such is the case with Bobin and Orcel. And though many of Richard's examples of Patrick Drevet's preoccupation with the minuscule are drawn from the fluid, meandering narrative prose of that writer's superb childhood autobiography, *La Micheline* (1990), the critic also highlights a poetics of the minuscule at work in Drevet's collection of essays, *Huit petites études sur le désir de voir* (1991). Drevet has since gone on to publish a second volume of such essays, *Petites études sur le désir de voir II* (1996), where once again the mere wording of a title is enough to activate a strong sense of allegiance to a contemporary paradigm: a paradigm whose intellectual roots lie in the work of Barthes and Lyotard in the mid-to-late 1970s, and whose first decisive literary articulation is proving with time to have been Pierre Michon's *Vies minuscules* (1984). That this paradigm continues to exercise a seductive pull on both writers and readers, that it continues to impart to French literature today what Brunel calls a 'freshness' and Richard a 'fertility', is underlined by the surprise success enjoyed in 1997 by a collection of short prose pieces from the pen of the novelist Philippe Delerm, entitled *La première gorgée de bière et autres plaisirs minuscules* (1997).

The paradigm of the minuscule is one of the key factors currently motivating both writers and readers to take an interest in the field of *formes brèves*, but without passing through one of the traditional centres of activity within that field, the *nouvelle*. Michon, for example, has expressed his frank dislike for the term *nouvelle*, preferring instead to think of himself, rather like Orcel, as a writer of short novels: 'La brièveté est essentielle. J'incline à penser que j'écris des romans courts—densifiés, resserrés, dégraissés—plutôt que des nouvelles.'[36] Michon seems to think that the short story cannot recount a life, mistaking for a generic essence the common practice within the modern or modernist short story of focusing on a 'slice' of life, or, more pointedly still, on a single incident or moment of crisis in a character's life. More generally, however, if there is a broad under-standing of the *nouvelle* from which contemporary writers infer their own exteriority to the genre, it would appear to be a very simple and not particularly tendentious one. The case of Philippe Delerm is representative in this respect. Slotted into a subtitle, the noun-phrase 'plaisirs minuscules' clearly operates in a very similar way to Michon's 'vies minuscules', christening a form as well as identifying a content. Less idiomatically, on the inside title-page of Delerm's book, the term *récits* appears as a kind of sub-subtitle. This I take to signify that, for their author, the texts in question are too narrative to be considered prose poems, yet not narrative enough, and probably not fictional enough, to be thought of as short stories proper. The reason for Delerm's avoidance of the term *nouvelle* is his understanding of it as denoting a short narrative fiction. And in this he is not alone. For if such is the simplest, commonest, and most portable definition of the *nouvelle*, then the judgements 'not narrative enough' and/or 'not fictional enough' will automatically exclude—or exempt—much of the most vibrant contemporary French writing from membership of the genre.

At the same time, there is no denying the constant approximation of such writing, as writing, to the strategies, techniques, and preoccupations historically associated with the art of short fiction. In other words, many of the short texts written by Michon, Macé, Roubaud, Bobin, Orcel, Delerm, and numerous others, are something *like* short stories, and, historically and technically, contain something *of* the short story. This point will click as soon as we take care to recall that the history of short fiction during the twentieth century, at least throughout the modernist period, has in itself been one of progressive erosion of faith in the capacity of *mise en intrigue*, fictional plotting, storytelling, to reflect what is understood to be most important, most relevant, most real, and most under threat, in modern experience. Attenuated narrativity, then, is arguably a feature shared by the modern *nouvelle* and the more generally labelled, or quite unlabelled, *forme brève*. Beyond narrativity, something 'like' or 'of' the short story can surface in a variety of ways: for example, in any manifestation of the thematics of the *fantastique*, itself indelibly associated with the history of the *nouvelle*; in the choice of a delimited temporal or spatial frame; in the decision to focus on a single character or a single event; in the preference for a stylized, non-psychological approach to character; or in the desire to highlight those local intensities of situation, experience, and feeling which, in the form of 'caractérisation paroxystique', are said by Florence Goyet to be one of the hallmarks of the *nouvelle*.[37]

The features in question are qualitatively diverse and quantitatively variable. In the kind of context I have in mind here, they take the form of constituent factors, or ingredients. Alongside other ingredients, they thus contribute to the overall make-up of a text which is not itself clearly identified, or clearly identifiable, as a *nouvelle*. Such features can appear pervasively or intermittently. They can occur in such a way as to trouble other ingredients of the text, or be troubled by them. In either case, they thereby contribute to a *récit incertain*. And, at another level of uncertainty, they can appear as effects for a reader without having to be attributed to an authorial cause. Because what appears is only ever something which smacks of the *nouvelle*, and only ever one textual ingredient among others, that something can never determine the overall formal status of the text in which it appears. The notion of genre loses its pertinence in such a situation. Indeed, in the case of these variable ingredients we are dealing less with a genre than with a mode, less with the *nouvelle* than—to use a term which has already begun to take root in French criticism—with the *nouvellistique*.

It is the *nouvellistique* which explains why one can find texts partially construable as short stories in the most unexpected of places. Nicole Bajulaz-Fessler has shown how short-text sequences as different from one another as Régine Detambel's *Graveurs d'enfance* (1993), which veers towards the prose poem, and Jean-Luc Benoziglio's *Peinture avec pistolet* (1993), officially a novel, both contain strong traces of 'structure nouvellistique'.[38] Having written several short stories in the 1940s and '50s, Marguerite Duras went on in the last decades of her life to produce numerous works made up of short texts such as interviews, essays, journalistic pieces, and reviews. Within the pages of these works, Duras constantly reflects on their status as acts of writing and as books, invoking the idea of genre only in the negative. As she writes of *La Vie matérielle*, in a comment which could well be applied to her other collections of short texts: 'aucune formation livresque prévue ou en cours n'aurait pu contenir cette écriture flottante.'[39] Indeed, a similar point could easily be made concerning the *generic* 'formation' of individual texts within these collections. Sanda Golopentia, for instance, has analysed one of the texts from *La Vie matérielle*, 'Le Coupeur d'eau', if not as a *nouvelle*, then as what she calls a 'récit émergent', but nonetheless within the context of an anthology of 'la nouvelle féminine'.[40] Our uncertainty as to the text's ultimate status is further compounded when we learn that, like all the other texts in this collection, its origin lies in an interview she gave to Jérôme Beaujour, whose words have been excised for the purposes of the book. But uncertainty for Duras is a distinctly positive virtue, both ethically and aesthetically, as James Williams demonstrates elsewhere in this volume in his analysis of Duras's text, 'La Mort du jeune aviateur anglais' (1993). According to Williams, this is a text whose motor-force lies in its very inability to identify its own status as writing. It thrives on not knowing what it is. As it moves uneasily through various stages of self-constitution and self-reflection, it shows in particular how 'Duras's emotional commitment to the facts of the story outstrips any attempt to contain them in the form of a *récit* or *nouvelle*'.[41] Where 'Le Coupeur d'eau' amounted to a 'récit émergent', the later text would seem to move in the opposite direction, away from narrativity. But each in its own way invokes the *nouvellistique* within a textual regime that can aptly be characterized as constituting a *récit incertain*.

In sustaining a focus on the outer limits of the *nouvelle*, I do not wish to suggest that the *nouvelle* proper, situated at the 'core' of the space mapped out by *131 Nouvellistes contemporains*, is about to shut up shop. The fact that established writers with no previous experience in the genre are still being drawn to it can only be regarded as a promising sign for the future. I am thinking here in particular of writers such as Ludovic Janvier, best known as a literary critic, and Michel Serres, one of France's foremost philosophers, both of whom have moved over to the *nouvelle* in the mid-1990s. Both writers have produced works of considerable interest and quality belonging to what I have just called the '*nouvelle* proper'. By this I mean a sense of generic identity prompted by one of two minimal conditions: namely, that a text be either readily identifiable as a *nouvelle* by a reader, and/or that it comes already externally identified as a *nouvelle* for the reader. Both conditions are satisfied by the works in question. Firstly, in each case, most of the texts tend to contain enough narrative ingredients to strike the reader as being stories or at least story-like, rather than poems or essays. In addition, these same texts tend to be confirmed as *nouvelles* by external markers. To take Janvier's *En mémoire du lit: Brèves d'amour 2* (1996), this is a volume which was awarded the 1996 Bourse Goncourt de la Nouvelle, and in which its companion volume, *Brèves d'amour* (1993), receives the label *nouvelles* on the page listing the author's previous works. As we shall see, however, neither of these conferrals of identity is in any way binding. In the case of Michel Serres, external identification occurs in a manner at once more direct and more oblique: more direct to the extent that the identifying term occurs in the very title of the book, *Nouvelles du monde* (1997); but more oblique in so far as the word in question is subject to a destabilizing play of meaning (between 'short stories' and 'news').

Whilst not wishing to sound pessimistic about the future of the *nouvelle*, I would stick to my contention, as previously expressed, that the idea of the *nouvelle* as a distinct genre has begun to slip. In this respect, I find it symptomatic that Serres's book, consisting of seventeen pairs of texts, each pair bearing a shared title, and each element of the pair its own separate title, should additionally specify that the first text of each pair is a 'récit' and the second a 'paysage'. As with Delerm, one term is too general and the other too particular to correspond to the *nouvelle*. Likewise, despite the apparently official generic status conferred on Janvier's book by external markers, the author himself has insisted in interview not only that his collection of stories is in many ways 'une autobiographie éclatée' filtered through 'la médiation de figures qui ne sont pas entièrement fictives', but that his chosen title is a repudiation of the notion of genre: 'Je n'aime pas la notion de genre. C'est pourquoi j'ai donné à mon dernier livre le sous-titre de *Brèves d'amour 2*. C'est un livre polymorphe, qui contient du poème, du récit, du théâtre.'[42] Slippage can be found, then, very close to the 'core' of the contemporary *nouvelle*, and this reinforces my view that no analyst of this area of writing can afford to disregard either the fact of generic indeterminacy or the aesthetic and ethical value placed on it by more and more writers. Besides examining cases of overlap between the novel and the *nouvelle* on the one hand, and autobiography and the *nouvelle* on the other, I have sought to highlight the instance of indeterminacy as reflected in the alternative

Notes

Introduction

1. Johnnie Gratton and Brigitte Le Juez, *Modern French Short Fiction* (Manchester and New York: Manchester University Press 1994). Hereafter Gratton and Le Juez.
2. René Godenne, *La Nouvelle française* (Paris: PUF, 1974), pp. 8 and 9.
3. Jean-Pierre Blin even talks of 'la tutelle stimulante et paralysante de Maupassant'. 'Nouvelle et narration du XXe siècle. La nouvelle, raconte-t-elle toujours une histoire?' in *La Nouvelle: définitions et transformations*, textes recueillis par Bernard Alluin et François Suard (Lille: Presses universitaires de Lille, 1990), p. 115.
4. M. Cottenet-Hage et J.-P. Imbert, *Parallèles* (Québec: L'Instant même, 1996), p. 8.
5. Regularly quoted by critics from a 'Philosophy of Composition' and 'Review of Twice-Told Tales', *Graham's Magazine*, May 1842.
6. Ian Reid, *The Short Story*, The Critical Idiom Series, (London and New York: Methuen, 1997), pp. 8 and 9.
7. Valerie Shaw, *The Short Story: a critical introduction* (London and New York: Longman, 1983), p. vi.
8. Allan H. Pasco, 'On defining short stoires', *New Literary History*, Vol. 22, Spring 1991. Quoted in Charles E. May (ed.), *The New Short Story Theories* (Athens: Ohio University Press, 1994), p. 114.
9. These requirements have been regularly cited by critics during the last two decades in particular; they borrow and adapt such phrases from one another regularly. See in particular the two collections of essays edited by Charles E. May, *Short Story Theories* (Athens: Ohio University Press, 1994) and *The New Short Story Theories*, (op. cit.); Valerie Shaw, op. cit. Ian Reid, op. cit. E. Current-García and W. Patrick, *What is the short story?* (Glenview, Illinois, and Brighton: Scott, Foresman &

Co., 1974); V. Engel (ed.), *Le genre de la nouvelle dans le monde francophone au tournant du XXIe siècle* (Frasne et Québec: Canevas et l'Instant même, 1995); J. P. Blin, op. cit.' René Godenne, op. cit.

10. Op. cit., pp. 16–18.

11. J.-P. Blin, op. cit. p. 117, claims that on account of such distillation the French story is running the risk of destroying itself.

12. Gratton and Le Juez, p. 18. Compare with Carmen Camero Perez's remark in 'Pour une poétique de la nouvelle française contemporaine', in V. Engel, op. cit., p. 140: 'textes qui font très très court, mais vont très très loin.'

13. Gratton and Le Juez, p. 10.

14. Some of the spartan forms now being produced are not entirely without precedent as the appearance in 1998 of Félix Fénéon's *Nouvelles en trois lignes* (first published in the daily newspaper *Le Matin* in 1906) reminds us. Much admired by the influential editor of the *N.R.F.*, Jean Paulhan (who himself experimented with short fiction), Fénéon produced these originally in the form of *faits divers*.

Chapter One

Bibliographical note

Readers who wish to pursue their interest in Sartre may find the following indications useful. Point of departure for any work on Sartre prior to 1970 is M. Contat & M. Rybalka, *Les Écrits de Sartre. Chronologie. Bibliographie commentée* (Paris: Gallimard, 1970). Where the prose fiction is concerned, much of the information contained in that admirable work of scholarship has subsequently been incorporated into J.-P. Sartre, *Œuvres romanesques* (Paris: Gallimard, Bibliothèque de la Pléiade, 1981), of which Contat and Rybalka, together with Geneviève Idt, are the editors. An enthusiastic, well-informed biography is that by Annie Cohen-Solal, *Sartre 1905–1980* (Paris: Gallimard, Folio, 1989). Unrivalled as a sustained piece of writing about the short stories is the monograph by Geneviève Idt, *Le Mur de Jean-Paul Sartre* (Paris: Larousse, Thèmes et textes, 1972). The same critic has written perceptively about the biographical dimension of our text: 'Des Mots à 'L'Enfance d'un chef: Autobiographie et psychanalyse', in M. Issacharoff & J.-C. Vilquin, *Sartre et la mise en signe*, (Paris: Klincksieck, 1982). Some of the most sensitive and intelligent writing on Sartre at the present time is being done by J.-F. Louette, whether for the general reader: *Jean-Paul Sartre* (Paris: Hachette, Portraits littéraires, 1993), or for a more academic audience: *Silences de Sartre* (Toulouse, Presses Universitaires du

Mirail, 1995). For an understanding of formal aspects of 'L'Enfance d'un chef', an article on which others have built but which continues to illuminate is that by Dorrit Cohn, 'Narrated Monologue; Definitions of a Fictional Style', *Comparative Literature*, vol. xviii, spring 1966, no. 2, pp. 97–112. (If I have said little about form, it is from a sense that Cohn and Idt have been there before me.) Finally, I would mention S. R. Suleiman, *Authoritarian Fictions* (New York: Columbia University Press, 1983), which situates 'L'Enfance d'un chef' as a kind of counter-example in the developing tradition of the *roman à thèse*.

1. To be exact, *L'Etre et le néant. Essai d'ontologie phénoménologique* (Paris: Gallimard, 1969 [1943]), 3ème partie, ch. I, iv, pp. 310–64.

2. Article-interview de Claudine Chonez, *Marianne*, 7 décembre 1938, described and summarized in M. Contat and M. Rybalka, *Les Ecrits de Sartre* (Paris: Gallimard, 1970), p. 65.

3. From the speech by Chorus, at the outset: 'Piece out our imperfections with your thoughts:/ . . . /For 'tis your thoughts that now must deck our kings,/Carry them here and there, jumping o'er times,/Turning the accomplishment of many years/Into an hour-glass . . .'.

4. Matthew 16:18.

5. A. Camus, *Le Mythe de Sisyphe* (Paris: Gallimard, 1942), p. 166.

6. J.-P. Sartre, *Œuvres romanesques* (Gallimard, Bibliothèque de la Pléiade, 1981), *Documents*, p. 1807.

7. J.-P. Sartre, *Le Mur* (Paris: Gallimard, Folio, 1989), p. 88.

8. Perhaps Massé has been reading Musset: 'Qu'ils m'appellent comme ils voudront, Brutus ou Érostate, il ne me plaît pas qu'ils m'oublient' (*Lorenzaccio*, Acte III, Sc. 3 [Paris: Eds du Seuil, 1963], p. 342).

9. Sartre, Pléiade, p. 1807.

10. See the headword: *chef*, in *Le Petit Robert* (Paris: Société du Nouveau Littré, 1979).

11. As, for example, in the concluding paragraph of Maurois's life of Disraeli. The biographer quotes a contemporary remark to the effect that Disraeli had been canonized as a saint, and then comments: 'As a saint? No, Disraeli was very far from being a saint. But perhaps as some old Spirit of Spring, ever vanquished and ever alive, and *as a symbol of what can be accomplished, in a cold and hostile universe, by a long youthfulness of heart*' (A. Maurois, trans. H. Miles, *Disraeli. A Picture of the Victorian Age* [London: Bodley Head, 1927], p. 325; my italics).

12. Chateaubriand, *De Buonaparte et des Bourbons* (Paris: J.-J. Pauvert, Libertés, 1966), p. 93. Chateaubriand is not a biographer of Napoleon in the conventional sense. Embedded in his autobiography there is, however, what amounts to a biography of the Emperor: see *Mémoires*

d'outre-tombe, Troisième partie, Livres 19–22. Chateaubriand's opinion of Napoleon changed over the years. At his most disapproving, he delivers a verdict which anticipates quite strikingly Sartre's conception of Lucien: 'Buonaparte est un faux grand homme (. . .) Mobile comme les hommes de son pays, il a quelque chose de l'histrion et du comédien' (*De Buonaparte et des Bourbons*, pp. 105–6). One should, perhaps, remember that Lucien Bonaparte played a key role in the *coup d'état* by which Napoleon rose to power (18 Brumaire [9 November], 1799). Described by Jean Tülard (*Napoleon*, London: Methuen, 1985, p. 236) as the most intelligent of Napoleon's brothers, he was the only one who never received a kingdom.

13. J.-P. Sartre, *Les Mots* (Paris: Gallimard, Folio, 1991), p. 163. All subsequent references are to the Folio edition.

14. Ibid., pp. 163–4.

15. The claim that Lucien's behaviour is previsible corresponds to a view on the part of Sartre as to what distinguishes the novella from the novel. If, however, we approach the story via a comparison between biography and biographical fiction, we are likely to get a different impression. The remark concerning Lucien is quoted in F. Jeanson, *Sartre par lui-même* (Paris: Seuil, 1960), p. 7; see also G. Idt, *'Le Mur' de Jean-Paul Sartre* (Paris: Larousse, 1972), p. 27.

16. See G. Idt, op. cit., pp. 20–30. Idt refines on an initial set of arguments by suggesting that the novella, because it is written from the standpoint of a completed action, establishes not real but false enigmas: 'énigmes (. . .) que la réflexion résout, mais qui permettent au texte de se constituer' (p. 28). Does 'L'Enfance d'un chef' conform to this theoretical model? One objection might be that the answer: 'Lucien est un chef', which is implicit in the title, turns out to be false. If that is so, it follows that enigmas of the kind: 'Lucien sera-t-il un chef?', are not false but real.

17. J.-P. Sartre, *Le Mur* (Paris: Gallimard, Folio, 1989), pp. 164–5. The Folio edition has been used for all quotations from 'L'Enfance d'un chef'; page references hereafter will be shown in the body of the text.

18. There are thirteen occurrences of the word *chef*, together with other fragments of text bearing on the subject of war, relations between *patrons* and *ouvriers*, and the whole notion of a match between role and qualities. The tone is set by the sentence in which the word *chef* first appears: 'M. Fleurier revint au mois de mars parce que c'était un chef et le général lui avait dit qu'il serait plus utile à la tête de son usine que dans les tranchées comme n'importe qui' (p. 160). Space prevents me from presenting all of the evidence.

19. I have taken the examples which came to mind and not worried

excessively about whether this or that novel is traditionally known as a *roman d'apprentissage*. Oysters for the respective pearls are: Voltaire, *Candide*; Balzac, *Le Père Goriot*; Nerval, *Sylvie*; Flaubert, *L'Éducation sentimentale*; Gide, *Les Faux-monnayeurs*; Dutourd, *Au Bon Beurre*.

20. We might of course take a stern view of the activities of Bergère, but the night that he and Lucien spend in the Rouen hotel scarcely reads like a case of child abuse. The fact is that Lucien—'je ne veux pas m'esquinter' (p. 195)—is much too prudent a young man to assume the mantle of Rimbaud. Sartre's way of putting him down is to allow him to remain unscathed.

21. Sartre, Pléiade, p. 81.

22. G. Idt, op. cit.; see also note 16, above.

23. Lamartine, 'L'Immortalité', *Méditations poétiques* (Paris: Gallimard, Poésie, 1981), p. 39. Sartre compares Lucien favourably with the protagonists of the other stories, while insisting that he too fails to confront the truth: 'Lucien Fleurier est le plus près de sentir qu'il existe mais il ne le veut pas, il s'évade, il se réfugie dans la contemplation de ses droits . . .' (Sartre, Pléiade, p. 1807).

24. It is tempting to see in the episode which follows yet another example of Sartre's subverting the classic texts of moral reflection. When Rousseau, in the *Rêveries*, announces his intention to keep a 'registre fidèle des mes promenades', he does so on the grounds that: 'Ces heures de solitude et de méditation sont les seules de la journée où je sois pleinement moi et à moi sans diversion, sans obstacle, et où je puisse véritablement dire être ce que la nature a voulu' (*Les Rêveries du promeneur solitaire* [Paris: Garnier-Flammarion, 1964], p. 45). Sartre mocks Rousseau by adopting the walk as the context of self-discovery and then presenting a very un-Rousseau-like set of conclusions.

25. The *larve blanche* metaphor is interesting in its failure to develop. The contingent life, it would seem, is a life without metamorphosis: all vegetables and caterpillars; not a butterfly in sight! Sartre is an exception to the rule. In the biography of Sartre by Annie Cohen-Solal, we read, at the beginning of the second part: 'Le Sartre de 1945 n'est plus le Sartre de 1939. C'est la grande mutation, la grande métamorphose de sa vie' (A. Cohen-Solal, *Sartre 1905–1980* [Paris: Gallimard, Folio/ Essais, 1989], p. 247).

26. J.-P. Sartre, *L'Etre et le néant. Essai d'ontologie phénoménologique* (Paris: Gallimard, 1969 [1943]), p. 97.

27. See, for example, the *Notice* to *Le Mur* in the Pléiade *Œuvres romanesques*: '"L'Enfance d'un chef" est un texte historiquement mieux situé, politiquement plus explicite que les nouvelles qui précèdent. Sartre n'hésite pas à prendre nettement position sur des problèmes de société,

ou de culture, tels que l'activité de groupes d'extrême droite, l'anti-sémitisme, la mode psychanalytique et un certain surréalisme. L'œuvre propose un bilan négatif de l'entre-deux-guerres *et annonce le Sartre engagé des années quarante'* (Pléiade, p. 1805; my italics). See also A. Cohen-Solal, op. cit., pp. 230–41 *passim.* Cohen-Solal nevertheless structures her narrative in ways which respect the force of Sartre's remark: 'La guerre a vraiment divisé ma vie en deux' (J.-P. Sartre, *Situations X* [Paris: Gallimard, 1976], p. 180).

28. A. Cohen-Solal, op. cit., p. 247.

29. Ibid., p. 239.

30. On the model of Charles Schweitzer, his maternal grandfather, whom Sartre describes as 'un homme du xixe siècle qui se prenait, comme tant d'autres, comme Victor Hugo lui-même, pour Victor Hugo' (J.-P. Sartre, *Les Mots*, p. 22). By analogy, Mme Thatcher serait une femme qui se prend pour Mme Thatcher; De Gaulle, un homme qui se prenait pour De Gaulle.

31. 'Tant de gens l'attendaient, au port d'armes: et lui [Lucien] il était, il serait toujours cette immense attente des autres' (p. 243).

32. A belief which found its echo on the other side of the Atlantic, in Chaplin's *The Great Dictator* (1940).

33. Pierre Drieu la Rochelle, 1893–1945. Only twelve years separate the two authors, but perhaps for all that the description 'near contemporary' is misleading. Drieu had seen service in the First World War and been wounded on three occasions. Arguably, that experience placed him in a different generation from Sartre.

34. For maximum effect, I present them in a single block, with commentary to follow. Page references are to the *La Comédie de Charleroi* Folio edition: Pierre Drieu la Rochelle (Paris: Gallimard, 1982), and are given in the body of the text.

35. S. de Beauvoir, *La Force de l'âge* (Paris: Gallimard, 1960), p. 142.

36. Sartre's views on Drieu's collaborationism are well known. For an account of 'Drieu la Rochelle ou la haine de soi', the unsigned piece which appeared, in April 1943, in *Les Lettres françaises* (clandestines), see M. Contat and M. Rybalka, *Les Ecrits de Sartre*, p. 93. The same authors remind us that Sartre develops a similar line of argument in *Qu'est-ce que la littérature?* (1947). According to Simone de Beauvoir, Sartre discussed with her, as early as February 1940, the possibility that he might take upon himself, post-war, a very different role from that which Drieu assumed relative to the *génération perdue* of 1914–18. See S. de Beauvoir, *La Force de l'âge*, pp. 442–3.

One further piece of evidence bears on the possibility of a Sartre/Drieu dialogue. There exists a play by Drieu, *Le Chef*, written in 1933 and given five performances in 1934 by the Pitoeff company. It presents striking similarities to Sartre's highly successful political thriller of 1948, *Les Mains sales*. Unlike 'La Comédie de Charleroi', it is sceptical in its handling of the subject of leadership.

37. The relationship between the young men and their victim (who may or may not be a Jew—we only have Lucien's word for it) is a relationship of power and privilege, the same kind of relationship as Dickens depicts, in *A Tale of Two Cities*, between the Marquis de St Evrémonde and Dr Manette. In this respect, the novella offers a faithful representation of the Marxist thesis whereby the bourgeoisie, a force for change and progress in the eighteenth century, becomes at some point in the nineteenth (1848 or 1851 or 1871) a reactionary, repressive force.

38. S. R. Suleiman, *Authoritarian Fictions* (New York: Columbia University Press, 1983), p. 253.

39. It is worth remembering that 1939 was the hundred-and-fiftieth anniversary of the Revolution. Sartre's critique was topical, whether or not it was logical or just.

40. See *La Nausée*, Pléiade, p. 121. Roquentin floats the proposition in the course of imagining what it must be like to be *le beau monsieur qui passe*, a well-heeled gent whose air of self-satisfaction inspires him to feats of poetic rage. The connection with Lucien is made by Contat and Rybalka in the notes to *Le Mur*/'L'Enfance d'un chef' (Pléiade, p. 1859).

Chapter Two

1. References in this article are taken from the 1958 edition of *Le Passe-Muraille* and given in the text.

2. J.-L. Dumont, *Marcel Aymé et le merveilleux* (Paris: Nouvelles éditions Debresse, 1970), p. 20.

3. P. Defresnoy, 'La Manipulation temporelle dans l'œuvre de Marcel Aymé', *Cahiers Marcel Aymé*, 3, (1984), pp. 83–93. For a fuller discussion of the concept of the fantastic in Aymé's work, see also my article 'Le Naturalisme merveilleux de Marcel Aymé: l'exemple de *La Vouivre*' in *Colloque Marcel Aymé et son temps*, ed. Y.-A. Favre and M. Lecureur (Paris: Société des Amis de Marcel Aymé, 1985), pp. 97–108. It is worth noting here that the well-known taxonomic categories of Todorov's *Introduction à la littérature fantastique* (Paris: Seuil, 1970), which are based on the concept of varying perceptual uncertainty and attempt to separate the fantastic, the marvellous and the uncanny, are singularly inappropriate to any discussion of Aymé's fictions, which are essentially posited on the certainty of the fantastic as a phenomenon

and its consequential disruptive effect on a reality otherwise governed by conventional laws.

4. Quoted by D. Veillon, *La Collaboration: textes et débats* (Paris: Le Livre de Poche, 1984), p. 47.

5. See for example P. Burrin, *La France à l'heure allemande* (Paris: Seuil, 1995) and J.-L. Bory, *Mon village à l'heure allemande* (Paris: J'ai lu, 1982).

6. *Histoires du temps* (1982), cited by Dufresnoy, op. cit. p. 85.

7. Dufresnoy, ibid., p. 84.

8. A. Juillard, *Marcel Aymé: Le Passe-Muraille* (Paris, Gallimard, Foliothèque, 1995), p. 74.

9. J. Guéhenno, *Journal des années noires* (Paris: Gallimard, Folio, 1973), p. 174, p. 56. See also J. Boal, *Journaux intimes sous l'Occupation* (Paris: Armand Colin, 1993).

10. While three obvious reference points for the treatment of time in 'La Carte' are Bergson's *Essai sur les données immédiates de la conscience* (1889), Einstein's general theory of relativity (elaborated from 1915), and Sartre's study of phenomenologicial ontology in *L'Etre et le néant* (1943), it strikes me as potentially more fruitful to compare Aymé as an inventor of fictions with other novelists who likewise combine science fiction with reflection on the historical consequences of World War Two. Kurt Vonnegut's *Slaughterhouse V* (1969) would be a famous example. In a more immediate French context, René Barjavel's splendid novel *Le Voyageur imprudent* (1944) seems to have been directly inspired by 'La Carte'. Barjavel remains largely unknown outside France.

11. Quoted from *Vagabondages*, ed. M. Lécureur (Besançon, La Manufacture, 1992), pp. 61, 75, 98.

12. Quoted in *Cahiers Marcel Aymé*, 3 (1984), p. 48.

13. R. Godenne, *La Nouvelle française* (Paris: PUF, 1974), p. 119.

Chapter Three

1. References to works by Camus denote the following editions, indicated by the accompanying abbreviations:
I—*Théâtre, Récits, Nouvelles* (Paris: Gallimard, Bibliothèque de la Pléiade, 1962)
II—*Essais* (Paris: Gallimard, Bibliothèque de la Pléiade, 1965)
C2—*Carnets, janvier 1942–mars 1951* (Paris: Gallimard, 1964).
Page references to 'La Pierre qui pousse', in I, appear in parentheses in the text.

2. See 'Albert Camus: the eye of the reporter', in David H. Walker, *Outrage*

and Insight: Modern French writers and the 'fait divers' (Oxford: Berg, 1995), pp. 139–53.

3. The expression is used by Camus in the preface he wrote for the re-publication of *L'Envers et l'endroit* in 1957: see II, p. 13. The motif of 'image' recurs repeatedly in *L'Envers et l'endroit* and in the later novel—which Camus was working on as he wrote the preface in question.

4. See Paul Viallaneix, *Le Premier Camus, suivi de Écrits de jeunesse d'Albert Camus* (Paris: Gallimard, Cahiers Albert Camus, 2, 1973), pp. 177–97.

5. *Le Mythe de Sisyphe*, in II, p. 101.

6. The way in which 'La Pierre qui pousse' makes subtle use of exoticism to effect the protagonist's renewal and induce the reader similarly to incorporate new perspectives is the subject of an interesting article by Joaquim Horacio, 'Exotopie: l'enjeu dans "La Pierre qui pousse" ', *Albert Camus 17, La Revue des Lettres modernes*, 1996, pp. 123–36.

7. Albert Camus, *Journaux de Voyage (États-Unis, 1946; Amérique du Sud, 1949)* (Paris: Gallimard, 1978).

8. Albert Camus, *Le Premier Homme* (Paris: Gallimard, 1994), pp. 172–3.

9. Commentators agree on this, while varying in their interpretations of the water imagery. Carina Gadourek, *Les Innocents et les coupables: essai d'exégèse de l'œuvre d'Albert Camus* (La Haye: Mouton, 1963), p. 218, sees water as an 'élément négatif', and quotes *L'Homme révolté*, II, p. 664, where Camus compares the instability of human reality to a river. Peter Cryle borrows this *rapprochement*, although it is of little real help in explaining the significance of the story's imagery: *L'Exil et le royaume: Bilan Critique* (Paris: Lettres Modernes, Minard, coll. 'Situation', 28, 1973) pp. 182–3. Donald Lazere makes no attempt to elucidate this point: 'Imagery of water is prominent throughout the story, but its significance is vague', he writes: *The Unique Creation of Albert Camus* (New Haven and London: Yale University Press, 1973), p. 209. Crochet shows how water is associated with a threat which hangs over Iguape, while she adds that it can be beneficial; but her analysis suffers from the imposition of an external framework of reference—'la tradition judéo-chrétienne'—which inhibits the development of the subtle interplay of symbols within the text itself: see *Les mythes dans l'œuvre de Camus* (Paris: Éditions universitaires, coll. Encyclopédie universitaire, 1973), pp. 201–2.

10. Olivier Todd, *Albert Camus, une vie* (Paris: Gallimard, 1996), pp. 504–5.

11. The term 'récit-mythe' is used by Roger Quilliot, I, p. 2056. Cryle, op. cit., pp. 180–1, assesses critical opinion on the possible symbolic nature of the story, and takes issue with this interpretation, particularly

with those versions of it proposed by Gaëtan Picon in '*Exile and the Kingdom*', *Camus: a collection of critical essays*, ed. by G. Brée (Englewood Cliffs: Prentice-Hall, 1962), p. 152, and by Alexander Fischler, in 'Camus's "La Pierre qui pousse": Saint George and the Protean dragon', *Symposium*, vol. 24, no. 3, Fall 1970, pp. 206–17. For Cryle, certain purely descriptive details which 'ne répondent pas à un dessein précis' bear witness to the realistic aims of the story. The details in question —the statue of the horned god, the Japanese colony, the incident with the policeman—are on the contrary all susceptible of interpretation in the general context of the story's thematic content. Fischler explains the Japanese colony (loc. cit., p. 210), and it is hoped that the thematic relevance of other elements pointed out by Cryle will emerge in the course of the present study. It must be added, moreover, that Cryle casts doubt on those who see symbolism and realism as mutually exclusive (op. cit., pp. 16–7); and elsewhere (p. 411, he refers to Camus's revealing comments on Melville: 'Melville a construit ses symboles sur le concret, non dans le matériau du rêve. Le créateur de mythes ne participe au génie que dans la mesure où il les inscrit dans l'épaisseur de la réalité et non dans les nuées fugitives de l'imagination [. . .] chez Melville le symbole sort de la réalité, l'image naît de la perception' (quoted in I, pp. 1901–2). The process here analysed by Camus is evident in 'La Pierre qui pousse', whose symbolism does indeed emerge from a series of real facts, events and descriptions noted by the author during his trip to Brazil. See *Journaux de Voyage*, op. cit., pp. 73–4, 84–90, 92–4, 105–6, 123–4, 125–7. For an archetypal reading, see Linda Forge Mellon, 'An Archetypal analysis of Albert Camus's "La Pierre qui pousse": the quest as process of individuation', *The French Review*, 64: 6 (1991), pp. 934–44.

12. See *La Peste*, in I, pp. 1239–40, 1308–10, 1409, 1411.
13. Ibid, p. 1424.
14. Lazere considers 'La Pierre qui pousse' to be 'one of Camus's weaker pieces of writing' because of the improbability of the story it tells (op. cit., p. 208), while Alfred Noyer-Weidner criticizes what he sees as the artistic flaws of the work ('Albert Camus im Stadium der Novelle [*L'Exil et le royaume*]', *Zeitschrift für französische Sprache und Literatur*, Band 70, 1960, pp. 9, 29, 31: reprinted as 'Albert Camus in his Short Story Phase' in Judith Suter, ed., *Essays on Camus's 'Exile and the Kingdom'* (Missouri: Missouri University Press, Romance Monographs, 1980), pp. 45–87.
15. This evocation of the pilgrims in the rain calls to mind a passage of Camus's notebooks in which the poetic connection between subjection to rainfall and submission to religion appears obliquely: 'Fin du roman.

'L'homme est un animal religieux,' dit-il. Et sur la terre cruelle tombait une pluie inexorable' (*C2*, p. 254).

16. On Camus's opposition to this view, see 'L'Incroyant et les chrétiens', *Actuelles II*, II, pp. 373–4.

17. Critics have asserted that there is a link without being able to explain it. Cryle admits that 'il y a [. . .] une certaine évolution du symbolisme qui permet de mieux comprendre la signification de la pierre qui pousse' (op. cit., p. 197): he points out (p. 199) the tenuous nature of the connection made by Gadourek—'De façon mystérieuse, la charge du coq devient *"la pierre qui pousse"* d'Arrast vers la rencontre attendue', she says (op. cit., pp. 220–1)—but is unable to establish any other link before the end of the story, where the stone 'à moitié enfouie dans les cendres et la terre' seems to recall the miraculous stone in the grotto as a focus of the people's attention (op. cit., p. 200). As far as any other similarity is concerned, says Cryle, the story of the origin of the growing stone 'rappelle vaguement le naufrage du coq, la promesse faite en mer, mais il n'y a aucun lien direct entre les deux pierres, l'une à moitié enfouie dans la terre, l'autre portée haut par le coq' (op. cit., p. 198). In fact, this rejection of any link is little more than a preparation for Cryle's later hypothesis, quoted above: the growing stone is not 'à moitié enfouie dans la terre', but grows in the waters of the grotto where the fishermen washed the statue of Christ.

18. Alexander Fischler highlights the water imagery in this passage: see loc. cit., p. 214.

19. The imagery which Camus uses here to achieve this aim is markedly less contrived than the devices he employs in *La Peste* to indicate Cottard's 'affinités' (I, p. 1332) with the plague: 'Il respirait fortement et les regardait avec des yeux congestionnés. Le docteur s'arrêta. Dans les intervalles de la respiration, il lui semblait entendre des petits cris de rats' (I, p. 1230; see also ibid., p. 1377, where Cottard is described as a 'complice' of the plague).

20. *C2*, p. 16.

21. Ibid., p. 112: 'Ce que je reproche au Christianisme, c'est qu'il est une doctrine de l'injustice.'

22. Loc. cit., pp. 211–4.

23. This is the term adopted by Gide to designate that technique whereby the artist transposes 'à l'échelle des personnages, le sujet même de l'œuvre': see André Gide, *Journal 1889–1939* (Paris: Gallimard, Bibliothèque de la Pléiade, 1951), p. 41.

24. It is perhaps significant that the only face Camus describes amongst the crowd of pilgrims waiting to acquire a piece of the growing stone is that of a 'gaucho maigre aux longues moustaches' (p. 1666); the face

of religious devotion and that of the dragon are shown to be not dissimilar.

25. It seems to be derived from the Spanish *arrastrar*, or Portuguese *arrastar*, to drag, or haul; the respective past participles *arrastrado* and *arrastado* can mean miserable, humble, living in distress.

26. See E. Bradford Burns, *A History of Brazil* (New York and London: Columbia University Press, 1970), pp. 332–3.

27. Socrate and the cook both think that d'Arrast is a 'seigneur'; the engineer insists that he is not, but that his grandfather was (1667)—hence, presumably, the 'nom à particule'. The moral and psychological qualities which d'Arrast's aristocratic ancestry may have conferred on him are examined by Cryle (op. cit., pp. 194–5); no mention has been made of its politico-historical significance on the continent of the *conquistadores*, and in particular in Iguape, where the Negro community is descended from those Africans whom the aristocratic Portuguese *fezendeiros* imported as slaves.

28. See Caio Prado Jr., *The Colonial Background of Modern Brazil*, tr. by Suzette Macedo (Berkeley and Los Angeles: University of California Press, 1967).

29. Cf. Cryle, op. cit., p. 190: 'On ne peut parler utilement des habitants d'Iguape sans distinguer entre ceux qui s'appellent les "notables" et ceux qui risquent de perdre dans la misère leur vie et leur identité.' For Jaime Castro Segovia, the social criticism implied in 'La Pierre qui pousse' is the story's most important element: see 'L'Image des réalités afro-brésiliennes dans "La Pierre qui pousse", nouvelle d'Albert Camus', *Présence Francophone* (Sherbrooke, Quebec), no. 1, automne 1970, pp. 109–114, 119. (Reprinted in English as 'Reflections of the Afro-Brazilian World in "The Growing Stone" ', in Judith Suter, ed. *Essays on Camus's 'Exile and the Kingdom'*, op. cit., pp. 171–188). It is all the more surprising, therefore, that Donald Lazere should maintain: 'The story reveals no lucid political consciousness of the colonial situation; its tone, on the contrary, is patronizing toward the noble savages' (op. cit., p. 208). In fact it will be seen that Camus attacks just such a patronizing attitude through his satire of the notables.

30. It is not inconceivable that this reworking and adaptation of what was the central element of *La Peste* is partly motivated by Sartre's criticism of the novel's symbolism during the dispute over *L'Homme révolté*: 'La lutte de l'homme contre la Nature est à la fois la cause et l'effet d'une autre lutte, aussi vieille et plus impitoyable: la lutte de l'homme contre l'homme. Vous vous revoltiez contre la mort mais, dans les ceintures de fer qui entourent les villes, d'autres hommes se révoltaient contre les conditions sociales qui augmentent le taux de la mortalité. Un enfant

mourait, vous accusiez l'absurdité du monde [. . .]; mais le père de l'enfant s'il était chômeur ou manœuvre, accusait les hommes: il savait bien que l'absurdité de notre condition n'est pas la même à Passy et à Billancourt. Et finalement les hommes lui masquaient presque les microbes: dans les quartiers misérables, les enfants meurent deux fois plus que dans les quartiers aisés et, puisqu'une autre répartition de revenus pourrait les sauver, la moitié des morts, chez les pauvres, paraissent des exécutions capitales dont le microbe n'est que le bourreau' ('Réponse à Camus', *Les Temps Modernes*, vol. 8, no. 82, août 1952, p. 349).

31. The hostility of the Blacks and the domination by force implicit in the 'ton impératif' of the harbourmaster are underlined by Camus through the interpolation of certain key phrases, which, though not in the second manuscript, appear in the final version of the story: 'Quand le commandant eut fini, personne ne bougea. Il parla de nouveau, d'une voix impatiente. Puis, il interpella un des hommes qui secoua la tête. Le commandant dit alors quelques mots brefs sur un ton impératif' (p. 1664). In the final text, the expression of the man who obeys the order becomes explicitly 'hostile' (ibid.) and the 'sorte de sourire' which he originally wore at the end of d'Arrast's visit is suppressed (see I, p. 2059, notes to pp. 1664 and 1665).

32. Monique Crochet, op. cit., pp. 203–4, makes this point: but by interpreting the forces in conflict strictly in accordance with Christian symbolism, she sees the leader as the embodiment of an evil spirit, called Echou in Camus's travel notes (see I, p. 2064). Hence Crochet arrives at an interpretation which is the inverse of the author's intention: the evidence to show that water is a deleterious element in the story is overwhelming, and Camus indicates in the second manuscript that the 'chef' is the 'père des saints' who calls down 'l'esprit de saint Georges' so that the 'enfants de religion' dancing round him may also become 'des saints' (I, p. 2060, notes to p. 1672). Fischler actually sees the dance leader as 'Saint George reincarnated' (loc. cit., p. 213).

33. 'Une macumba, au Brésil', I, p. 2063.

34. I, p. 2031.

35. Cf. 'Avant-propos' to *Actuelles III*, in relation to Algeria: 'Le premier bénéficiaire du système colonial est la nation française tout entière' (II, p. 897). Similarly, Camus makes it quite clear who are the 'profiteurs de la colonisation' in an article entitled 'La Bonne Conscience': 'le niveau de vie des Français, si insuffisant qu'il fût, n'aurait-il pas été moindre sans la misère de millions d'Arabes? La France entière s'est engraissée de cette faim, voilà la vérité' (ibid., p. 974).

36. It has been argued by Peter Cryle that this 'sans savoir pourquoi' shows

that d'Arrast's actions are spontaneous and unpremeditated, and therefore do not admit of ideological or symbolic interpretation (op. cit., p. 202). But this phrase is a device which Camus uses deliberately. It is also 'sans savoir pourquoi' that d'Arrast has a vision of the young Negress when he accepts the cook's request for help (1669): and comparison with the second manuscript reveals that these two details were inserted together in the final version of the story (cf. I, pp. 2059, 2062, notes to pp. 1169 and 1682). When d'Arrast descends from the balcony, it is 'sans qu'il sût comment' that he finds himself beside the cook (p. 1681). This repetitive reminder, at key moments of the plot, that d'Arrast does not understand what motivates him, paradoxically indicates that a force which is coherently purposive, if unrecognized by him, governs his actions.

Chapter Four

1. *Les Yeux ouverts*, p. 60.
2. *Les Yeux ouverts*, p. 90
3. Her mother died ten days after her birth leaving her father to bring her up with the help of a series of maids and tutors.
4. In an interview with Yourcenar, Matthieu Galey asks her: 'Est-ce que cette absence [d'une mère] vous pesait?' Yourcenar replies, 'Pas le moins du monde. On ne m'a jamais montré un portrait de ma mère dans mon, enfance [. . .]. mon père était fort entouré de femmes' (*Les Yeux ouverts*, p. 16). In *Souvenirs pieux*, the first part of her autobiographical trilogy, Yourcenar asserts: 'je m'inscris en faux contre l'assertion souvent entendue, que la perte prématurée d'une mère est toujours un désastre [. . .] mon premier déchirement ne fut pas la mort de Fernande, mais le départ de ma bonne' (p. 65).

   Both examples suggest an apparent rejection of the mother-figure. Reasons for such a rejection are unconvincing: her mother lacked sophistication; was naive and unworthy of Yourcenar's admiration according to Yourcenar's accounts of her in *Souvenirs pieux*.
5. See my essay 'The Adoptive Mother in Marguerite Yourcenar's *Quoi? L'Éternité*' in *Thirty Voices in the Feminine* (Amsterdam–Atlanta: Rodopi, 1996).
6. In *Quoi? L'Éternité* (the third part of her autobiographical trilogy), Yourcenar remembers being on the beach at Scheveningue as a child and being led down to the sea by her mother's friend (and father's lover), Jeanne de Reval: 'C'est peut-être parce que je veux que cette promenade ait été une sorte d'enlèvement loin du petit monde

domestique connu, une espèce d'adoption, que j'ai préféré imaginer ce beau visage penché sur moi' (*Quoi? L'Éternité*, pp. 127–8).

The imagined adoption reveals firstly that Yourcenar did indeed feel the lack of a mother-figure despite her assertions to the contrary and secondly that Jeanne incarnated for her the perfect adoptive mother: loving, beautiful and intelligent.

7. In *Souvenirs pieux*, Yourcenar is scathing of her mother's superstitions: the desire to dress the baby in blue for the first seven years of its life in memory of the Virgin Mary (p. 33); having everything blessed before the baby was born; her dying wish that the baby be allowed to become a nun should she wish (p. 51).

8. The critics, and in particular the feminist critics, frequently lament her masculine style of writing and the female stereotypes which are everywhere in her work.

9. See her interview with Patrick de Rosbo in *Entretiens radiophoniques*, p. 96.

10. Yourcenar comments on the ambiguity of the title in *Les Yeux ouverts*: 'Le titre est un peu ambigu: j'avais sans doute pensé aux *Nouvelles occidentales* de Gobineau; mais après tout la Grèce et les Balkans, c'est déjà l'Orient, du moins pour le XVIIIe ou le XIXe siècle. Pour Delacroix, pour Byron, en effet, les Balkans se ressentent d'avoir été longtemps terre d'Islam' (p. 108).

11. *Œuvres* (Paris: Bordas, 1991, p. 233).

12. *Entretiens radiophoniques avec Marguerite Yourcenar*, Patrick de Rosbo, p. 146.

13. See *Le Coup de grâce*, p. 148 where Yourcenar's description of Conrad testifies to a belief in universal patterns of behaviour which transcend temporal limits by alluding to Greek myth, Teutonic knights, Racine and Ibsen in the same breath.

14. Her punishment for disobeying the king's orders was to be buried alive in a vault where she hung herself. Her lover, Haemon followed her to his death.

15. Griselda, a simple peasant girl, marries the Marquis of Saluzzo and bears him two children. He then allows her to believe that he has put them to death. Later on, pretending that she has displeased him and that he has remarried, he arranges for his own daughter to return home where he passes her off as his new wife, having meanwhile turned his wife out in only the shift she is wearing. But on finding that she endures it all with patience, he cherishes her all the more deeply, brings her back to the house, shows her their children and honours her as the Marchioness, causing others to honour her likewise.

16. Isolde falls in love with Tristan, her husband's nephew, as the result of

a love philtre they have drunk unawares. They are conscious of the tie of kinship and loyalty that binds them to Isolde's husband, yet dominated by their passion, which finally wears off causing them to repent and separate.

17. Aude is the sister of Olivier who rescues her from Roland who has fallen in love with her. Roland and Olivier fight a duel to decide who should win the war and the duel is stopped by divine intervention. The two swear eternal friendship and Aude is betrothed to Roland.

18. *Mémoires d'Hadrien*, p. 314

19. See Colette Gaudin, 'Marguerite Yourcenar's Prefaces: Genesis as Self-effacement', *Studies in Twentieth-Century Literature*, 10(1) (Fall, 1985), pp. 31–55 for an excellent analysis of Yourcenar's prefaces.

20. *From Violence to Vision: Sacrifice in the Works of Marguerite Yourcenar* (Carbondale and Edwardsville: Southern Illinois University Press, 1992)

21. 'Influencée par elle, ou irritée par elle, mon adolescence eût versé davantage dans la soumission ou dans la révolte, et la révolte eût presque inévitablement prévalu vers 1920 chez une fille de dix-sept ans. (*Souvenirs pieux*, p. 66).

22. See Postface to *Anna, soror . . .* , p. 246.

Chapter Five

1. References in the article are to the French edition of *La Femme rompue* (Paris: Gallimard, 1967). The English translation by O'Brian was first published by Collins in 1969, subsequently by Fontana in 1971 and is currently in its fifth edition since 1984 with Flamingo.

2. The other stories are 'L'âge de discrétion' (75 pages) and 'Monologue' (31 pages). 'La Femme rompue' itself is 130 pages.

3. Cf. Claude Francis et Fernande Gontier, *Les Écrits de Simone de Beauvoir* (Paris: Gallimard, 1979), pp. 39–40.

4. Ibid, pp. 410–12. Here Beauvoir discusses the perdurable fascination of Perrault but does not discuss the stories generically or relate them to her own theory of concrete particulars and abstraction.

5. The title page of *La Femme rompue* refers to the three short stories as *récits*, whilst Beauvoir, in *Tout Compte fait*, always refers to the text as 'mon roman'.

6. Printed in Francis et Gontier, op cit pp. 439–57.

7. *L'Existentialisme et la sagesse des nations* (Paris: Nagel, 1948), pp. 103–24.

8. 'Mon Expérience d'écrivain', p. 447.

9. Beauvoir particularly felt that *Le Sang des autres* suffered from abstraction.

10. 'Mon Expérience d'écrivain', pp. 448–9.

11. Beauvoir uses the adjective 'anecdotique' to describe concrete particulars which simply remain interesting or amusing but do not achieve expressive universality or meaning beyond their naturalistic, referential frame.

12. *Tout Compte fait* (Paris: Gallimard, 1972), p. 141.

13. Ibid, p. 141.

14. Ibid, p. 142.

15. 'Prière d'insérer de *La Femme rompue*' in Francis et Gontier, op cit, pp. 231–2.

16. In Francis et Gontier, op cit, pp. 422–38.

17. *Tout Compte fait*, p. 144.

18. Ibid, pp. 143–5.

19. Elizabeth Fallaize, *The Novels of Simone de Beauvoir* (London and New York: Routledge, 1988), p. 171.

20. Terry Keefe, *La Femme rompue* (Glasgow: University Press, Introductory Guide to French literature 12, 1991) pp. 64–6.

21. As an epigraph to *Le Deuxième Sexe*, Vol II.

22. Clamence in *La Chute* (Paris: Gallimard, 1956), p. 89.

23. Toril Moi, *Simone de Beauvoir*, The Making of an Intellectual Woman (Oxford: Blackwell, 1994) pp. 106–10 and pp. 244–7.

24. Ibid, p. 108.

25. Ibid, pp. 217–18.

26. Fallaize, op cit, p. 167.

27. Moi, op cit, p. 167.

28. Ibid, p. 244.

29. Simone de Beauvoir, *Journal de guerre*, septembre 1934–janvier 1941 (Paris: Gallimard, 1990) pp. 275–6.

30. I am aware that the extract quoted refers to separation in war and comes from a Simone de Beauvoir some twenty years younger than the author of 'La Femme rompue' and that much water has flowed under the bridge in her personal life over that period. However, the various diary excerpts used in Beauvoir's memoirs at different times, including 1940 (*La Force de l'âge* [Paris: Gallimard, Collection Folio, 1960], pp. 689–90, *La Force des choses*, 2 Vols [Paris: Gallimard, 1963], I, pp. 103–27 and II, pp. 161–244) all reveal a person highly vulnerable to anxiety and depression and expressing herself in a manner which would not be out of place in Monique's diary.

31. Moi, op cit, pp. 250–1.

32. Ibid, p. 251.

33. Ibid, pp. 250–2.

34. Simone de Beauvoir, *Lettres à Nelson Algren: un amour transatlantique* (Paris: Gallimard, 1997). To anyone really familiar with Beauvoir's

work, the 'revelation' of an emotionally dependent dimension to her attachments should have come as no surprise (and it might be argued that such an attribute should not be seen as a real surprise in anybody). However, reaction in the British press in particular, was typically dramatic and rather silly. (Cf Susannah Herbert (sic), 'Simone's true confessions, France's feminist icon had a soppy side', *Daily Telegraph* (Wednesday, 26 February, 1997), p. 17 and Ben MacIntyre, 'Love letters show submissive side of feminist icon', *The Times* (Friday, 21 February, 1997), p. 11.

35. Francis et Gontier, op cit, p. 578.
36. Ibid, pp. 577–9.
37. Of course, if one assumes that people are free and that we invent ourselves anew at every moment, then Monique, by an act of will, could theoretically welcome Maurice's departure as a thankful relief from oppression, marital bonds and from patriarchy, and as an invitation to start a new independent life. Emotional wounds do not appear to be so readily transcended in Beauvoir.

Chapter Six

1. *Le Coq de bruyère* simply takes its title from the longest story in the collection. Whilst the narratives are not directly connected to each other some critics do consider them to be organized according to certain themes. See, for example, David Gascoigne's *Michel Tournier* (Oxford: Berg, 1996) pp. 20–1. Susan Petit, in her *Michel Tournier's Metaphysical Fictions* (Amsterdam: John Benjamins, 1991) pp. 101–9, has gone one step further and sees the first seven narratives as being emblematic of the seven cardinal virtues and the last seven as representing the seven deadly sins.
2. See the chapter entitled '*Barbe-Bleue* ou le secret du conte', in Michel Tournier, *Le Vol du vampire* (Paris: Mercure de France, 1981). Further references to this work will be included in the text where possible.
3. Michel Mansuy, 'Trois chercheurs de paradis: Bosco, Tournier, Cayrol', *Travaux de linguistique et de littérature*, XVI, 2 (1978), p. 211.
4. 'Les Suaires de Véronique' in *Le Coq de bruyère* (Paris: Folio, 1978). Further references are to this edition and will be parenthetically included in the text.
5. Michel Tournier, *Le Crépuscule des masques* (Paris: Editions Hoëbeke, 1992), p. 171.
6. Jean Calvin, *Traité des reliques*, in *Three French Treaties*, ed Francis M. Higman (London: The Athlone Press, 1970), p. 68.
7. In March 1996 Thomas Hamilton opened fire on a group of four- and

five-year-olds in a primary school in Dunblane, Scotland. Sixteen children and their teacher were killed. Tiffauges's actions here seem like a macabre premonition of this event.

8. Michel Tournier, 'Je copie, et j'en suis fier!', *Femme* (mai, 1990).

9. For Lévi-Strauss's analysis of myth in terms of *bricolage* see his *La Pensée Sauvage* (Paris: Plon, 1962).

10. Martin Roberts in *Michel Tournier: Bricolage and Cultural Mythology*, Stanford French and Italian Studies, 79 (Saratoga, CA: Anma Libri, 1994), p. 99. Further references to Roberts are to this work and will be included in the text.

11. Walter Redfern, *Michel Tournier: Le Coq de bruyère* (Madison, NJ: Fairleigh Dickinson University Press; London and Toronto: Associated University Presses, 1996), p. 70. Further references to Redfern are to this work and will be included in the text where possible.

12. Régis Debray, *L'Œil naïf* (Paris: Editions du Seuil, 1994), p. 141.

13. Michel Tournier, *Le Roi des aulnes* (Paris: Folio, 1970), p. 167. Further references to this novel will be parenthetically included in the text.

14. Two of the best examples of initiation are found in *Le Coq de bruyère* in the stories of 'Tupik' and 'Amandine ou les deux jardins'. For a detailed examination of initiation in the latter see Rachel Edwards, 'Initiation and Menstruation: Michel Tournier's "Amandine ou les deux jardins" ', in *Essays in French Literature*, no 27 (November, 1990), pp. 75–90.

15. For an analysis of the role of the narrator, see Nicole Bourbonnais, ' "Les Suaires de Véronique": présences du narrateur', in *Incidences: analyse plurielle*: 'Les Suaires de Véronique' *de Michel Tournier*, 2–3 (1979), pp. 51–74.

16. Françoise Kaye, 'Ce petit Hector, on aimerait en faire quelque chose', in *Incidences: analyse plurielle*: 'Les Suaires de Véronique' *de Michel Tournier*, 2–3 (1979), p. 26.

17. See especially Alexandre's 'Esthétique du dandy des gadoues' in Michel Tournier *Les Métréores* (Paris: Folio, 1975), pp. 101–3.

18. Michel Tournier, *Vendredi ou les limbes du Pacifique* (Paris: Folio, 1972), p. 46.

19. Michel Tournier, *Des Clefs et des serrures: images et proses* (Paris: Chêne, Hachette, 1979), p. 112. Further references to this work will be parenthetically included in the text.

Chapter Seven

(NB All references to 'Aviateur' are from the original 1993 Gallimard edition of *Ecrire*.)

1. See the collection *Des Journées entières dans les arbres, suivi de Le Boa, Madame Dodin, Les Chantiers* (Paris: Gallimard, 1954).

2. This claim is made in 'Marguerite Duras: "Ce qui arrive tous les jours n'arrive qu'une seule fois" ': interview with G. Costaz, *Le Matin*, 28 September 1984.

3. See E. A. Poe, 'Review of *Twice-told Tales*', in C. E. May (ed), *Short Story Theories* (Columbus, OH: Ohio University Press, 1976), pp. 45–51 (p. 47).

4. See R. Godenne, *Etudes sur la nouvelle française* (Geneva and Paris: Editions Slatkine, 1985), in particular, chapter 24, 'La nouvelle selon Marcel Arland' (pp. 253–81). See also M. Viegnes, *L'Ésthétique de la nouvelle française au vingtième siècle* (Bern: Peter Lang, 1989), in particular chapter 2, 'Panorama historique' (pp. 47–73).

5. See J. Barnes, 'Evermore', in *Cross Channel* [1996] (London: Picador, 1997), pp. 89–111. Another obvious point of difference is that the dead soldier, Private Sam Moss, was Jewish, and his grave displays the Star of David. I would like to thank Bill Bell for introducing me to this text.

6. See M. Duras, *L'Amant* (Paris: Editions de Minuit, 1984), pp. 126–9. See also in this regard 'L'horreur d'un pareil amour', in M. Duras, *Outside: Papiers d'un Jour* (Paris: Albin Michel, 1981), pp. 280–2, where the stillborn child is described as 'mort d'une mort séparée' (p. 281).

7. Ibid, p. 85.

8. For a brief but valuable summary of the different ways in which the play has been received politically, both as a tribute to the spirit of the Resistance and as a call to collaboration (depending on whether one prioritizes Antigone or Créon), see W. M. Landers, (ed). Jean Anouilh, *Antigone*, (London: George Harrap and Co, 1957), pp. 23–6.

9. *Pearl: A new verse translation*, trans. and ed. by M. Borroff, (New York: W. W. Norton and Company, 1977), p. 31. Like 'Aviateur', *Pearl* develops the theme of childhood innocence but in a specifically Christian context: a dead infant who has been baptized is unspoiled by sin and thus has a soul as immaculate and eternal as the Heavenly Kingdom.

10. M. Duras, *Des Journées entières dans les arbres*, pp. 101–2.

11. M. Duras, *L'Amant*, p. 15.

12. I have explored the different chiastic formations in Duras's film-work in *The Erotics of Passage: Pleasure, Politics, and Form in the later work of Marguerite Duras* (Liverpool: Liverpool University Press, 1997), in particular chapter 3, 'Every Which Way but Loose: Duras and the Erotic Crimes of Montage'.

13. See R. Barthes, *S/Z* (Paris: Éditions du Seuil, 1970), p. 35.

14. *Pearl*, p. 5.
15. See T. Weiskel, *The Romantic Sublime: Studies in the Structure and Psychology of Transcendence* (Baltimore: Johns Hopkins University Press, 1978), pp. 22-5.
16. See 'Duras tout entière: Un écrivain au-dessus de tout Goncourt': interview with P. Bénichou and H. Le Masson, *Le Nouvel Observateur*, 14–20 November 1986, pp. 56–9 (p. 58).
17. In S. Lamy, and A. Roy, (eds), *Marguerite Duras à Montréal* (Montreal: Editions Spirale, 1981), Duras states the following: 'Moi, j'écris avec Diderot, j'en suis sûre, avec Pascal, avec les grands hommes de ma vie, avec Kierkegaard, avec Rousseau, j'en suis sûre, avec Stendhal, pas avec Balzac, avec les autres, mais totalement à mon insu, c'est ma première nourriture que je lis avidement' (p. 23).
18. See M. Duras, 'Sublime, forcément sublime Christine V.', *Libération*, 17 July 1985, pp. 4–6. The article was commissioned by *Libération* and published on the 273rd day of the 'Petit Grégory' affair.
19. Ibid, p. 4.
20. See A. Smock, 'Learn to Read, She Said', *October* 41 (1987) pp. 53–60 (p. 60).
21. In her preface to the title-text of *La Douleur* Duras declares that the very term 'literature' would be shameful in the case of describing painful, 'sacred' writing, writing that results directly from personal experience and which produces 'un désordre phénoménal de la pensée et du sentiment auquel je n'ai pas osé toucher et au regard de quoi la littérature m'a fait honte' (*La Douleur* [Paris: Editions POL, 1985], p. 10). She proposes instead the term *anti-littérature*.
22. For an excellent analysis of this social process of reclamation, see S. Felman, and D. Laub, *Testimony: Crises of Witnessing in Literature, Psychoanalysis, and History* (London and New York: Routledge, 1992), in particular chapter 7, 'The Return of the Voice: Claude Lanzmann's *Shoah*'.

Chapter Eight

1. John Taylor, 'France', in *The Oxford Guide to Contemporary World Literature*, ed by John Sturrock (Oxford: Oxford University Press, 1997), pp. 142–64 (p. 142).
2. Taylor, p. 143.
3. Pierre Brunel, *La Littérature française aujourd'hui: Essai sur la littérature française dans la seconde moitié du XXe siècle* (Paris: Vuibert, 1997), p. 206.
4. Brunel, p. 206.

5. See *Les voilà quel bonheur* (Paris: Julliard, 1993; also available as a 'Pocket' paperback), pp. 81–103.

6. For 'Taggers taggez' and 'Un Régime pour Régine', see *Les voilà quel bonheur*, pp. 73–80 and 37–48 respectively. For 'La Bâche', 'Les Enfants s'ennuient le dimanche', and 'Une Semaine comme les autres', see *Après* (Paris: Julliard, 1996), pp. 7–9, 33–40, and 11–22 respectively.

7. 'Il revenait de Chicago, Papa', *Les voilà quel bonheur*, pp. 105–9 (pp. 108–9).

8. 'Une Semaine comme les autres', *Après*, pp. 11–22 (pp. 21–2).

9. 'Les voilà quel bonheur', *Les voilà quel bonheur*, pp. 155–60 (p. 155).

10. Ibid, p. 155.

11. See Claude Pujade-Renaud and Daniel Zimmermann (eds), *131 Nouvellistes par eux-mêmes* (Levallois-Perret: Ed. Manya, 1993), p. 276.

12. Ibid, p. 276.

13. *131 Nouvellistes*, p. 253.

14. *131 Nouvellistes*, p. 158.

15. René Godenne, 'Les Années 90 de la nouvelle française et suisse: retour à la case départ', in Vincent Engel (ed.), *Le Genre de la nouvelle dans le monde francophone au tournant du XXIe siècle: Actes du colloque de L'Année Nouvelle à Louvain-la-Neuve, 26–28 avril 1994* (Canevas éditeur/ L'Instant même/Editions Phi, 1995), pp. 15–22 (p. 19).

16. Claude Burgelin, *Georges Perec* (Paris: Seuil, 1988), p. 174.

17. The evolution of the modern French short story towards and beyond the *nouvelle-instant* is discussed in Johnnie Gratton and Brigitte Le Juez, *Modern French Short Fiction* (Manchester: Manchester University Press, 1994), pp. 7–12.

18. *131 Nouvellistes*, p. 50. See also Jean-Noël Blanc, 'Pour une petite histoire du "roman-par-nouvelles" et de ses malentendus', in Vincent Engel (ed.), *Le Genre de la nouvelle*, op. cit., pp. 173–83.

19. *131 Nouvellistes*, pp. 207–8.

20. Jean-François Lyotard, *La Condition postmoderne: rapport sur le savoir* (Paris: Minuit 1979), pp. 7–8.

21. Gilbert Lascault, *Gens ordinaires de Sore-les-Sept-Jardins* (Paris: Gallimard, coll. L'Arpenteur, 1994), p. 13.

22. *131 Nouvellistes*, p. 141.

23. Jean-Christophe Duchon-Doris, *Les Lettres du Baron* (Paris: Julliard, 1994), p. 12. Further page references to this work are given in the text, following the abbreviation 'LB'.

24. *131 Nouvellistes*, p. 141.

25. Daniel Grojnowski, *Lire la nouvelle* (Paris: Dunod, 1993), pp. 103–4.

26. *131 Nouvellistes*, p. 78.

27. See the back cover of Louis Calaferte, *Ebauche d'un autoportrait* (Paris: Denoël, 1983).
28. Patrick Modiano, *Livret de famille* (Paris: Folio, 1981; first publ 1977), back cover and p. 5 respectively.
29. See Jean-Claude Pirotte, *Récits incertains* (Cognac: Le temps qu'il fait, 1992).
30. See Daniel Delas and Tristan Hordé, 'Nouvelles, vies et récits d'aujourd'hui: entretiens et lectures', in *Le Français aujourd'hui*, 87, 1989, pp. 75–85 (p. 76).
31. Arlette Farge and Pierre Michon, 'Entretien', in *Villa Gillet*, 3, 1995, pp. 151–64 (p. 152). The Foucault essay in question was in fact published in the *Cahiers du chemin* in 1977.
32. Michel Foucault, *La Vie des hommes infâmes*, quoted in Farge and Michon, 'Entretien', pp. 151–2.
33. Pierre Michon, *Vies minuscules* (Paris: Gallimard, 1984), p. 11. This text was finally issued as a Folio paperback in 1996. Further page references to this the Gallimard edition are given in the text, following the abbreviation 'VM'.
34. From an interview given in July 1993 to Marianne Alphant, in 'Rencontre avec Pierre Michon', a leaflet published by the bookshop collective 'L'œil de la lettre' (no further details given).
35. Jean-Pierre Richard, 'Du Sang sur la neige', in *Terrains de lecture* (Paris: Gallimard, 1996), p. 46. Further references to this work appear between parentheses in the text.
36. Pierre Michon, as interviewed in 'Nouvelles, vies et récits d'aujourd'hui', op. cit., p. 77.
37. See Florence Goyet, *La Nouvelle 1870–1925: Description d'un genre à son apogée* (Paris: PUF, 1993), pp. 15–27.
38. Nicole Bajulaz-Fessier, 'Quand on aime il faut partir . . . un peu', in Vincent Engel (ed), *Le Genre de la nouvelle*, op. cit., pp. 141–8.
39. Marguerite Duras, *La Vie matérielle* (Paris: Folio, 1994; first publ. in 1987), p. 9.
40. Sanda Golopentia, 'Les Silences du récit', in Madelaine Cottenet-Hage and Jean-Philippe Imbert (eds), *Parallèles: Anthologie de la nouvelle féminine de langue française* (Québec: L'Instant même, 1996), pp. 156–71.
41. See the present volume, p. 119.
42. Janvier, quoted in Monique Petillon, 'Ludovic Janvier, le beau parleur', *Le Monde des livres*, 9 Feb 1996, p. 5.

Notes on Contributors

William Bell teaches French language and literature at the University of Kent at Canterbury. His research interests include the history of republican ideas and the poetry and prose of the nineteenth and twentieth centuries. In the field of twentieth-century prose, he has recently contributed essays on Julian Barnes and on André Gide, to *Imitating Art* (edited by David Ellis) and to *André Gide* (edited by David Walker) respectively.

Ray Davison is Senior Lecturer in French at the University of Exeter, where he specializes in modern French literature and thought. His published work includes editions of Albert Camus's *L'Étranger* and Simone de Beauvoir's *Une Mort très douce*, as well as the critical study *Camus: The Challenge of Dostoevsky*.

Rachel Edwards is lecturer in French Studies at the University of Newcastle upon Tyne. She wrote her thesis on Myth in Contemporary French Fiction and is currently working on Michel Tournier and Patrick Grainville. She is also carrying out research on the Papin sisters and the role their crime continues to play in French culture. She has published on contemporary French fiction including that of Michel Tournier.

John Flower is Professor of French at the University of Kent at Canterbury. He has published widely on the twentieth-century French novel and in particular on the relationship between imaginative writing and politics and religion. His books include studies of Mauriac, Vailland and Pierre Courtade. He is currently preparing an edition of the correspondence between Jean Paulhan and François Mauriac and an essay on Paul Nizan's novel *La Conspiration*. He is editor of the *Journal of European Studies* and of Berg's French Studies series.

Johnnie Gratton is a Statutory Lecturer in French at the National University of Ireland, Dublin. His main research interest is in the area of contemporary French autobiography, fiction and short fiction. He is co-editor with Brigitte Le Juez of *Modern French Short Fiction*, and with Jean-Philippe Imbert of *La Nouvelle hier et aujourd'hui*. He has published articles on Roland Barthes, Colette, Marcel Proust, Nathalie Sarraute, Jean-Loup Trassard, and postmodern French fiction.

Christopher Lloyd is Chairman of Modern European Languages and senior lecturer in French at Durham University. His publications include books on Aymé, Maupassant, Huysmans and Mirbeau.

David Walker is Professor of French at the University of Sheffield, where he is also Director of the 'André Gide Editions Project'. His previous publications include *André Gide*, and *Modern French Writers and the 'Fait Divers'*. In addition to publications on Genet, the *nouveau roman* and aspects of French theatre, he has published numerous articles on the fiction and thought of Camus, including studies of *L'Exil et le royaume* and *Le Premier Homme*. He is a member of the editorial team for the series *Albert Camus* published by the *Revue des Lettres Modernes*.

Sally Wallis has worked as a lecturer in French at the Universities of Strathclyde and Exeter. She presently works for the Open University and holds the position of Honorary Research Fellow at the University of Kent in Canterbury. Her PhD was on the novels of Marguerite Yourcenar and she has published many introductions to, and articles and conference papers on, Yourcenar's work.

James Williams teaches French and comparative literature and film at the University of Kent at Canterbury. He has published on Marguerite Duras, Roland Barthes and Jean-Luc Godard, and is the author of *The Erotics of Passage: Pleasure, Politics and Form in the Later Work of Marguerite Duras*. He has also co-edited the recent collection entitled *Gay Signatures: Gay and Lesbian Theory, Fiction and Film, 1945–1995*, and his critical guide to Camus's *La Peste* is forthcoming.

Selective Index